THE MYTH OF AUNT JEMIMA

Representations of Race and Region

Diane Roberts

London and New York

First published 1994
by Routledge
11 New Fetter Lane, London EC4P 4EE

Simultaneously published in the USA and Canada
by Routledge
29 West 35th Street, New York, NY 10001

Typeset in Palatino by the EPPP Group at Routledge

Printed and bound in Great Britain by Clays Ltd. St. Ives, plc

British Library Cataloguing in Publication Data
A catalogue record for this book is available from the British Library

Library of Congress Cataloging in Publication Data
A catalog record for this book has been requested

ISBN 0–415–04918–0 (hbk)
ISBN 0–415–04919–9 (pbk)

for Sarah Jackson, Philip Plowden and Adam Sampson

CONTENTS

ACKNOWLEDGEMENTS

This book got written on two continents, in six libraries, in seven houses and at three universities. A lot of people helped with reading, conversation, book lists, criticism or just looking on more or less approvingly. I want to thank Sue Roe, who commissioned the book and encouraged me throughout, and Talia Rodgers, my editor at Routledge, who has been a tower of strength, a pearl of wisdom and a monument of patience. An editor who actually cares for style is a rare being. I am exceedingly grateful to Helen Taylor of Warwick University who read the manuscript in several versions and offered excellent, generous advice on it – as she has been doing with my work for years. I am also grateful to Margaret Ferguson of the University of Colorado who offered much help on *Oroonoko* and *Uncle Tom*, and to my colleagues Hero Chalmers of Worcester College, Oxford, and Mary Finn, Harold Weber and Elizabeth Meese of the University of Alabama, and Bruce Boehrer, W. T. Lhamon, Jr and C. Peter Ripley of the Florida State University, who read, criticized, and therefore bettered the book all through the process. I had helpful conversations with Peter Stallybrass, Karen Newman, Jerome Stern and Alan Sinfield about issues from the construction of the South as "low" to the ways Aunt Jemima has altered her look on the pancake box. George Starbuck wrote the most elegant comments in his Carolingian hand all over one version; all scholars ought to seek out poets to read work: they improve it at all levels. Just being around George is a kind of postdoc in itself.

I would like to thank the Principal and Fellows of Brasenose College, Oxford for welcoming me, the pupil who won't go away, back every summer, especially my former tutor Bernard Richards, my former moral tutor Leighton Reynolds, and my friend John Rowett – as liberal with his knowledge of American history as he is with the Tallisker. The staff of the Brasenose College Library have been very kind and helpful: the college has a collection of books on Southern American politics, race, and women's history which proved better for my purposes than the holdings of many American libraries of far greater size and resources. Ewen Green of Reading University and Clare Brant of King's College, London, shared knowledge of the Confederacy, Aphra Behn, old movies, new movies, Screaming Jay Hawkins, pets and Lebanese wine. In Oxford, Emma Holden and Sandra Richards have been exemplary friends. In London, Russell Celyn Jones, Barbara Bayliss, Alyson Coates, Fred Ponsonby, Penny Smith, David Bedingfield and Deborah Postgate also shared their houses, alcohol, children, blues tapes and cats. In Barnard Castle, Deborah Jenkins proffered virtually unlimited hospitality and Rebecca Jenkins showed willing to talk about Fanny Kemble indefinitely.

In Tallahassee, Fita Ferguson, Mark Hinson, Ben Wilcox, Maxine Stern, Michael McClelland and the *Florida Flambeau* newsroom, Charlotte Williams, Barbara Petersen and Bob Shacochis have patiently listened to me talk about the South, the gothic, the oriental and the death of Little Eva without complaint, cooked gorgeous dinners, loaned computers, played George Jones – whatever I wanted. Betty Roberts and Brad Roberts let me come back to the house any time. In Tuscaloosa, Francesca Kazan, Joe Hornsby and Kathy Starbuck have been supportive and charming throughout a manic writing process. Our former department chair, Claudia Johnson, gave me the encouragement, the research assistance and the *time* to make this book happen – every writer's happy daydream. Our new department chair, Sara de Saussure Davis, has also been very supportive. I should also thank the American Council of Learned Societies for a grant which enabled me to finish the research for the book in 1992, as well as the staffs of the British Library and the Bodleian Library, and my seminar students who argue with me, challenge me, fuss at me and insist on getting a word in edgewise: I learn so much from them.

INTRODUCTION

This is not a story to pass on.
> Toni Morrison, *Beloved*

Who knows but that, on the lower frequencies,
I speak for you?
> Ralph Ellison, *Invisible Man*

It is over thirty-five years since Autherine Lucy walked a gauntlet of white students screaming "Kill her!" to enter a classroom at the University of Alabama; over thirty-five years since Rosa Parks sparked the Montgomery bus boycott by refusing to give her seat to a white man; thirty years since Fannie Lou Hamer was shot at by Mississippi nightriders for registering to vote. We in the United States have had at least three decades of powerful, passionate images of black women (and men) to complicate and challenge three hundred years of stereotypes, and yet the best-known black woman's face in the land looks out from a box of pancake mix.

Aunt Jemima is so familiar she is practically invisible, part of America's racial background noise. Aunt Jemima flourished in minstrel shows before she became a corporate brand name: the archetypal "mammy," her shiny, scrubbed black face beaming, her crimson head-rag tied smartly in a square knot. The mammy typifies the mythic Old South of benign slavery, grace and abundance; she rules the kitchen or she instructs the young ladies in decorum or she buries the family silver in the orchard so the Yankees won't steal it. Now she presides over the great American breakfast, the head-rag gone, the face slimmer, the outfit changed to what a businesswoman might wear, a Black Urban Professional, or Buppie, Jemima.[1] But the name on the pancake-mix box is still "Aunt Jemima" – we are still haunted by titles of slavery and minstrelsy, even in our bright egalitarian supermarkets.

1

INTRODUCTION

Aunt Jemima has an opposite, Jezebel, as sexy as the mammy is sexless, figured not by the treats of the kitchen but the delights of the bedroom (or the barn or the ditch), not mother but prostitute. Aunt Jemima's enormous bosom signifies her maternal feeding function: she is a nurturing body. But Jezebel does not feed, she entices, she is to be used, penetrated, had, impregnated. Jezebel can act wicked as a razorblade or sweet as sugar cane, but she is always the willing receptacle, the hip-grinding blues woman, the almond-eyed mulatta, the overblown "wench" who always says yes to men.

In between, there are other images, other names for black women (and men) which divide, categorize and circumscribe them: Sapphire, Brown Sugar, Prissy, Buck, Sambo, Bad Nigger, Uncle Tom. Hortense Spillers says these names "are markers so loaded with mythic prepossession that there is no easy way for the agents buried beneath them to come clean" ("Mama's Baby" 65). I will not attempt to excavate the humans beneath those weighted, white-given names; only to show how the marking itself constitutes a battle over how whites and blacks, women and men, defined themselves and each other in America. This book is concerned with the writings of white women during times when it was hard for blacks to be heard in their attempts to name themselves. How white women endorse, reinforce or deny those names – Jemima and Jezebel and every one in between – speaks to how Americans understood race, gender and class from the 1830s to the beginning of the Civil Rights movement. Not that we have solved the problem of representation, but in order to move forward, to hear the new names that marginalized groups and minorities utter, we must understand what superfluous veils, what ugly appellations, what aliases, they have to discard.

> *What is socially peripheral is often symbolically central*
> Barbara Babcock, *The Reversible World:*
> *Symbolic Inversion in Art and Society*

Representations of whites and blacks fuel a war over the body: the black body, the white body, the female body. The body is defined and circumscribed according to gender, race, and class. The ante-bellum South represented the middle-class white woman as asexual, spiritual, morally elevated and angelic. If she deviated from certain codes, trespassing into the realm of behaviours relegated to black women (sexuality, "dirt," passion), she lost her value in the white economy. Some bodies are "high," like the statue on the pedestal that so often represents white women in Southern culture,

2

while some, like black women (and black men) are "low," represented by the unspeakable, "unclean" elements official culture
would repress. I use Bakhtin's model for the "classical body" and
the "grotesque body" to express these extremes: "The essential
principle of grotesque realism is degradation, that is, the lowering
of all that is high, spiritual, ideal, abstract; it is a transfer to the
material level, to the sphere of earth and body in their indissoluble
unity" (Bakhtin 19–20). The grotesque body is

> multiple, bulging, over- or under-sized, protuberant and in-
> complete. The openings and orifices of this carnival body are
> emphasized, not its closure and finish. It is an image of impure
> corporeal bulk with its orifices (mouth, flared nostrils, anus)
> yawning wide and its lower regions (belly, legs, feet, buttocks
> and genitals) given priority over its upper regions (head,
> "spirit," reason).
>
> (Stallybrass and White 9)

The classical body is, on the other hand, single, ethereal, sanctioned
and official. It

> presents an entirely finished, completed, strictly limited body,
> which is shown from the outside as something individual.
> That which protrudes, bulges, sprouts, or branches off (when
> a body transgresses its limits and a new one begins) is elimi-
> nated, hidden or moderated. All orifices of the body are closed.
>
> (Bakhtin 320)

One problem with Bakhtin's grotesque/classical opposition is, as
Peter Stallybrass observes ("Patriarchal Territories," 123–25), that
it "concentrates on the body as a *locus* of class conflict to the
exclusion of gender," assuming an "ungendered," that is, male,
body. Yet western culture has always been obsessed with controlling women's bodies. Stallybrass argues (126) that Elizabethans
assumed the female body was "naturally 'grotesque,'" requiring
constant vigilance and control lest it overreach ("Patriarchal
Territories," 126). Nineteenth-century American culture inherited
these early modern attitudes.

When race is introduced into the Bakhtinian scheme, the imper-
ative for control becomes at once more visible and more complex.
If the female body tended toward the grotesque unless sternly
regulated, the black body could never, in the mind of the slave
South, be *anything but* grotesque. Vigilance was required to keep

white bodies from slipping toward blackness. So the slaveholders of the American South represented white women (at least of the middle and upper classes) and black women as high and low, pure and polluted, bodies. This opposition became part of the ideology of slavery itself: the sexual availability of slave women (who could not without danger refuse the Master), their ability to perform hard physical labour, their exposed bodies, their dark skin itself served to make the lady in the big house more ladylike: more untouchable, more angelic, more *white*. Like the characters Aunt Jemima and Jezebel, these constructed categories reinforce a set of discourses which should not be confused with how people actually lived their day-to-day lives. The stories that slave society (and postwar segregated America) created about women and blacks are partial, warped or fantastic, yet always revealing. In Faulkner's *Absalom, Absalom!*, Mr Compson, a notorious theorizer of the feminine, imagines the Old South gender map. Women are

> separated into three sharp divisions, separated (two of them) by a chasm which could be crossed but one time and in but one direction – ladies, women, females – the virgins whom gentlemen someday married, the courtesans to whom they went while on sabbaticals to the cities, the slave girls and women upon whom that first caste rested and to whom in certain cases it doubtless owed the very fact of its virginity –
> (Faulkner, *Absalom, Absalom!* 109)

America's racial representations were built on reinventions of European racial representations where *blackness* was a sign of lasciviousness and excess. When Europeans enslaved Africans, blackness came to mean not only easy sexuality but laziness, bestiality, savagery and violence, all of which had to be contained. The colonial encounter, the plantation and Jim Crow laws in turn *created* race as an immutable state of being. As Henry Louis Gates reminds us, "race" is a metaphor, not "an objective term of classification:"

> Race has become a trope of ultimate, irreducible difference between cultures, linguistic groups, or adherents of specific belief systems which – more often than not – also have fundamentally opposed economic interests. Race is the ultimate trope of difference because it is so very arbitrary in its application.
> (Gates, *"Race," Writing* 5)

4

White culture tried to place Africans at the losing end of every scale upon which they measured themselves. The Enlightenment chain of being ranged from the "lowliest Hottentot" up to Newton and Milton (ibid. 8). Race is one category of definition: class and gender also figure centrally in American hierarchies. Class and gender, too, get treated as fixed situations. Yet all three are fluid. Teresa de Lauretis remarks "gender represents not an individual but a relation, and a social relation" (2–3). An individual can occupy more than one class position at a time, more than one race (as mulattoes do) and more than one gender. As I discuss in detail later, Harriet Beecher Stowe was seen at various times as both ladylike and "common," both female and male, depending on the politics of the beholder. Race, class and gender can be "understood as historically contingent and relational:" cut loose from their short moorings as "foundational concepts," race, class and gender become dynamic categories of analysis (Ferguson, "Juggling" 163). I will not claim to deal with them equally in this book; *class* often lurks masked inside *gender* and *race*.[2] The cultivated mulatta Cassy and the barely literate Tom in *Uncle Tom's Cabin* are both defined by race, both black, both slaves, yet Tom calls Cassy "Missis" and understands her as being of a different class than himself. And in *Oroonoko*, Aphra Behn distinguishes between "the royal slave" Prince Oroonoko and the ordinary field hands in Surinam, though, in the end, all are subject to white rule.

The ideology of slavery was based on an ever-refining set of hierarchies demonstrating the radical difference between black and white bodies. The black female body often stands for sexuality, based on old understandings of African "lust" and eighteenth- and nineteenth-century racialist physiognomy which held, among other things, that black women were lascivious because they had more highly developed sexual organs than whites (Sander Gilman 231–32). A black woman called Sarah Bateman, "the Hottentot Venus," was depicted naked in many illustrations and "exhibited" in Europe from 1810–1815, displaying her enormous breasts, buttocks and genitalia (ibid. 235). Engravings of her show the grotesque body objectified, its orifices evident, its protuberances vital. The white world drew the black woman's body as excessive and flagrantly sexual, quite different from the emerging ideology of purity and modesty which defined the white woman's body.

The trouble with the opposition of classical *white* body and grotesque *black* body is that they are, in fact, interdependent. Blacks in a slave society were powerless and marginal yet the whites who owned them built their culture around *not* being black.[3] The stories they subscribed to about the meaning of black skin (or "black blood," since hue was not always a reliable indicator of racial definition) shaped their construction of what whiteness meant. The white world had to be vigilant and creative, constantly reinventing racial categories and redrawing racial boundaries. Offspring of white fathers and slave mothers, (officially "black"), the abolition movement, Emancipation and the liberalisation of race laws demonstrated the precariousness of the proclaimed absolutes of race and class. Conservative whites insisted that blackness was low and therefore antithetical to the "civilization," morality and elevation represented by whiteness, yet the fascination betrayed with every nuance associated with "the African" and the many ways to slip "down," speaks to the instability of the hierarchy:

> A recurrent pattern emerges: the "top" attempts to reject and eliminate the "bottom" for reasons of prestige and status, only to discover, not only that it is in some way frequently dependent upon that low-Other . . . but also that the top *includes* that low symbolically, as a primary eroticized constituent of its own fantasy life.
>
> (Stallybrass and White 5)

Race, class, sexuality and gender are divided into opposing extremes; it is no wonder that women were closely concerned with these hierarchies – they were imprisoned in them. White women in particular, because until comparatively recently they had greater access than blacks to literacy and publishing, addressed these representations in their writing. Not that black women ignored them. From Phyllis Wheatley's poems, published in 1773, and Harriet E. Wilson's novel, *Our Nig*, published in 1859, to slave narratives, to the feminist work of Anna Julia Cooper and Ida B. Wells, to writers and critics like Hazel Carby, June Jordan and Toni Morrison, to name but a very few, black women confront the dominant culture's representations of them, insisting on dignity and autonomy, interrogating stereotypes, challenging the categorizations which had oppressed them. Henry Louis Gates says, "We black people tried to write ourselves out of slavery, a slavery even more profound than mere physical bondage" (Gates, *"Race," Writing* 12).

We white women have also tried to write ourselves out of a kind of slavery – and sometimes tried to write black slaves out of slavery

as well.[4] We have also, on occasion, tried to solidify our position at
the top of that lonely pedestal, designated work of art of our
culture. I investigate the ways white women write about race in this
book because I am interested in the resistance of writers at once
part of the ruling elite – and marginalized. As white, they were
instantly privileged; as women, they were often silenced. I have
chosen to focus in this study on texts by white women, mostly from
the nineteenth century with some from the first half of the twentieth, for several reasons. One, because white women's books –
Uncle Tom's Cabin, Gone With the Wind, and many in between – have
been elaborators and transmitters of many of the most powerful
representations of blacks in western culture. And because the
debate over slavery, and later the debate over segregation, has been
argued by men publicly, in government, in speeches, but as often
(and perhaps with more power) by women in published appeals
and in fiction. Women were officially limited to fiction reflecting
"feminine" concerns, like the home and the family; it was deemed
inappropriate for them to take on central political (or religious or
even social) issues. True to the "classical" body that represented
the lady, silence, especially on political questions, implied goodness. The Elizabethan attitude Stallybrass describes flourished
amongst American and British Victorians: "The signs of the 'harlot'
are her linguistic 'fullness' and her frequenting of public space"
(Stallybrass 127). Therefore many women writers developed a
strategy of making fiction out of and about their private space
which none the less engaged the vital issues of their world. Their
books sold and their influence was enormous. Perhaps *Uncle Tom's
Cabin* did not make the "great war" as Lincoln says in the apocry-
phal story, but it did offer representations of the South and of blacks
there which ran counter to the dominant assumptions of both South
and North. That novel had a power that all of Calhoun's or Sum-
ner's speeches on Capitol Hill could not match. *Uncle Tom* ignited
a firestorm of responses and counter-responses, not entirely but
largely by women; after the Civil War, a revisionist cartload of
diaries reinventing the Old South as Eden and slavery as virtuous,
answered *Uncle Tom's Cabin* anew. In the twentieth century,
women still talk back to it: Margaret Mitchell saw *Gone With the
Wind* as a retort to Stowe while Toni Morrison's *Beloved* responds
to and revises Stowe. Controlling the representation means controlling the culture: if blacks are the ignorant, over-sexed savages
of pro-slavery literature, then laws must be made to keep them

separate from the whites they might harm – or seduce. If they are Christlike, loving, innocent souls, they must be educated and brought along slowly to citizenship; and if they are intelligent, resourceful, mature beings, then they must be granted the full rights of citizenship. Representation is intimately involved with power.

In *Playing in the Dark*, Toni Morrison says: "The scholarship that looks into the mind, imagination and behavior of slaves is valuable. But equally valuable is a serious intellectual effort to see what racial ideology does to the mind, imagination and behavior of masters" (11–12). Or mistresses. I mean this book to be an exploration, though not, of course, a comprehensive one, of the ways white women write about race. I start with Aphra Behn's *Oroonoko*, a text which stands at the beginning of white women's confrontations with race in British America. Then I move ahead to *Uncle Tom's Cabin*, the seminal, even if not the first, American text on race, considering how Harriet Beecher Stowe constructs a gothic and oriental South to demonstrate the evils and temptations of slavery. Chapter 2 looks at Stowe's pro-slavery opponents, women whose writings engage Stowe on her own terms while attempting to wrest from her the moral high ground. Chapters 3 and 4 explore the British women – Frances Trollope, Frances Wright, Harriet Martineau and Frances Kemble – who embraced abolitionism, seeing so clearly its relation to breaking down class and gender barriers. In Chapter 5, I study the often overlooked American radical, Lydia Maria Child, an early advocate of race-mixing as a way to solve race problems. Finally, in Chapter 6, I look at twentieth-century writers such as Willa Cather, Margaret Mitchell and Lillian Smith who return to the past, to the racial decorum of the South, either to uphold segregation as their grandmothers did or to explore new racial and gender paradigms.

My choice of writers is necessarily selective and incomplete. Some, like Stowe and Mitchell, produced books so influential that they shaped national, even international, understandings of blackness, whiteness and the history of slavery in America. Others, like Trollope, Child, Louisa McCord and Lillian Smith, are not themselves so culturally central, yet they form part of a continuing dialogue about race in which women participated from the very beginning of the nation.[5] All the writers I study have in common a political, as well as a literary, purpose in writing, a sense of urgency over the question of race and its importance in the invention of the nation.

Finally, I am interested in white women's racial writings because white women themselves have such a stake in racial representations: the understanding of what it means to be a white woman in the United States, particularly in the South, is still largely predicated on what it means to be black. Stallybrass says the classical and the grotesque relate diacritically, each "formed by the redrawing of the boundaries of the other" (Stallybrass 124). The same is true of race. For women who challenged *ladyhood*, with all the aspects of the classical body that ladyhood implied, and the furnishings of class division, it was essential that blackness be shown to partake of that elevation, or that white women could move toward the position of blacks, or that "universal" female principles outweighed colour. For women like Frances Kemble, Harriet Martineau, Harriet Beecher Stowe, Lydia Maria Child and Lillian Smith, class was the determining factor in how the culture defined purity. But for women like Louisa McCord, Mary H. Eastman and Caroline Gilman, colour was absolute. They defined their position as elevated because they firmly believed that blackness was a *class*, carrying degradation, dirt, savagery, stupidity and vice within it like a virus. For both conservative and progressive women writers, class, race and gender become the categories through which the body is defined and controlled: who can dispose of women's bodies? Who controls them? The war over representations of race shapes the struggle for women's rights: feminism and abolitionism began as linked causes. Along the way they became divided and now, sometimes, divisive. Black feminists accuse white feminists of having parochial, white-centred views of women's struggle. White feminists have sometimes seen the fight against racism as a separate issue. But the very images of what a *woman* is in our culture have depended upon how we think about race, and what representations govern our assumptions. Uncle Tom and Jezebel and Aunt Jemima remain with us still in fiction and popular culture, and with them a tangle of invisible fetters impeding women – black and white.[6]

> *There's no racism without a language.*
> Jacques Derrida, "Racism's Last Word"

The black body in white America bears the marks both of desire and disgust. As "blackness" is invented (and reinvented) in the Old World's New World, it becomes invested with so many anxieties: pollution, violence, sexuality, primitivism. Or "blackness" is invested with romantic exaggerations: athleticism, childlikeness, maternal devotion, uncritical fidelity. Even before the first African slaves were pushed ashore at Jamestown in 1619 to help build the British American empire, Europeans had in place a number of (often competing) ideas on what black skin meant, especially when contrasted with white skin. Even before the sixteenth century, *black* denoted stain, evil, dirt. As Winthrop Jordan puts it, "No other color except white conveyed as much emotional impact" (Jordan 7).

British encounters with Africans fulfilled a set of already-constructed metaphors: colonisers polarized white and black as embodiments of good and evil, purity and pollution, virtue and sin, Christianity and paganism, God and the devil, angels and demons, virginity and vice, cleanliness and filth. *White* became more significant when an embodied *black* appeared in contrast. Removing African slaves to the Atlantic colonies proceeded from both fiscal expediency and a growing sense of racial superiority: white over black. The economics of the slave trade framed white encounters with Africans; the discourses of blackness reinforced the building of the "New World."

The knot of fictions surrounding blacks in the eyes of whites is overwhelmingly erotic. *Blackness* is loaded with sexuality. Early maps of Africa were illustrated by naked black men with huge genitalia. Sixteenth- and seventeenth-century travellers assumed a close biological relationship between Africans and apes, even that African women copulated with apes.[7] Even before Europeans journeyed in substantial numbers to Africa, the continent's association with heat implied licentiousness; Leo Africanus says that Africans "have great swarmes of Harlots among them whereupon a man may easily conjecture their manner of living" (quoted in Jordan 34). The anonymous *Golden Coast* of 1665 characterizes black men as "lustful and impudent, especially, when they come to hide their nakedness, (for a *Negroes* hiding his Members, their extraordinary greatness) is a token of their Lust" (ibid. 35). Europeans saw black women as sexually ravenous: they had "hot constitutions," they delighted in seducing white men, they showed no European "female modesty." Once slavery was firmly established in Britain's American colonies these attitudes settled into dogma. Black women were represented as willing sexual receptacles. In the poem *Jamaica* (1777), African women of every shade, "Samboe dark, and the Mulattoe brown/The Mestize fair, the well-limb'd Quaderoon" are all "well vers'd in Venus' school" and "To love each thought, to lust each nerve is strung" (ibid. 150). In Richard Ligon's *True and Exact History of the Island of Barbados* (1657), young black women disturbingly display their legs, backs and breasts, inclining the beholder to see this as, if not an invitation, at least provocation (16).

European insistence on African lust, wantonness and passion sprang from several cultural discourses explaining racial difference. One tradition held that black skin was a curse resulting from Ham's "looking upon the nakedness of his father", Noah. George Best's 1578 commentary explains blackness as an active breaking of a sexual taboo: Ham did not obey Noah's order to abstain from sex with his wife on board the ark and the child resulting from their union was "blacke and cursed" (Newman 147). If the origin of the "negro race" itself resulted from sexual transgression, it is no wonder that white representations of blacks were obsessed with sexuality. The British built and regulated slavery in the American colonies according to the assumption that black women were incorrigibly seductive and that black men inclined to rape, especially to rape white women. Colonial fears of slave rebellions were framed in sexual terms: it was assumed that slaves would revolt *in order to* rape the wives and daughters of their white masters (Jordan 150–54). Therefore, whites erected elaborate legal and social codes to regulate and control black bodies, both male and female, circumscribing sexual expression for the putative aggressors – black men – and their alleged intended victims – white women. Black men were enslaved, castrated, beaten, chained, hanged and burned. Black women were raped, separated from their children, abused and whipped. White women were not so much physically brutalized as hemmed in by rules of "virtue," "chastity," "purity" and "modesty." White men, committed to the creation of wealth and the spread of Christian civilization in the New World, feared outbreaks of "barbarism" or disorder. Indeed, such fears contributed to the urgency of colonization. By violence and by ideological imprisonment, black and white Americans in a slave society – and after Emancipation – were forced to conform to a racial decorum that insisted that black and white were opposite, as different as night and day.

"Race is a product of history, not of nature" (Fields 152). "Race" is also a product of literary texts. Alongside the history of British involvement in Africa, the slave trade, and the plantations of the Caribbean and the Southern states, fiction about race emerged. And women were involved from the beginning. Aphra Behn's novella

Oroonoko (1688) was the first important English fiction dealing with race in the "New World," "a crucial early text in the sentimental antislavery tradition that grew steadily throughout the eighteenth century" (Laura Brown 42). It is not hard to see the relationship between Behn's story of the African prince Oroonoko, cruelly enslaved and ready to die for his freedom, and later important works of the abolitionist movement, such as *Uncle Tom's Cabin*.[8]

Behn suffered many of the same attacks on her character that Stowe did a century and a half later. Because she did not confine herself to officially apolitical, "feminine" subjects, Stowe was accused of being vulgar, unladylike, irreligious and, most devastatingly, of being sexually attracted to black men (see Chapter 1 below). Because she wrote for money, Behn was called a prostitute, "revealing" herself through her writing, displaying her opinions as a writer as a whore displays her body. Pope, in his "Epistle to Augustus," says nastily, "The stage how loosely does Astraea tread/Who safely puts all characters to bed." She was satirized in a 1676 poem that brands her a whore and refers to female genitalia as a "black Ace" (Ferguson, "Whose Dominion" 9).[9]

The conjunction of blackness and female sexuality defines an important moment: cultural myths of African lasciviousness and cultural myths of matching female lust were given powerful play both in Behn's text and her life. Behn herself insists on her closeness to the African prince in *Oroonoko*, a titillating juxtaposition that evokes *Othello*. Indeed, when Thomas Southerne adapted *Oroonoko* for the stage in 1695, he cashed in on the implication by making Imoinda *white*. Gossip persisted that the model for Oroonoko was Behn's lover when she visited the then-English colony of Surinam some time in 1663–64.[10] The "History of the Life and Memoirs" of Aphra Behn, "Written by One of the Fair Sex" (possibly Behn herself) denied the rumours: "there was no Affair between that Prince and Astraea, but what the whole Plantation were witnesses of" (Behn, *All the Histories* 3).

None the less, Behn's career was dogged with sexual innuendo, marking the beginning of the long association in conservative minds with abolitionism and transgressive sexual ideologies such as "free love," women's rights, divorce and egalitarianism. I want to return to the issues raised by women writing about race in general and slavery in particular later on. But first I shall consider the story of *Oroonoko* and what it has to say about blackness in British America.

Oroonoko embodies the ambivalence white writers betray when representing black heroes. He is African but better than ordinary Africans, "adorn'd with a native beauty, so transcending all those of his gloomy race, that he struck an awe and reverence, even into those that knew not his quality" (*Oroonoko* 32). His features are attractive in European eyes, which is to say they *are* European: his nose is "Roman, instead of African" and his mouth is "far from those great turn'd lips, which are so natural to the rest of the Negroes" (33). Imoinda, his beloved, appears equally pleasing to the western gaze, "the beautiful black Venus to our young Mars" (34). The appropriation of western classical terms to describe Africans becomes standard for those insisting on the nobility of the savage. In M. R. Ridley's 1958 Arden *Othello*, he hastens to distinguish the hero from what "a great many people" think of as "a 'nigger,' the woolly hair, thick lips, round skull, blunt features, and burnt-cork blackness of the traditional nigger minstrel" (Ridley li, quoted in Newman 143). Othello is not the "veritable negro" that Coleridge recoiled from, certain that "this beautiful Venetian girl" could not love a real African, that is, a dark man.[11] Ridley goes on to say,

> One of the finest heads I have ever seen on any human being was that of a negro conductor on an American Pullman car. He had lips slightly thicker than an ordinary European's, and he had somewhat curly hair; for the rest he had a long head, a magnificent forehead, a keenly chiselled nose. . . . He was coal black, but he might have sat to a sculptor for a statue of Caesar.

The rhetoric of 1688 and that of 1958 seem very close: the negro conductor provides proof for Ridley of occasional African superiority, rising above the ordinary "nigger." The focus is on the lips, nose and hair as the features which display the African's otherness. It is no accident that Iago calls Othello "thick lips." Identifying Oroonoko and the Pullman conductor with "European" traits is meant as a compliment; connecting them to a western model of leadership and grandeur is meant as a compliment as well: Oroonoko's white owner renames him "Caesar," following a practice of assigning blacks Roman and Greek names that continued until after Emancipation. Later abolitionist writers gained their white audience's sympathy by depicting slaves who looked very white; indeed, the genre of "Tragic Mulatto" fiction depends on heroes and heroines with European features, light skin and straight hair, yet who are legally black. Emmeline, Cassy, Eliza and George in *Uncle Tom's Cabin* are slaves but can "pass" for white. Clearly the white reader identifies with these sensitive, cultivated people whose bodies are at others' disposal; this works particularly powerfully when a woman slave finds herself sexually menaced by a white man. Uncle Tom himself provides a notable exception to the European face – he *is* a "veritable negro," and one of Stowe's most important political gestures identifies him, black and African-featured, with both Victorian motherhood and the white Christ.

Oroonoko and Imoinda are quite dark, "ebony," and so combine European "refinement" of face with African skin; they bear both the European signs of beauty and the European signs of the erotic. *Othello* displays some of the same ambivalence: the hero's blackness proceeds from British understanding of Africans as savages, lascivious and "dirty," as well as noble, sexually-exciting beings that an upper-class Venetian like Desdemona *could* fall in love with. As Ferguson points out, there emerged in the seventeenth century a "minority" discourse that saw beauty in blackness, paralleling "an emergent cultural narrative of proto-feminist protest against the subordinate role prescribed for women" ("Whose Dominion" 6). Behn's portrayal of Oroonoko as princely, attractive, cultivated and yet always Other, provides a counter-story to African pollution and bestiality.

Behn goes to great lengths to assert Oroonoko's and Imoinda's virtues, European virtues as well as virtue beyond what Europeans practise. Oroonoko feels much proper princely outrage at the execution of Charles I, and is, for many critics, identified with the Stuarts himself.[12] He is "well-bred" and "civil," obviously comprehendible as a *gentleman* by his British audience. He falls in love as a European should, languishing like a follower of Petrarch over Imoinda and remaining faithful to her. Imoinda is also a pattern of goodness, displaying the official European female morality – modesty, chastity, beauty, grace and obedience – as well as an admired willingness to die at her husband's hand. In this, she resembles Desdemona, an identification amplified in Southerne's adaptation. Imoinda is, as Ferguson points out, an "amalgam of European ideals of wifely subservience and European fantasies about wives of oriental despots" ("Whose Dominion" 28).

Complicating Oroonoko and Imoinda's intersection with European ideals of princeliness, beauty, goodness and love are the discourses of the erotic and the "oriental" as understood by British culture at the time. Oroonoko has many western courtly qualities, but he comes from a kingdom in Africa ruled by a tyrant who keeps a harem. The association of unlicensed sexuality with "eastern" cultures includes the identification of dark skin with lust central to European views of Africans; Africa, like the near east and the far east, was considered "oriental," and while in the late seventeenth century there was not yet a full-blown literature of orientalism, a set of discourses defining Arabs, Africans and Asians as excessively sexual had already emerged. As the British empire expanded both westward and eastward, stories of oriental sexuality burgeoned, both as justification for missionary Christianity and as fodder for the fascination with the Other. Edward Said has analysed the stories of oriental sexuality, showing how the Orient is represented by a pervasive, pliant, mysterious and dark feminine: the woman in the harem. Said points out that Flaubert makes "an almost uniform association between the Orient and sex" (Said, *Orientalism* 188). But Flaubert was hardly the first to do so – a kingdom of the erotic, with flexible geographical boundaries, was in place two hundred years before Flaubert had his encounter with the Egyptian courtesan (ibid. 6).

Both Coramantien, Oroonoko's country, and Surinam are erotic, oriental landscapes.[13] Coramantien is figured by the harem where Imoinda becomes the object of "the dalliance of the King" and must learn "all those wanton arts of love" (*Oroonoko* 42–43). In Surinam, Imoinda has escaped being owned by the impotent king only to be owned by the white man Trefry who could rape her with impunity. Oroonoko, in Africa a slave owner himself, points out that Trefry could "oblige her to yield" (ibid. 66). Her "modesty and weeping" overcome Trefry's lust, proving his essential decency, but Behn's point is made: slavery, either of powerless women in an African harem or on a British plantation, encourages a climate of sexual abuse. Imoinda is a body in danger whether in Africa or in Surinam. Slavery exists in all three cultures in the novel, European, African and Caribbean, the difference being who, what "race," is enslaved; perhaps Behn wants to stress that women are subordinated no matter where they find themselves, no matter what colour their skin.

The conjunction of Europeans, Africans and the native Carib Indians creates both dangerous and pleasurable possibilities, implying various erotic combinations in a landscape of "eternal spring" with opulent plant life: "groves of oranges, lemons, citrons, figs, nutmegs and noble aromaticks . . . flowers of different kinds, some . . . all white, some purple, some blue, some yellow" and valuable woods and beautiful birds (ibid. 72). The different colours of the flowers, various fruits, woods and fauna echo the different skin tones and nationalities in Surinam, as well as the different "products" of the empire feeding demand in a growing consumer society.[14] The potential and actual sexual encounters include Imoinda and all the young slaves "undone in love" with her, Imoinda and Trefry, the deputy governor and his Carib mistress, the narrator and a Carib and the narrator and Oroonoko. Imoinda and Oroonoko's official marriage (as Caesar and Clemene, the western names underlining their intersection with European fictions) is the certified and consummated romance of the story, but the miscegenic subtext of the white deputy governor and his native lover, and the erotic subtext of the (fatherless and therefore "masterless") narrator's encounters with people of colour, imagine Surinam as a world of fluid racial and sexual possibilities. The narrator, (over) dressed in European clothes, none the less has a body fascinating to the Caribs who want to touch European faces, breasts and arms, to take up petticoats and look (ibid. 78). The narrator singles out one young man in particular, a prophet, who is "a youth of about sixteen years old, as handsom as nature could make a man," who kisses her after he sees her brother kiss his wife (ibid. 79). But the most important potential sexual relationship is between the narrator and Oroonoko, white woman and black man, the combination most fraught with European racial projections and taboos. Imoinda is relegated to a passive background for much of the story as the narrator constructs the character of the "royal slave" and her intimate friendship with him. She is so taken with him that she promises him (with small chance of delivering on it) freedom when the governor arrives, and tells him stories about the Romans (talking of the white Caesar to the black Caesar) and other "great men" (she tells Imoinda about nuns and sermonizes for "the true God"). Yet as a white person, she is also implicated in keeping Oroonoko a slave; she boasts that Oroonoko calls her his "great mistress" (a double-edged use of "mistress"), insisting on her influence with him.

But alongside this suggestive friendship exists the suspicion that Oroonoko is dangerous. The narrator says she does not much trust him (ibid. 71). Fear of black insurrection and rape compromises their relationship:

> You must know, that when the news was brought on Monday morning, that Caesar had betaken himself to the woods, and carry'd with him all the Negroes, we were possess'd with extreme fear, which no persuasions could dissipate, that he would secure himself till night, and then, that he would come down and cut all our throats. This apprehension made all the females of us fly.
>
> (Behn, *Oroonoko* 89–90)

The narrator believes in her power of influence over her friend, the house-trained African prince Caesar, yet fears ravishment from the rebel Oroonoko. This contradictory set of white responses to blackness uneasily informed the ideology of slaveholding in British America. Ambivalence flourished on all sides; even those most committed to ending black slavery were not free of anxieties over black violence and sexuality. Behn's story rehearses these contradictions so overtly that it is hard to claim *Oroonoko* wholeheartedly for the canon of abolitionist texts. Yet anxieties over blackness and ambivalence over slavery's part in furnishing the new middle class with the goods of the colonies (sugar, feathers, fruit) are still found in later works, especially by women. Harriet Beecher Stowe and Lydia Maria Child frequently privileged the plight of the European-looking slave over that of the African-looking slave; Frances Trollope and Frances Kemble analysed colour prejudice as a class problem yet were still committed to a set of genteel values and standards that tended to exclude blacks. Certainly, much of Behn's sympathy for Oroonoko depends on his status as a *prince*: she is less sanguine about emancipation for field hands. Behn finds herself both a critic of slavery and a servant of the empire it funds. As Ferguson puts it, Behn is a "female author oscillating among multiple subject positions and between complicity with and critique of the emergent institution of New World slavery" ("Whose Dominion" 11).

This raises questions of white women writers' paradoxical collaboration with and resistance to slavery. *Oroonoko* demonstrates that class and race are not adequate as categories through which to read writing about slavery: gender is also central. Black men and women and white women all experienced powerlessness in a slave society in some similar, and some quite different ways. Behn illustrates this when she says in the "Epistle Dedicatory" for *Oroonoko* that in Surinam "I had none above me in that country;" then in the next breath, "yet I wanted power to preserve this great man" (Behn,

17

Oroonoko 25). She boasts of her influence with the African prince yet fears him as a rebellious black slave and potential rapist. Oroonoko himself is feminized; he can sit about story-telling with the white women but he cannot go drinking with the white men: "he liked the company of us women much above the men" (ibid. 69). As the narrator navigates between poles of power (as white, as author) and powerlessness (as a woman, as a protester), Oroonoko also veers between subject positions as masculine, relating tales of his military prowess in Africa, killing tigers, and feminine, engaging in conversation with ladies, and, of course, having no power over his own body.

These oscillations between opposing states and social positions performed by the narrator and Oroonoko bring the two of them together. Ferguson sees in Behn's self-conscious (though partial) identification of the plight of African slaves with the plight of white women as creating a kind of miscegenic realm where the text of *Oroonoko* is

> a safe sex substitute for the potentially mutinous, economically valuable black slave child Oroonoko might have had with Imoinda – or indeed with Aphra Behn had she given physical rather than verbal 'satisfaction,' playing Tamora, as it were, to Oroonoko's Aaron and thereby activating long-standing English anxieties about the 'genetic' strength of blackness, since babies born of mixed unions were thought inevitably to follow the darker and 'lower' hue.
>
> (Ferguson, "Whose Dominion" 32)

Even though the narrator and Oroonoko do not produce the dangerous child they might have, the potential has been uttered; the text's engagement with its subject, the white woman narrator's engagement with the black man Oroonoko, trouble the binary of white over black in place since before the British slave trade. In the midst of this "emergent market in which books and bodies and bodily ornaments all jostled as commodities," Ferguson focuses on "the 'other' black slave in the story," Imoinda, whose body she sees as being even more dangerous than Oroonoko's to white hegemony (ibid. 23, 28, 33). While this is a judicious recovery of Imoinda's centrality to the story, I think that the kind of threat posed by a black woman, despite her attractiveness to white men, despite her possible bearing of dark children, in a white-run society is not as great as the threat posed by a black man. Ferguson reads Imoinda's

18

agency in the text astutely: Imoinda is the only person to wound the representative of white power, the deputy governor (with an arrow), while Oroonoko succumbs to "European codes of masculine honor and Petrarchan romance" when he murders her and their unborn child (ibid. 33). None the less, the erotic charge between Oroonoko and Imoinda's potential rival, the narrator, could have a more disruptive result than the offspring of the mostly-passive oriental heroine Imoinda.

While the discourses of taboo governing miscegenation – like laws against miscegenation – were still somewhat fluid in the seventeenth century, racial purity not yet being the full-blown obsession it became in the slave South, enforcement of laws was mostly aimed at white women who slept with black men for, as one Maryland law of 1681 put it, "the Satisfaccion of theire Lascivious and Lustfull desires" (Jordan 79). The threat of pollution for white women who sleep with black men appeared greater than for white men with black women. For a white woman to have a miscegenic affair endangered the transmission of property; she also forfeited her place within the discourse of "pure" white female bodies, though, as Bertram Wyatt-Brown points out, most women who had relationships with black men were of low social standing (314– 18).[15] So the eroticized narrative, closely associating the white female writer with her black male hero, enters the realm of miscegenation, bearing the capacity to retell *Othello*. But the narrator does not act Desdemona's part (though, as Ferguson points out, Southerne's adaptation of *Oroonoko* for the stage explicitly pushes the plot closer to *Othello* by making Imoinda white, raising implicit connections between Behn and Imoinda). Instead, "the white woman's book is born, quite starkly, from a self-willed (albeit partial) censoring of her own sexuality and from the death and suffering of black persons, one of them pregnant" (Ferguson, "Whose Dominion" 33). The text becomes the resistant, protesting product of a kind of miscegenation after all: it would seem that those conservative critics who accused white women authors such as Behn or Stowe or Kemble or Wright of sexual attraction to blacks had a point. Behn's story, as well as her anti-slavery sensibility, proceed from the tragic deaths of her black hero and black heroine; Stowe's novel, and her politics, are shaped by Eliza's suffering, Cassy's rage and Tom's martyrdom. The white woman writing about race is necessarily a double agent, both acting as "mistress" in controlling her characters and her plot, and identifying with them. The

relationship between the black and the feminine does not escape
the paradigm of Othello and Desdemona or the narrator of
Oroonoko and Oroonoko: "femininity is not opposed to blackness
and monstrosity, as white is to black, but identified with the
monstrous, an identification that makes miscegenation doubly
fearful" (Newman 145). The white woman writer amplifies this
sense of the *unnatural* in her dealings with blacks. If a woman
writer was seen in some quarters as a prostitute, displaying
herself for her male patrons, then a woman writer who involves
herself with the issue of race becomes doubly tainted. She commits literary miscegenation.

> *Among them the casual Yankees and the poor whites and even the
> Southerners who had lived for a while in the North, who believed
> aloud that it was an anonymous negro crime committed not by a
> negro but by Negro and who knew, believed, and hoped that she
> had been ravished too: at least once before her throat was cut and
> at least once afterward.*
>
> William Faulkner, *Light in August*

Oroonoko ends the way so many stories about Africans in
America end: with a violent death, with a lynching.[16] When
Oroonoko rebels against white authority, he casts off his European
name, Caesar, asserting his position as a prince and his African
identity: "Oroonoko scorns to live with the indignity that was put
on Caesar" (Behn, *Oroonoko* 91). As part of his defiance, he kills
Imoinda to protect her, he thinks, from the "nasty lusts" of his white
enemies, and to keep his child from being born into bondage, a
story acted out over and over again in the history of slavery and
rehearsed most recently in Toni Morrison's *Beloved*. Oroonoko cuts
Imoinda's throat and then decapitates her, prefiguring the dis-
memberment he will begin to inflict on himself, and which will be
finished by his white captors.

Oroonoko's lynching is distressingly familiar to anyone who
knows accounts of the executions of black men, both legal and
vigilante, in the United States from the seventeenth century to the
1960s:

> the executioner came, and first cut off his members, and threw
> them into the fire; after that, with an ill-favour'd knife, they cut
> off his ears and his nose, and burned them . . . then they hacked
> off one of his arms, and still he bore up, and held his pipe; but
> at the cutting off the other arm, his head sunk, and his pipe

dropt and he gave up the ghost, without a groan or a reproach. My mother and sister were by him all the while, but not suffer'd to save him; so rude and wild were the rabble.

(Behn, *Oroonoko* 98–99)

Oroonoko's lynching becomes a public occasion, community violence serving to cleanse the community. In the southern colonies during the seventeenth and eighteenth centuries, the severing of an ear, a hand or a foot was legally prescribed for minor offences such as talking back to a white person or running away (Jordan 154ff.). Some colonial legislatures mandated castration as punishment for running away or striking a white person. Social control was equated with control of the black body. By the middle of the eighteenth century, most of these *legal* tortures had been done away with. But their freelance application never died out. The lynching of Claud Neal in Marianna, Florida in 1934 followed a common pattern. The lynch mob cut off his penis and his testicles, burned and stabbed him, and cut off his fingers (for souvenirs). He surprised the mob by asking calmly for a cigarette and died without protest (McGovern 79–84). The similarities between Oroonoko's death, quietly smoking his pipe while a white mob cuts him into pieces, and Neal's death, are striking, even though Neal was lynched for the rape and murder of a white girl and Oroonoko was executed for rebellion. In the end the root causes are the same: both black men transgressed community codes.[17] And both had to be reduced to fragments because the terrors of the black male body – particularly the sexual terrors – must be contained.

White culture divides black bodies, male and female, into useful – or dangerous – parts. Imoinda is a collection of beautiful carved skin and a pretty face, but she also possesses sexual organs and a womb. Oroonoko worries about her as something of *his* that might be stolen or defiled, a body to be raped and the carrier of a child to be enslaved, and so he kills her, disposing of his possession himself. His own body rebels against white authority, a body which might itself rape white women, and so he is lynched and quartered, "a mangled king" (Behn, *Oroonoko* 99). While that image obviously connects him to the beheaded Charles I, it is also a paradigmatic picture of the black body tamed, the result of violent social control that lasted in the former plantation colonies until just a few years ago. *Oroonoko* may seem far removed from the world of race in the United States, and Aphra Behn might not have met with the approval of such stern moralists as Harriet Beecher Stowe, Frances

Trollope or Lydia Maria Child, yet Behn's novella stands at the beginning of a powerful literary and social tradition. Behn's understanding of blackness in a British America that insisted on seeing itself as white, a culture prepared to use violence to enforce its definitions of purity, informs the reading of later racial texts. *Oroonoko* is not abolitionist fiction in the sense that *Uncle Tom's Cabin* is, but it gives us a pattern of representations, of blackness, in the New World. Representations of blackness still govern responses to blackness in America. Blacks still fight white assumptions of their violence: young black men are the designated criminals of this culture; and blacks still suffer under white assumptions about their sexuality: Anita Hill's verbal whipping by the white men on the Senate Judiciary Committee was a graphic illustration of how the black woman as whore has not gone with the wind in this culture.[18] America lives still with its martyred Oroonokos and Uncle Toms, its Imoindas, its Jezebels, its Aunt Jemimas. They are the ghosts of a crippling past, and only by naming them can we exorcize them.

1

UNCLE TOM'S CABIN
An authentic ghost story

> *After all, let a man take what pains he may to hush it down, a*
> *human soul is an awful ghostly, unquiet possession for a bad man*
> *to have.*
>
> Harriet Beecher Stowe, *Uncle Tom's Cabin*

Uncle Tom's Cabin (1851) is a novel of sexual crises. It is also a novel
of religious, social, economic and ethical crises galvanized by the
overwhelming issue of race, a warning that slavery not only oppressed blacks but degraded whites, endangering the cherished
ideal of participatory democracy that both inspired and eluded
nineteenth-century Americans. Harriet Beecher Stowe said that the
worst of slavery was "its outrage upon the family" (*Key* 257). For
the white family, the outrage lay in slaveholding men committing
adultery with their female slaves, available and officially submissive. Slavery made sin easy. For the black family, the outrage
was manifested in the torture, humiliation and violation of the
slaves' minds and bodies. Children were separated from their
mothers, black men and women were denied sanctified marriage,
husbands were sold away from wives, women were kept as concubines or used as breeders.

The *sub rosa* truth, the skeleton in the South's closet, was that the
black family and the white family were often the *same* family;
slavery created criminal situations where the powerful members
of the family betrayed the weak. Two definitions of family com-
peted for dominance: the sentimental, bourgeois ideal of the father,
mother and children in a discrete domestic package, and the
broader, patriarchal, almost Biblical sense of a household.[1] Engels
reminds us that *family* refers etymologically to ownership, not
kinship; Southern planters spoke of wives, children, land and
slaves as their "family" or "household." Abolitionists rejected this

proprietorial, hierarchical notion of family for the more compact and, as they saw it, more egalitarian domestic version. As Angelina Grimké indignantly demands, "But do the *fathers of the South ever sell their daughters?*" (6, her emphasis). Stowe answers yes, and their sons, too. The slave's body is not her or his own: the slave's sexuality, like the slave's ability to work, is just another commodity.

To Stowe, slavery produces sexual anarchy. White men evade moral responsibility to women: in *Uncle Tom's Cabin*, none of the mulatta Cassy's owners, fathers of her children, would even consider marrying her: it would be illegal, anyway. In Stowe's second abolitionist novel, *Dred* (1856), the mulatta Cora Gordon's white brother Tom threatens her with rape. Not only does slavery attack women, it attacks the maternal. Where white men sexually enslave women, the unexamined elevation of motherhood, to which nineteenth-century middle-class culture was committed, is impossible: "Under these arrangements, the customary lexis of sexuality, including 'reproduction,' 'motherhood,' 'pleasure,' and 'desire' are thrown into unrelieved crisis" (Spillers, "Mama's Baby" 76).[2] Uncle Tom who, as Stowe says of Jesus, has "more of the purely feminine element in him than any other man," falls victim to this antimaternalism (Stowe, *Religious Studies* 36). Leslie Fiedler sees him as the central sufferer of the novel, the "heroine" in the violent clutches of the ravisher: "We do not remember the turncoat Puritan Legree squeezing the virginal breast of Emmeline, eyeing her lustfully; he is frozen forever... at his purest moment of passion, himself the slave of his need to destroy the Christian slave Tom" (Fiedler, *Love and Death* 265–66).

Legree acts "the archetypal seducer, ready for the final violation" of Tom in a scene that represents the power relations of the slave South in gendered terms: masculine aggression and power over feminine victimization and self-sacrifice. I would argue that Tom's subjugation should be read as part of a general pattern that includes Cassy and Emmeline: they suffer the slave South's all-out assault on the feminine and the maternal. The "violation" of Tom, the "outrage" threatening Emmeline, Cassy's history of abuse, as well as the menace directed at Eliza, and George Harris' pain over his sister's sale as "fancy goods" in the New Orleans slave market, constitute a sexual context which, in Stowe's eyes, reduces women's humanity. The slave South denies the sacredness of the maternal hearthside altar (while paying elaborate and, to Stowe, unconvincing, lip service to a useless idol, the white woman on the

24

pedestal): the slave South is therefore an assault on the central moral institution of the nation – the female-centred family.

George Eliot proclaimed "Mrs Stowe has *invented* the negro novel," that is, she exploited the rich thematic possibilities of the *"conflict* of *races"* (571–73). Fiedler echoes this, saying Stowe "invented American blacks for the imagination of the whole world" (Fiedler, *Inadvertent Epic* 26). It is troubling that a white novelist should be credited with creating blacks for fiction; where is the "negro" in the negro novel? Displaced. Stowe constructed a white-generated, white-directed vision of black slavery meant to ignite white political change. She was not the first white writer to become notorious using the "conflict of races" in fiction; Aphra Behn did it a hundred and sixty-odd years earlier, and Frances Trollope did it sixteen years earlier. Others such as Richard Hildreth, John Pendleton Kennedy, Harriet Martineau, Caroline Gilman, Lydia Maria Child and J. H. Ingraham, produced fiction representing various sides of the race issue before *Uncle Tom's Cabin*.[3] And black writers like Frederick Douglass and Mary Prince recounted stories of black struggle. But Stowe was fortunate in her moment: the Fugitive Slave Law had been passed in 1850, the Free Soil movement was loudly questioning the future of the United States as a slaveholding nation and the Nullification furor – the attempt by slave states to void federal legislation – was kicking up again. Though black and white abolitionists were publishing in Britain and America, *Uncle Tom's Cabin*, a work its author saw as conciliatory, grabbed the lion's share of publicity. Here is a salient irony in the battle over racial representation: that a novel by a white woman of colonizationist leanings could be said to "invent" the African American as a fictional subject.

This can be looked at another way. Toni Morrison makes the point that an "invented Africa" and "invented Africans" lie at the root of American nation-building; we have been shaped "by the four-hundred-year-old presence of, first, Africans and then African-Americans" (Morrison, *Playing in the Dark* 4–5). So it would have to be a white writer creating the "negro novel" just as white colonisers created "blackness" for the imagination of power. Therefore, arguing back again, George Eliot was quite right – Stowe distilled a set of racial constructions for the world and exploited them.

Stowe also "invented" the slave South, the ambivalent South which has fuelled American popular culture and driven America's sense of its regions ever since. Stowe's South combines an Edenic landscape with infernal immorality; her South is at once seductive, idyllic, tormented and vicious. Of course, *Uncle Tom's Cabin* was not the first novel ever to depict the South in such contradictory language: Frances Trollope's *Jonathan Jefferson Whitlaw*, published in 1836, raises images of both heaven and hell, as does Frances Kemble's Georgia journal of 1838–39 (see Chapters 3 and 4). Indeed, early European accounts of southern colonies from Virginia to Guiana toy with theological imagery crossed with anxiety over what passions such warm climates might enkindle in their inhabitants. In *Oroonoko*, Behn compares Surinam to Eden when she likens the Carib Indians to "our first parents before the fall" (then describes the violent episodes of Oroonoko's slavery and lynching in the flower-filled "paradise"). In *Uncle Tom*, Stowe manipulates older literary and popular discourses and characters at a moment when the novel-reading world was fascinated with Southern slavery to create the South as American Other. We still see the vestiges of, responses to, revisions of and homages to that South in the fiction of William Faulkner, Eudora Welty, Ralph Ellison, Erskine Caldwell, Charles Chesnutt, Flannery O'Connor, Carson McCullers, Alice Walker, Cormac McCarthy and Toni Morrison, a realm of anarchic eroticism, grotesquely shot through with violence: in other words, the "Southern gothic."[4]

In Stowe's fiction, the South is populated by insistent, clamorous bodies who, like poltergeists, are more felt than seen. The masses of slaves are as "invisible" as ghosts compared to the dominant, visible whites who own them. It is as if Stowe is determined to utter the spell that will force these shades into visibility, to assert their physical being. Slave bodies are not single and sacrosanct, like white bodies; they are multiple and expendable. But Stowe defies their official subterranean status and focuses on the harms done to their bodies as well as to their minds.

Southerners bought slaves, worked them, housed them, fed them, slept with them, chained them, beat them and sometimes killed them. The slave is "historically, North America's most *coveted* body, that is, the *captivated* man/woman-child who fulfills a variety of functions at the master's behest" (Spillers, "Changing the Letter" 27). The slave's body is the goods and that which produces the goods. It is also a forbidden body: polluted and polluting. The discourses of the slave body are paradoxical. White culture feels great anxiety over black and white touching, yet the plantation produces mulattoes. Laws are written more stringently defining the opposition between the black body and the white body, yet some bodies move dangerously between the insisted-upon poles. George and Eliza, Cassy and Mme de Thoux, mask their "blackness" with "whiteness," while legally the children of slave masters are forced to mask their "whiteness" with "blackness." The white South is obsessed with the body; in order for its "peculiar institution" to work at all, it must be ever-vigilant of the alien, threatening, subtly-hued bodies that inhabit it. In the gothic South, the suppressed, the *sub rosa*, the subterranean, that which is locked up in cellars and attics, or forced to live in the Quarters or kept discreetly in little houses in New Orleans, will necessarily return to destroy what Faulkner called "the eggshell shibboleth of caste and color" (Faulkner, *Absalom, Absalom!* 139). The writer participates in this play of secrets and disguises. Toni Morrison's minstrel show metaphor applies to the world Stowe makes in *Uncle Tom's Cabin*: "In minstrelsy, a layer of blackness applied to a white face released it from law. . . so American writers were able to employ an imagined Africanist persona to articulate and imaginatively act out the forbidden in American culture" (Morrison, *Playing in the Dark* 66). Stowe's strategy is to force a communion of black and white, allowing white readers, however partially and safely, to figure themselves as slaves through the characters in her novel.

Stowe uses images of lawless, excessive sexuality to construct her sinning South. For her, North America can be represented as an uneasy composite of Bakhtin's classical and grotesque bodies with the rational, righteous, liberal intelligence at the top – that is, New England, Ohio and Canada, the homes of order and liberty – while the "dirty," unspeakable, irrational parts – that is, the slave South – seethe at the bottom. The bottom, the "low-Other," in Bakhtin's term, is ruled by the appetites, not enlightenment. The South is "down there" the way the stomach, the bowels and the genitals are "down there." The South has always been eroticized in white American minds. Even before it became a slave society, the South was represented in early narratives as a female body to be penetrated, ravished, exploited and impregnated, a landscape of breasts and genitals displayed for the "use" and "enjoyment" of the European coloniser, much as the female slave's body was to be used and enjoyed at will by the European American master.[5] In Robert Johnson's "Nova Britannia" (1609), Virginia's streams and springs are "like veynes in a naturall bodie"; Virginia has "hills and mountains making sensible proffer of hidden treasure, neuer yet searched" (Kolodny 11). John Hammond's treatise, "Leah and Rachel; or The Two Fruitfull Sisters Virginia and Mary-land" (1656), presents the colonies as two ripe, amorous women (ibid. 13). The very naming of the first Southern colonies after women demonstrates the colonisers' commitment to seeing the "New World" as a feminine space to be "taken": *Virginia* implies not only a compliment to Elizabeth I but an ideology: virgin land to be possessed, to be made fruitful.

The institution of slavery reinforced the representation of the South as erotic since, to Europeans, Africans had always been associated with sexuality. *Uncle Tom's Cabin* juxtaposes the erotic with the infernal in Stowe's moralized geography; the further South slaves go, the worse conditions get. From the comparatively tolerable Kentucky plantation of the Shelbys, Aunt Chloe laments: "'Nobody ever comes up that goes down thar!'" (163). "Down there" is the lower South of Louisiana, and "down there" is the kingdom of the damned, mysterious and horrible – like the gothic dungeon or the forbidden regions of the body. Spillers reminds us of the 1853 children's abridgment of Stowe's novel called *A Peep into Uncle Tom's Cabin*: "The prurient, voyeuristic suggestion of 'peep' is quite appropriate to a national mentality that wants to 'steal' a look at the genitals in vague consciousness that they are covered by an interdiction" (Spillers, "Changing the Letter" 30). Looking at slavery is looking at a taboo, covered, "shameful" part of the national body; the slave South represents at once the sinful regions of the body, the oubliette with the nasty secret, and hell.

Stowe's South weaves the Calvinist surety of sin with the Romantic strands of the gothic and the orientalist; she insists on revealing slavery's sexual crises.[6] Stowe's Calvinism has been much discussed: I shall concentrate on her use of orientalist and gothic representations in *Uncle Tom's Cabin*.[7] The gothic's emphasis on family degeneracy, guilt and the supernatural combines with the orientalist obsession with captive sexuality, rich surroundings and pleasure, providing Stowe with a familiar popular and literary vocabulary for discussing what she saw as the sins of slavery: rape, incest, miscegenation, adultery, dead children, stolen children, absent spouses, split families, broken marriages. Stowe's South is not just culturally Other but morally alien. Of course, in declaring this so, Stowe steers perilously close to romanticizing the very passions she abhors. The moral of her story demands the exhibition of uncontrolled desire that is the heart of Southern darkness; but the uttering of that desire threatens to drown out the Christian revelation that is supposed to redeem the South's soul.[8]

VOLUPTUOUS GARDENS: THE ORIENTAL SOUTH

Edward Said remarks that the white westerner sees "the Orient as a sort of surrogate and even underground self" (Said, *Orientalism* 103). The slave South is America's domestic Orient, its secret self, its Other, as the African and the female – so involved in representations of the South – are Other. The feminized, receptive, seductive metaphorical landscape of the South owes much to the seductive, secretive metaphorical landscape of the Orient. The geography of the Other is a cultural production: the west makes the east in the image of its "dark" self as the American North constructs the slave South as its "dark" self. Said reminds us that

> geographical sectors such as "Orient" and "Occident" are man-made. Therefore as much as the West itself, the Orient is an idea that has a history, a tradition of thought, imagery and vocabulary that have given it reality and presence in and for the West. The two geographical entities thus support and to an extent reflect each other.
>
> (Said, *Orientalism* 5)

Orient and Occident depend on each other for definition; the values of the North (defined for Stowe and many other abolitionists as New England) depend on the sins of the South, just as the conventions of being white take shape against the conventions of being black.

Representations of the South in a number of nineteenth-century texts intersect with representations of the Orient. In this symbolic geography, North=West and South=East. By inventing an "eastern," erotically-charged, pagan, authoritarian, chaotic Other *within* the occidental, quotidian, Christian, chaste, orderly democracy of the United States, abolitionist writers could insist that slavery threatens the country's domestic decorum. In *Uncle Tom's Cabin* Stowe draws upon literary orientalism to imagine a New Orleans where the putative "jungles" of "darkest Africa" meet Islamic Spain. In English writing from the seventeenth century on, the various "Orients" of Arabia, Turkey, Greece, India, Africa, even Spain and China merged as landscapes for fiction. The actual histories, customs, religions and governments of these nations

29

mattered less than a titillating exoticism: they were tyrannical, cruel, luxurious (in both senses), and they had harems. Sexual licence combined with male control of women's bodies made the "Orient" fatally fascinating (if officially repellent) to European and American readers.[9] Inventing an Oriental South became a powerful abolitionist tactic, demanding that the American public recognize a despotic kingdom where men have sexual access to women slaves within the borders of their democratic republic, decadent poison weakening the national body.

In *The Key to Uncle Tom's Cabin* (1853), Stowe says Africans are "oriental" characters whose "whole bodily system sympathizes with the movement of their minds" (*Key* 45, Spillers, "Changing the Letter" 26). Stowe's serious orientalizing of the South begins with Tom's sojourn in New Orleans and the St Clares' "East Indian cottage" on Lake Pontchartrain. The Shelby plantation in Kentucky is innocent of the oriental: perhaps it is too near the antiseptic North. Stowe actually visited Kentucky while living in Cincinnatti in the 1830s, but she had to improvise her ornate, decadent Louisiana. The rose-covered cottage where Uncle Tom and Aunt Chloe raise their children in Christian goodness suggests more a prefigurement of heaven than a threat of hell: still, the oriental is latent in Tom himself. Once he is in Louisiana, it begins to appear: "the negro, it must be remembered, is an exotic of the most gorgeous and superb countries of the world, and he has, deep in his heart, a passion for all that is splendid, rich and fanciful" (Stowe, *Uncle Tom's Cabin* 253). The African presence orientalizes the South: slaves are necessary to its "gorgeousness" (Stowe uses this word often) yet the South must be purged of orientalism to be redeemed. This fits, albeit uncomfortably, with Stowe's belief that the Africans who had been brought unwillingly out of their "Orient" should be sent back there, despite their potential for Christian perfection in adversity. America would then be cleansed of slavery – and of the erotic suggestiveness of African flesh, purged from the national body as middle-class Victorians were always trying to rid themselves of desire.

Stowe is not subtle in her conflation of New Orleans with the omnibus "East" of romance. The St Clare mansion looks like "Aladdin's palace," "built in that mixture of Spanish and French style" as well as "in the Moorish fashion" (ibid. 275, 252). Its design gratifies "a picturesque and voluptuous ideality. Wide galleries ran all around the four sides, whose Moorish arches, slender pillars and

Arabesque ornaments, carried the mind back, as in a dream, to the reign of oriental romance in Spain" (ibid. 252). This sort of description echoes Washington Irving's Alhambra stories, so popular in the 1830s. The St Clare fountains and mosaics are surrounded by orange trees, "dark-leaved Arabian jessamines" and a "mystic old aloe with its strange massive leaves ... looking like some old enchanter" (ibid. 253). All the gardens in New Orleans are lush, bright and covered in the kind of tropical flora familiar in the oriental tale. The caliph's garden in *Vathek* has

> a hundred arbours of roses, entwined with jessamine and honey-suckle; as many clumps of orange trees, cedar and citron; whose branches, interwoven with the palm, the pomegranate, and the vine presented every luxury that could regale the eye or the taste.
>
> (Beckford 13)

The St Clare garden also has pomegranate trees, but where the caliph Vathek's garden is supposed to conjure up heaven, Stowe reminds us that this South is a lower region, an underworld. J. C. Furnas, in his *ad feminam* attack *Goodbye to Uncle Tom* (1956), ridicules Stowe because she never went to Louisiana and so would not know "whether houses in New Orleans were really so like stage sets for *Lalla Rookh*" (Furnas, *Goodbye to Uncle Tom* 25). In demanding documentary accuracy, Furnas both misses Stowe's point and betrays an accidental acuity. Stowe invents an oriental New Orleans for political reasons: her readers, familiar with oriental fiction by English and American writers, would understand that Thomas Moore's *Lalla Rookh* (1817), with its charming but despotic sultans and submissive harem beauties, is precisely what she wants them to see. The exotic, the sensual and the sinful combine in the oriental South, a fit setting for both the "poetical voluptuary" Augustine St Clare and the African saint Uncle Tom. Stowe tries to work through the attractiveness of this oriental landscape to focus on its distinguishing social feature, slavery. As Spillers points out, Stowe "reinforces a semantics of 'oriental romance'" here, marking the South as criminal: "In Puritan terms, we might imagine, the landscape of this scene is 'heathen' in its excess, openly deranging the senses" (Spillers, "Changing the Letter" 26).

Stowe resolves Africa's oriental opulence and Tom's exemplary selflessness by transforming the excessive and pagan into the orderly and Christian. Africa's orientalism, while not a positive moral

31

trait, will energize the church just as slavery, while abhorrent, creates the Christlike Tom.[10] In the future,

> Africa shall show an elevated and cultivated race . . . life will awake there with a gorgeousness and a splendour of which our cold western tribes faintly have conceived. In that far-off mystic land of gold and gems, and spices and waving palms and wondrous flowers and miraculous fertility, will awake new forms of art, new styles of splendour.
>
> (Stowe, *Uncle Tom's Cabin* 275)

More importantly, Africa "will exhibit the highest form of the peculiarly *Christian* life" (ibid. 275). Stowe almost pulls back from the seductiveness of "splendid" Africa (just as the warm beauty of the South threatens to subvert the argument against slavery), correcting her own excessive descriptions with the claim that Africa will produce the most Christian of nations, and comparing Tom with a black Bishop of Carthage: a little missionary work will trim this lush growth of chaotic flora into an orderly garden.

Stowe has it both ways: oriental Africa (and the oriental South) embody pagan excess and Christian virtue. But the North is the necessary agent of restraint. As Said puts it: "The Oriental is irrational, depraved (fallen), childlike, 'different;' thus the European [or the Northern] is rational, virtuous, mature, 'normal'" (Said, *Orientalism* 40). "Happy the nations of the moral North!" Byron sneers in *Don Juan*, clearly preferring disordered passions of the immoral South: in his terms, northern and southern Europe. But the pattern holds: the qualities of the oriental South are not necessarily consistent (covered under the "irrational"); thus it can encode the potential for Christian redemption and regeneration while exhibiting pagan excess and degeneration. It is also true that the catalogue of attributes ascribed to the oriental (Southern) and occidental (Northern) corresponds to the feminine and the masculine, or to the grotesque and classical bodies in Bakhtin's scheme: the low Other and high official culture. The oriental, feminine South is multiple, fecund and polluted by slavery; it is marked by "undifferentiated sexual desire." Like the Europeans' Orient, it cannot sustain a "civilisation," just appetite (ibid. 310ff.). Like the insistent, omnivorous grotesque body, the slave South acts to gratify desire, not to exercise good reason or sound religion. Like Dinah's kitchen at the St Clare mansion, where the food is overdressed, over-sauced and often wasted, drawers and cabinets disorganized, the South is guilty of what Gillian Brown calls "promiscuous housekeeping" (Brown, "Getting in the Kitchen" 503).

Indeed, *promiscuity*, in its multiple meanings, is central. The most compelling "orientalist" image is the harem; the most effective image from the oriental South, as used by abolitionist writers, is also the harem. The twinned reactions of fascination and horror at polygyny explain the popularity of oriental romances like *Vathek*, *Lalla Rookh* and *The Arabian Nights* as well as anti-slavery texts. Theodore Weld's *American Slavery As It Is* (1839) contains testimony after testimony of masters sexually exploiting their female slaves.[11] Texts from the 1830s to the time of the Civil War, including Richard Hildreth's *The White Slave* (1836), Frances Kemble's 1838–39 Georgia Journal (see Chapter 4), Lydia Maria Child's "The Quadroons" (1842), William Wells Brown's *Clotel* (1853), Harriet Jacobs' *Incidents in the Life of a Slave Girl* (1861) as well as slaveholding women's private writings, describe the sexual "use" of slaves by masters in terms of the harem. Mary Boykin Chesnut's famous condemnation of the slaveholder who runs a "hideous black harem" on the plantation where his chaste wife and daughters live is not an eccentric remark. Chesnut is fully aware of so many of her culture's hypocrisies. She goes on:

> [That slaveholder] holds his head as high and poses as a model of all human virtues to these poor women whom God and the laws have given him. From the height of his awful majesty he scolds and thunders at them, as if he never did wrong in his life.
>
> Fancy such a man finding his daughter reading *Don Juan*. "You with that immoral book!" And he orders her out of his sight.
>
> (Woodward 168)[12]

One of the (many) "immoral" elements in *Don Juan* is the hero's sojourn in a Turkish harem.

Both Northern and Southern women read *Don Juan* and Byron's other orientalist poems *The Giaour* (1813) and *The Bride of Abydos* (1813). Mary Chesnut refers constantly to Byron in her diary, and Byron was Harriet Beecher's great guilty literary pleasure when young: her father wanted to convert him to Christianity, and Harriet fantasized along those same lines (Gossett 11). The harem was common cultural currency. In one of the most delicious ironies of slaveholding culture, Thomas Moore's *Lalla Rookh* was a favourite book in the South as well as a perennial subject for *tableaux vivants* performed by plantation ladies. Given the way many slaveholding women participated in Southern orientalizing by referring to the collection of slave women on the plantation as a harem, I have to wonder if they were not making a sly, subversive point in dressing up as members of the seraglio for their husbands' "entertainment" in these *tableaux vivants*.[13] Perhaps in wearing the veils and kohl of oriental women they were subtly arraigning their husbands for sexual misconduct out in the *real* harem, the Quarters; or perhaps they were toying with a dangerous sexuality officially out of bounds for them: playing "black." Certainly there is a risky (and *risqué*) element of inversion here: along with the fiction popular at the time about oriental women in oriental harems there was a school of near- and actual pornography about *white* women in oriental harems. *The Female Captive* (1769) and *The Fair Syrian* (1787) breathlessly recount tales of white slavery in Ottoman Turkey. One of the most famous works of nineteenth-century pornography, *The Lustful Turk* (1828), plays titillation off against cultural anxiety: a young Englishwoman becomes the sex-slave of a sultan and ends up enjoying it. A different sort of white slave was still more famous in America: Hiram Powers' statue *The Greek Slave* became one of the best known pieces of Victorian American art. Powers made six full-size versions and a vast number of three-quarter-size replicas and busts between 1844 and 1869 of the fragile-looking white marble nude, standing as if trying to hide her "shame," hands chained before her (Kasson 174). Powers provided a narrative to go along with the statue, characterizing her as a maiden sold into captivity to the Muslim Turks, a model of Christian fortitude and resignation. Whatever her spiritual qualities, *The Greek Slave* fits into American orientalism as an emblem of the nation's conflicting feelings about slavery and sexuality.[14] Powers himself had anti-slavery sympathies (ibid. 185). The complex inversions in play when audiences in a slaveholding United States gazed on the vulnerable *white* body in chains were not lost on abolitionist commentators. When Powers showed *The Greek Slave* at the 1851 Great Exhibition at Crystal Palace in London, the satirical magazine *Punch* published an engraving lampooning the statue, showing a black woman in chains, captioned "The Virginian Slave" (ibid. 185). Abolitionists used sensational harem images to indict the morality of slavery; but Americans in general, for or against slavery, participated in fantasies of sexually-subjugated women.

As Mary Chesnut and Harriet Beecher Stowe knew, there were real harems and real sex-slaves in the South: New Orleans, the South's most "oriental" city, was most closely associated with them. Travellers from the North and abroad wrote scandalized accounts of the Quadroon Balls where mixed-race girls were paraded before white men looking for a *placée*, or concubine, set up in an apartment or house and funded by (*owned* by) the man until he chose to sell her. In *Absalom, Absalom!* a Southern gentleman describes the *placée* as "the eighth part negromistress ... as much a part of a wealthy young New Orleansian's social and fashionable equipment as his dancing slippers" (100). The *placée* is a valuable commodity (she could cost tens of thousands of dollars), marketed

> through a system more formal than any that white girls are sold under since they are more valuable than white girls, raised and trained to fulfill a woman's sole end and purpose: to love, to be beautiful and divert; never to see a man's face hardly until brought to the ball and offered to and chosen by some man.
>
> (Faulkner, *Absalom, Absalom!* 117)

Plaçage is simultaneously attacked and romanticized in Tragic Mulatta novels like J. H. Ingraham's *The Quadroone* (1840) in which the tormented heroine Azélie wants to be properly married, not live in sin. The British actress Frances Kemble uses *plaçage* to undermine whites' declarations that the races were naturally antipathetic to each other: "while the slave owners of the Southern states insist vehemently on the mental and physical inferiority of the blacks, they are benevolently doing their best, in one way at least, to raise and improve the degraded race" (Kemble 10). Indeed these mixed-race women got so "improved" that many were nearly white. A class of legally black women who could none the less "pass," creates a more complex image of the harem. These women were, as Alice Parker points out, "cultural products, created to serve white male interests," a harem oscillating between fantasies about black women's seductiveness and white women's "morality," jeopardized by sexual slavery (Parker 76). The fair complexion of the *placée* (like Cassy or Mme de Thoux) works as a specular counterpoint of her socially-defined darkness: she is both the resisting white captive in the sultan's harem and the compliant dusky Nouronihar, Zuleika or Lalla who has always belonged there.

The harem lurks in the background in Stowe's Louisiana: she does not bring it to the fore the way Tragic Mulatta *romanciers* like

J. H. Ingraham, Lydia Maria Child and Dion Boucicault do. Perhaps
Stowe relies on popular knowledge of New Orleans as site of one
of the largest slave markets in the nation as well as the notorious
home of *plaçage*. Certainly antebellum journalists and travel writers
had covered the subject thoroughly. On the subject of New Orleans
"fancy girls," Frederick Law Olmsted says "I have described this
custom as it was described to me; I need hardly say, in only its best
aspects. The crime and heart-breaking sorrow that must frequently
result from it, must be evident to every reflective reader" (Olmsted I,
305).[15] Curiously enough in *Uncle Tom's Cabin*, actual sexual menace
diminishes in New Orleans. The terror of the harem is displaced onto
the slave traders or to Legree's plantation, not located in the heart of
plaçage. I think there are several reasons why: one is that Augustine St
Clare shows Stowe being conciliatory toward the South, as she was in
describing the kindly Shelby household. St Clare is stereotypically
indolent and charming, as Southerners were (and are) held to be, but
he has had the moral advantage of contact with the North. He spent
time in New England, loved a lady of New England and has New
England family. He is an attractive, if weak, master. He is not, in
Stowe's scheme, a candidate for owning a *placee*. Another reason is
Stowe's own ambivalence toward the orientalist South she creates.
The danger of such a "gorgeous," seductive, orange-and-jasmine
scented world is that the moralist herself is partially seduced by it.
Stowe exhibits this ambivalence over her reading of Byron: she was
both carried away by his orientalist excesses and desirous of purifying
him.

Mainly, though, I think Stowe depends on her readers to recognize how the delightful Augustine has merely papered over the rot
of slavery: it stains his house the minute he dies. The discourse of
the harem, partially suppressed by the master's goodness, returns.
Just after his funeral, his slaves are marched off to market. Despite
Augustine's good intentions, trade in human bodies is the bottom
line in New Orleans. Slaves like Jane and Rosa, with their light skin,
could easily be sold as "fancy goods." The undercurrent of illicit
desire is never absent from New Orleans: Stowe invites the reader
to think about how Jane and Rosa got to be so light. On the block,
Jane, Rosa and Emmeline, Legree's "prize article," might well recall
more *The Greek Slave* than "The Virginian Slave," their pale bodies,
like that of Power's statue, vulnerable to the gazes and touch of
men. Yet no societal outrage greets *their* sale. Powers exhibited *The
Greek Slave* in antebellum New Orleans to great acclaim: "much of

its audience was apparently oblivious to the ironies of driving past slave marts to shed tears over the white marble captive" (Kasson 185).

Stowe plays with an inversion of the usual sexual dynamic of white man and black woman in the slave South to suggest that disordered desire also taints the "innocent." A white girl says of a black man: "I want him" (Stowe, *Uncle Tom's Cabin* 236). True, the white girl is Little Eva, usually read as an emblem of purity, and the black man is Uncle Tom, the slave Christ, yet their juxtaposition mounts a challenge to white female chastity. We are accustomed to reading these two as the apex of Stowe's "pious sentimentalism:" a child and slave too good for this world.[16] It is possible to question the assumed sexlessness of Tom and Eva's companionship. Despite later minstrel-show depictions of Uncle Tom as old, the novel makes clear that he is not; he is a strong man in the prime of his life. And Eva may be pre-pubescent, but she is old enough to be attractive to her Byronic cousin Henrique. Eva herself is implicated in the orientalism, with its implied sexuality, tinting the Southern landscape she inhabits. Spillers suggests she is "fatally marked by a lush sensuality;" to Miss Ophelia's horror, Eva is always touching the forbidden, "low," bodies of slaves: kissing Mammy, cuddling Topsy, sitting on Tom's lap or walking with him in secluded corners and secret places among the St Clare flower-beds like a pair of lovers (Spillers,"Changing the Letter" 42). The perfumed oriental garden, with its suggestive "invaginated" violet borders, enclosures and recesses, "threatens to overcome the planned and precise geometrics of landscape gardening," symbolically overturning the imposed order and implied virginity of the *hortus conclusus*, a central symbol of the "Edenic" plantation (ibid. 41).

I would push Spillers' argument further. The virgin body is a *hortus conclusus*, sealed off from intruders, pollution or violation. Yet the black body in the form of Tom, according to Southern ideology an unclean element, is *already inside* the walls. He moves in the space that represents Eva the pure. Eden is double: both unfallen and "soiled." Lynn Wardley suggests that "Tom's Christianization is arguably matched by Eva's Africanization" – Lake Pontchartrain, where the St Clares have their cottage, was the site of voodoo rituals performed by the two Marie Laveaus, New Orleans' famous priestesses (213). The physical licence and sensual freedom allowed in the oriental space of the St Clare garden attacks the South's defining opposition of white and black at the roots, proving that racial and cultural borders can be transgressed.

Marie St Clare's conversation rings with familiar race theory on how "they" cannot participate in white morals, manners, discipline or intelligence. Absurdly (and viciously) Marie attempts to enforce difference by punishing slaves for imitating the behaviour of their owners: having Rosa whipped for trying on one of her dresses, for example. She fails to comprehend Mammy's anguished longing for her own husband and children: "'Mammy couldn't have the feelings that I should. It's a different thing altogether, of course it is – '" (Stowe, *Uncle Tom's Cabin* 268). Yet Mammy embodies the "white" ideal of motherhood far better than the neurasthenic Marie, and Rosa, beaten for acting white, nearly *is* white. Insisting on the violent binary of black and white is futile. The loving relationship of Little Eva and Tom, in both its spiritual and sensual aspects, further disables the binary. Little Eva manifests "daring and impermissible desire" for the black body which, though she is a child, reveals "a disturbed female sexuality that American women of Stowe's era could neither articulate nor cancel, only loudly proclaim in ornamental language which counterfeits the 'sacrificial' of disguise and substitution" (Spillers, "Changing the Letter" 44). The potential of this forbidden desire to disrupt white over black goes, of course, unrealized; when slavery ended whites began an even more rigid programme of racial separation than existed before. None the less, my point remains that the language of the oriental, the discourse of harem and garden, *does* articulate white women's desire. Stowe reveals ambivalence toward the slave body and the slave – seduced by it one moment, sanctifying it the next. The political consequence of Little Eva's touching Tom is not impotent: in this bold connection of the saintly and the sexual, the Christian and the oriental, the white and the black, Stowe forces a kind of textual miscegenation, rather as Aphra Behn does in *Oroonoko*. The living evidence of white desire for the black body (in most cases mixed-race women) populates the novel; by orientalizing the South, Stowe creates a space in which desire can be spoken to challenge racial oppositions and so the very foundation of slavery itself.

LE ROMAN NOIR: THE GOTHIC SOUTH

As Uncle Tom lies dying in his squalid hut on Legree's plantation, the mulatta Cassy fashions herself into the literal "madwoman in the attic" of the big house, haunting her evil former lover, driving him to the brink of insanity. Two stories operate in this section of the novel: the Christian narrative of Tom's faith and martyrdom and the gothic narrative of Cassy's revenge and escape. While Tom dies passively in Christian *caritas*, Cassy acts out her rage, waging pitiless psychological war against Legree, last and most monstrous in the series of white men who have owned and used her. Ultimately the redemptive Passion story defeats the nihilistic ghost story: Tom's death is a victory, Cassy reunites with her family and becomes a Christian. Hope dawns east in Africa.

None the less, the gothic is central to Stowe's representation of the slave South, offering her a vocabulary for sin, abuse, guilt, rage and vengeance. As the oriental provides *Uncle Tom's Cabin* with a means to articulate desire, the gothic provides a complementary discourse expressing the perversion of love, of order, of democracy and of the family. Stowe exhibits the sentimental's sphere of concern – the young, the poor, the chained – yet lets the gothic invade every episode from Little Eva's death to the ex-slaves' final family reunions. As Sundquist remarks, "Gothic was the psychic nightmare of sentimentality, whose central novelistic strategy was the elicitation of compassion for the marginalized" (*To Wake the Nations* 108). Stowe employs the sentimental as a strategy to demand attention for the emotional and sexual crimes of the slave South. *Uncle Tom's Cabin* places slavery's "worst horrors in a haunted house" (Halttunen 107). And as in so many gothic tales, the ghosts are women.

Stowe was not the first (or the last) to represent the slave South as haunted. Sarah Grimké testifies in *American Slavery As It Is* that she fled South Carolina, "the home of my fathers to escape the sound of the lash and the shrieks of tortured victims. . . they came over my memory like gory spectres" (23). Grimké raises the gothic image of the ancestral mansion infested with suffering ghosts from which she and her sister Angelina (gothic heroines) must escape.[17] The haunted house is a metaphor for the blood-curdling moral and psychological effects of slavery. Grimké constructs the South as a prison that the virtuous should flee as Emily St Aubert flees the cursed castles in Ann Radcliffe's gothic classic *The Mysteries of Udolpho* (1794). Yet like the monomanias and persistent delusions suffered in the gothic fictions of Matthew Lewis and Edgar Allan Poe, witnesses to the evil carry with them the taint got from looking on the heart of darkness. Sarah and Angelina Grimké cannot forget. For their work as abolitionists, it is important that the curse be named for the ghost to be exorcized. Angelina Grimké writes:

> It seemed to me that all the cruelty and unkindness which I had from infancy seen practised toward [slaves] came back to my mind. . . . Night and day they were before me and yet my hands were bound as with chains of iron. . . . If only I could be the means of exposing the cruelty and injustice, of bringing to light the hidden things of darkness.
>
> (Lerner 79)

Slaveholders are haunted, too. Sarah Grimké remembers visiting the deathbed of an aristocratic, vicious slave owner:

> The girl on whom he had so often inflicted punishment haunted his dying hours; and when at last the King of Terrors approached, he shrieked in utter agony of spirit "Oh the blackness of darkness, the black imps, I can see them all around me – take them away!" and amid such exclamations he expired.
>
> (Weld 23)

This histrionic scene is more than merely reminiscent of Poe, it recalls many gothic villains' deaths: Lewis' Faustian Monk, for example, destroyed by a literal fiend. Grimké's "King of Terrors" conjures up a picture of both death and the devil: hell for white men who abuse their slaves is stocked with "black imps" to needle their guilty souls. Similar demons terrorize Simon Legree when Cassy appears by his bed in the night – not a deathbed but, given his heavy drinking and slipping hold on reality, certainly a sickbed – draped in a white sheet. Legree guiltily thinks it is his dead white mother's spirit; instead it is his abused black lover in the flesh. The world of the slaveholder is infernal, expressed for the abolitionist with maximum political and affective power in the language of the gothic with its outraged dead, unquiet spirits, sexual perversion, paranoia and madness.

Representing America's racial history as a "curse" is a commonplace in American fiction. The mixed-race Cora Munro in *The Last of the Mohicans* despairs, "The curse of my ancestors has fallen heavily on their child;" in *Benito Cereno*, Captain Delano exclaims to Benito, "You are saved: what has cast such a shadow over you?" and the answer comes, "The negro." And in *Light in August*, Joanna Burden Calvinizes the gothic curse, bemoaning the "black shadow," the "black cross" all whites must bear. It is both useful and elegantly appropriate that the name for the gothic novel in French is *le roman noir*. Stowe uses *black* in two ways: black as the occult colour of mystery, night – the gothic – and black as the colour of America's oppressed and unseen. Blacks haunt the officially-optimistic story America tells about itself: opportunity, equality, wealth, freedom. The wails of beaten slaves are never quite erased in the loud proclamations of democracy. Often invisible (like ghosts), blacks manifest themselves at uncomfortable moments as reminders of past crimes: the return of America's racial repressed. *Uncle Tom's Cabin* is a *roman noir* in every sense: a novel of black life and a gothic tale of blacks' deaths.

The discourses of the gothic proved useful to abolitionist writers. In *The Slave* (1836), Richard Hildreth translates the yoked fascination with and fear of incest, prominent in *The Mysteries of Udolpho*, *The Monk* and American gothic fiction by Charles Brockden Brown, into a sensational exposé of how, in answer to Angelina Grimké's original question, the fathers of the South not only sell their daughters but sleep with them as well.[18] Frederick Douglass uses gothic imagery to describe the torments of slavery: dungeons, "bloody whips," and "iron chains" (Sundquist, *To Wake the Nations* 107). Frances Trollope pictures the Usher-like desolation of a crumbling plantation. Fleeing the horror (incest, murder, curse or ghost), the essential gothic movement, is also the central action of abolitionist fiction: Eliza runs from the bounty hunters, and Cassy and Emmeline escape Legree's decaying mansion. Stowe integrates gothic forms and gothic trappings with her thematic attention to the sentimental and its refocus on the powerless and the suffering, "the madman, the child, the very old, the animal and the slave," as critics, most notably Philip Fisher, have noticed (Fisher 99). In Stowe's South, as in the gothic landscape, evil is always present, though often hidden or disguised. The St Clare mansion masks its gothicness in its orientalism, though, as we come to see, the full horror of slavery is kept at bay only by Augustine St Clare's fragile life. St Clare's name itself is a gothic sign: the evil convent in *The Monk* is dedicated to St Clare (ironically, an associate of St Francis who preached the sacredness of all life and the virtues of poverty). "St Clare" sounds like a standard gothic name, echoing Radcliffe's "St Aubert" in *The Mysteries of Udolpho*; it also sounds dangerously Catholic – the New England branch of the family uses the more Protestant (Scots) sounding "Sinclair."

41

The radical horror of the slave South, like the radical horror of gothic Europe, lies in discovering that the ordinariness of home, family and self is a tissue-thin veneer, vulnerable to puncture, veiling a crude, violent reality. Things are never what they seem. Even at the Shelby plantation in Kentucky, slavery's "mildest" manifestation, and, as illustrated by Uncle Tom's and Aunt Chloe's flower-bedecked, food-filled cabin, the South's nearest brush with the domestic ideal central to Stowe's vision of a redeemed America, there is always the danger of decay, of the activation of a lurking curse:

> over and above the scene there broods a portentous shadow –
> the shadow of *law*. So long as the law considers all these human
> beings, with beating hearts and living affections, only as so
> many *things* belonging to a master, – so long as the fortune, or
> misfortune, or imprudence, or death of the kindest owner,
> may cause them any day to exchange a life of kind protection
> and indulgence for one of hopeless misery and toil, – so long
> it is impossible to make anything beautiful or desirable in the
> best-regulated administrations of slavery.
>
> *(Uncle Tom's Cabin* 51)

The subversiveness of this passage comes from the idea that *law*, the force that should banish the gothic's anarchic, dangerous ambivalence through the democratic power of the state, is itself gothicized. The duly-elected Congress of the United States, in failing to do away with slavery (and in passing the Fugitive Slave Law), creates the "shadow" which allows the trader Haley to chase runaway slaves like animals, to traffic in flesh, to reduce Eliza, almost a foster-daughter to the Shelbys, to a mere commodity: "Her dress was of the neatest possible fit, and set off to advantage her finely moulded shape; a delicately formed hand and a trim foot and ankle were items of appearance that did not escape the quick eye of the trader, well used to run up at a glance the points of a fine female article" (ibid. 45). This is shocking language, revealing the way the slave economy regards a woman as a checklist of selling points: the slave economy "values" Eliza for her torso, her hands, her ankles. It is pornographic language, making a woman a thing. Haley's gaze, both lustful and avaricious, sees Eliza as sexual merchandise: he or Shelby might make a "'fortune on that ar gal in Orleans'" (ibid. 45).[19] Almost in the next breath, as Haley talks Shelby into parting with Eliza's son Harry, he tells of a slave woman

42

who went mad and died when her child was taken from her. Clearly, the merchandise is sometimes faulty.

Good mothers like Mrs Shelby, Mrs Bird, Aunt Chloe, the Quaker Rachel Halliday (and, to some extent, Uncle Tom) form the moral *foci* of the novel. Elizabeth Ammons remarks, Stowe "heartily embraced the Victorian idealization of motherhood and channeled it into an argument for widespread social change." Stowe felt that "rather than segregate maternal ethics into some private domestic realm, motherhood – the morality of women – should be made the ethical and structural model for all of American life" (Ammons, "Stowe's Dream" 159). That reformist model of motherhood is possible in the free North; in the South, mothers lack the necessary power. Marie St Clare is self-obsessed: Mammy must care for her like a baby, poor Prue dies of cruelty, St Clare's mother Evangeline is long dead. Eva, Miss Ophelia and Tom act as substitute mothers. If the maternal is the soul of "sacred womanhood," as Stowe saw it, heart of the ethical home and *omphalos* of democratic government, the South is missing a vital organ. In gothic convention, mothers also disappear or die: Poe, Brockden Brown, Lewis, Maturin and especially Radcliffe hurl their young heroes and heroines into a hostile world where the mother lives only as a memory of virtue and nurture. Much menace derives from the protagonists' lack of maternal protection or moral guidance; the gothic world suppresses actual mothers and tries to destroy potential mothers. Slavery attacks the maternal body in which Stowe (though not as all-encompassingly as her sister Isabella) located redemption, reducing it to a mere breeding animal or sexual receptacle.[20] Invoking both the Bible and the gothic novel, Mrs Shelby exclaims "'This is God's curse on slavery!'" The Shelby household, once a refuge and a home for Eliza and her child, has become a dangerous place they must, like their European antecedents in Radcliffe or Lewis, flee. Once across the Ohio, her feet sacrificially bleeding, Eliza's progress North takes her farther and farther away from the gothic prison of the South with its language of curses, perversion and shadows. Stowe tracks Eliza's escape north to the cold, ungothic, unoriental nation of Canada – its very coldness a sign of purity – as she chronicles Tom's descent south into the *oubliette* of slaves, "down there." While Eliza finds refuge in the Quakers' ideal community, homes with no secrets *or* servants, homes that seem all cozy kitchen, Tom is taken "down river" towards New Orleans, centre of the traffic in human flesh, witnessing dreadful scenes such as the slave Lucy's suicide after her child is sold. While Eliza dreams of "a beautiful country. . . there, in a house which kind voices told her was her home, she saw her boy playing, a free and happy child," a landscape increasingly egalitarian, Tom encounters new levels of class division, hardly dreamt of in Kentucky, and will never see his family again (Stowe, *Uncle Tom's Cabin* 222). Eliza has a vision of heaven; Tom is dragged to hell.

While the St Clare place in New Orleans is as flower-filled as the Shelby plantation, it is also, as we have seen, an orientalized garden, bearing signs of the excessive passion and disordered sexuality that characterize slavery. The St Clare house encodes illness and decay. Marie St Clare is a hypochondriac, ancestress of generations of neurasthenic Southern white women prostrate with mysterious headaches, "sickly" and "fragile" but also vicious and violent. She complains to Miss Ophelia "'we mistresses. . . are the slaves down here,'" while bemoaning the ingratitude of her personal servant, Mammy, "sulking" over her distant husband and children and misuse by her owner: "'She never was whipped more than once or twice in her life'" (ibid. 263). Slavery has perverted Marie's "womanly" nature; she is a monster who would like Topsy "'whipped till she couldn't stand!'" (ibid. 407). She does order the refined mulatta Rosa beaten by "the master of a whipping establishment." Whipping and rape merge here in Miss Ophelia's outraged mind: "women and young girls" put in "the hands of the lowest of men – men vile enough to make this their profession" (ibid. 460). In the whipping houses, a woman is "subjected to brutal exposure and shameful correction" that will "'deprave her very fast'" (ibid. 461). The orientalist and the gothic intersect in the voyeuristic shock produced by punishing women. The threat of physical chastisement or death characterizes the harem, where the women are under the despotic rule of a man who regulates all aspects of their behaviour. Torture is also part of the gothic: young women were brutalized and confined in the terrible convent in *The Monk*. Marie St Clare is not as imaginative in her cruelty as the Abbess of St Clare in *The Monk*, but, in the absence of her husband and her saintly child, she seems quite capable of turning her home into a more upmarket version of Legree's house of torments where all slaves are "brought under" and "'kept in order'" (ibid. 461).

The gothic manifests itself at the St Clare house in the "curse" of slavery. Augustine St Clare cries: "'Talk of the *abuses* of slavery! Humbug! The *thing itself* is the essence of all abuse!'" (ibid. 332). Of course, the curse falls hardest on the slaves themselves, but it also makes virtuous white people mentally and physically ill. St Clare tells how slaveowning exacerbated his father's authoritarian temper to the despair of his devout mother Evangeline: "'It will never be known, till the last account, what noble and sensitive natures like hers have felt, cast, utterly helpless, into what seems to them an abyss of injustice and cruelty which seems so to nobody but them'" (ibid. 337). We witness what the evils of slavery do to the second Evangeline: "Little Eva sickens and dies from hearing and seeing the slavery around her" (Fisher 103).[21] When told of Prue's imprisonment and death by starvation, she is stricken as if by disease, the information working like poison in "the spirit-like form of Evangeline, her large mystic eyes dilated with horror, and every drop of blood driven from her lips and cheeks" (Stowe, *Uncle Tom's Cabin* 327). Eva is fast becoming a corpse, murdered by slavery. If one reads *Uncle Tom's Cabin* as a Christian epic, Eva is heading for sainthood; if one reads *Uncle Tom's Cabin* as a *roman noir*, she seems already a ghost, her "spirit-like" self echoing Lewis' Bleeding Nun, the ghost who walks with a symbolic dagger in stained white robes, an emblem of suffering.

Slavery itself tortures Eva: "'these things *sink into my heart*,'" she says, as if speaking of a knife-wound. In Eva's fragile, fading body, the gothic exists alongside the Christian: not only is she nearly incorporeal herself, she says spirits "'come to me sometimes in my sleep'" (ibid. 382). They are at once the blessed spirits of heaven who will soon descend to carry her "home" and the agonized ghosts of slavery haunting her. Eva is at once Christ (like Tom), wanting, as she says, to die *for* the slaves, and a victim of the South's great sin against humanity, its curse, dying *because* of slavery. As Tom says, "'She's got the Lord's mark in her forehead'" (ibid. 401). In Eva, the Christian, the oriental and the gothic converge. The mark signifies her sanctity, but it also signifies her *femaleness*, the sexual possibilities latent in her touching of black bodies, and it signifies the curse – the mark of blackness.[22] In her gradually-disappearing body, Eva bears the signs of victim, woman and, though she is not black as Tom is black, she has "touched" blackness, she bears, in a sense, its inscription. She cannot live. Finally, like both a Christian saint and one of Poe's heroines, she is most beautiful in death.

Stowe's gothic reading of slavery intensifies after Little Eva dies, and Simon Legree buys Tom. Tom's Mississippi River trip represented one stage in his journey to the underworld; travelling the

Red River takes him still further "down there" to hell. As Karen Halttunen, in her excellent essay, points out, the red clay banks suggest blood: they also (along with the name of the river) suggest flames. Moreover, the name of this chapter, "The Middle Passage," refers to slave ships bringing captured Africans to be sold in America, a symbolic (and what must have felt to many like a literal) descent into hell. The next chapter is "Dark Places;" Tom goes from the fire to the abyss, down a "wild forsaken road" under "long wreaths of funeral black moss" (ibid. 488). Legree's plantation proves as ruinous and rotten as the Usher mansion, a place of "utter decay," a swamp of "shattered branches that lay here and there, rotting up the water," where the once "smooth-shaven lawn" is full of litter, the garden choked with weeds and the windows boarded up (ibid. 488).

The crumbling plantation house is the most familiar emblem of the Southern gothic. Legree's house is a "dark place:" in the 1930s, Faulkner initially gave the title "Dark House" to two of his most gothic fictions, *Light in August* and *Absalom, Absalom!*. Representing the plantation South as a fallen mansion becomes a moralizing trope carrying with it the gothic burden of guilt, sin and cruelty inherent in slavery. For the modernist Faulkner, the fallen mansion signifies a warped relationship with the past; for Victorian abolitionists, the fallen mansion betokens spiritual *malaise*. Frances Trollope's *Adventures of Jonathan Jefferson Whitlaw* (1836) begins by describing a wrecked estate, a prophecy for the slave South; and in her journal, Fanny Kemble tells of living in a squalid overseer's cottage while visiting her husband's Georgia holdings because the once-grand seat of the Butlers had decayed into uninhabitability.

The ruin of Legree's house encompasses more than the physical: it is haunted. Stowe shows her debt to Charlotte Brontë in the narrative of Cassy, the "madwoman" who eventually masters the master from her attic. Yet the attic is not a prison for her, it is a means to escape. Cassy is passionate in the Brontesque manner: "A dark, wild face was seen, for a moment, to glance at the window of the house" (ibid. 494).[23] She embodies the gothic fear of the skeleton in the closet, the family secret, the terror that "something" is "living in that house," as Faulkner puts it in *Absalom, Absalom!*. She is the wronged mulatta, the "black" woman in a "white" skin (as she eventually wears a white sheet, impersonating a ghost). She becomes a "ghost of her own dead self" (Gilbert and Gubar 534). Significantly, the spectral face at the window, "a face that, once seen, could not be forgotten," belongs to a woman with "a wild, painful and romantic history" (Stowe, *Uncle Tom's Cabin* 501). Stowe's representation of Cassy veers between gothic monster and conventional heroine: Cassy's face partakes of both the beautiful and the frightening.

Here at Legree's swamp-castle, Stowe constructs her most graphic sexual crises. Nightmarish as it is for Tom, denied his hymns, his Bible and his mementoes of Little Eva, beaten, tortured and finally killed, Legree's plantation seems most terrible for women. Tom's integrity of self cannot be touched; but Legree can threaten Emmeline's integrity of self while Cassy's has nearly been destroyed. Legree commits his most awful crimes against women: "his denial of his mother, of mother love and of mother right" (Gilbert and Gubar 535). Legree is "guilty of matricide;" he is also guilty of rape. In the past, he has forced Cassy. Now, he intends to force Emmeline (whose similarity of name to *Evangeline*, *Emily* de Thoux and *Emily* Shelby helps create a network of feminine experience and suffering in the novel) to become his concubine. He exhibits his lustful, contemptuous, vicious attitude toward all women in the slave market, running his hands over Emmeline's body. He has used and abused Cassy (whose life has been an accumulation of pain at the hands of white men) and, as master, he abuses his female slaves, ignoring what Stowe would have called their true "womanly" feelings, giving the mulatta Lucy to Sambo, even though she protests she is already married (Stowe, *Uncle Tom's Cabin* 493). Life on Legree's plantation attacks the principles of Christian womanhood and Christian marriage; Legree's very existence is dedicated to violence against the feminine.

While Legree's plantation might not be, say, literally farther South than New Orleans, according to the symbolic geography Stowe sets up, it is the most alien, the most Other, the most "down there." Stowe's sense of descending, both morally and physically, to the South, is evident in her first book, a geography text for children, written with her sister Catherine and published twenty years before *Uncle Tom's Cabin*. The Beecher sisters speak with great disapproval of the South's defining institution, describing overseers whipping slaves, characterizing the South as "shiftless and indolent," sometimes "severe and cruel" (Stowe and Beecher, *A First Geography for Children* 73). The gothic mansion, the dark place, figures the South. While Legree's plantation is a gothic realm where women are abused, it is also represented in "genital" language, identifying it with the female body. In the gothic castle, the dungeons or cellars signify female genitalia, the "dark places," the recesses of the body. Stowe's ambivalent language reveals conflicting attitudes toward the sexuality inherent in the South (the genital region of the American nation-body): as with the oriental, both seduction and repulsion are in play. The Red River leads Tom and Emmeline not only to hell but to a monstrous womb; it is not only a tunnel to the underworld, but a "red" uterine canal. Like the St Clare garden, the ruined nature of Legree's plantation is also (to borrow Spillers' term) "invaginated," ringed about by "funeral wreaths of black moss" and infested with poisonous snakes as if to underscore the sexual threat. The swamps, the dim rooms of Legree's mansion, the dark garret itself suggest the enclosure of the female body. Stowe does not reconcile the geography of the gothic and the geography of the body: Legree's plantation bears the signs of both the sexual and the violent as the St Clare mansion partakes of both the oriental and the gothic. Indeed, Legree's house "suggests what St Clare's magnificent New Orleans establishment may one day become under the ruinous influence of the slave system" (Halttunen 119). The attractive scent of the jasmines and orange blossoms changes into a "peculiar sickening, unwholesome smell . . . damp, dirt and decay" at the Legree place (Stowe, *Uncle Tom's Cabin* 524).

Harriet was not the only Beecher to use the haunted house as a metaphor for corruption. Her father Lyman, as Karen Halttunen tells us, employs it in his *Six Sermons on Intemperance* (1826), and her brother, the notorious Henry Ward Beecher, creates a "palace" right out of "The Masque of the Red Death" in his 1844 lecture against prostitution, "The Strange Woman." Henry Ward Beecher conducts a tour of "the prostitute's 'house of death'," moving from a lush (quite orientalized) garden inside into a series of chambers tantalizingly called *Wards* of "Pleasure," "Satiety," "Discovery," "Disease" and "Death" through which the young man, in the toils of "the strange woman," passes (Halttunen 113). The Wards or chambers express "a sexual nausea whose implicit focus was not the prostitute but female anatomy itself" (ibid. 115). As in Lewis, Radcliffe and Poe, the home, sometimes figured as castle, convent or monastery, normally a "safe" bounded, domestic space, is transformed into a realm of the Other, of danger.[24] Stowe represents the ambivalence of Legree's plantation as a polluted space, sinful and violent, as well as a suggestion of a female body, but her gothic and sexual discourses do not resolve the paradoxes. Disgust and desire depend on each other in her South.

Halttunen is most convincing in her analysis of Lyman Beecher's and Henry Ward Beecher's gothic construction of sin and its misogynist underpinnings. However, she is missing the point when she says "the haunted houses of Lyman and Henry had represented ruined bodies, the haunted house in *Uncle Tom's Cabin* represented a ruined mind" (ibid. 124). Certainly, Legree's mind is ruined, but Cassy's *body* is also ruined; Stowe uses the gothic association of house with body, the wrecked and decaying garden, the seductive flowers smelling not sweet but rotten, to figure sexuality, morality and authority corrupted. Legree's haunted house does represent his disordered consciousness; at the same time it figures, maybe not a body "ruined" by wilful transgression, but a body violated, "ruined" without consent and without redress. Women killed or wronged by slavery haunt the house. Little Eva, dead of the "disease" of the South, joins the spectres when the lock of her hair "like a living thing, twined itself around Legree's fingers" (Stowe, *Uncle Tom's Cabin* 527). Eva's fair hair reminds him of his rejected mother who, on her deathbed, forgave her drunken, profane, slave-owning son, sending him "a lock of long, curling hair" that wrapped itself eerily around his fingers (ibid. 529). In addition to these two virtuous spirits, there is the slave woman beaten to death in the attic when she "incurred Legree's displeasure," the supposed house ghost (ibid. 565). How did she "displease" Legree? A plausible guess might be that she resisted his sexual advances. It is only a matter of time before Emmeline finally "displeases" Legree, risking rape, torture or death.

Finally there is Cassy, the actual ghost. She is like the house itself: once beautiful, elegant and refined, now frayed, neglected and maltreated. Slavery has inscribed itself on the house as slavery inscribed itself on her body. In the once-luxurious parlour, the very walls bear the text of slavery: "The wallpaper was defaced in spots, by slops of beer or wine; or garnished with chalk memorandums and long sums footed up, as if somebody had been practising arithmetic there" (ibid. 524). Alcohol, decay, illness and the accounts for the labour and sale of slave bodies: the writing of exploitation is literally on the wall, as evocative of the evils of slavery as the lines on Cassy's face.

As the haunted house is both a space where women are violated and abused and a representation of the woman's body itself, the haunted house becomes both the emblem of the slave woman's damaged body and a site of resistance to slavery. The feminine stands in opposition to the masculine at Legree's plantation. At the St Clare house, Eva engaged in a feminine campaign against slavery, trying to use spirituality, example and "influence" (the appropriate power for women, according to Ruskin and other Victorian theorists of "woman's sphere") in a powerful, if short-lived, struggle to bring about salvation and liberation for both black and white. Tom, Lucy, Cassy and Emmeline also engage in a feminine challenge to slavery. In refusing to break her vow to her "husband" (slave marriages had no legal status), Lucy resists the reduction of slave relationships to random, meaningless, unsanctioned sexual encounters for the purpose of breeding more slaves. In refusing to beat Lucy, Tom resists the power of the master through disobedience and denies that kind of "masculinity" himself.

A number of critics have pointed out that Tom is a feminized character, a male mammy, a rape victim, Stowe's Christ.[25] It is important, then, to see Tom's Christ-like struggle as part of a network of feminine resistance to Legree: Tom and Cassy participate in the same potent, maternal revolution though, in some ways, Tom's passivity and Christian submission to his fate seem far more traditionally "womanly" than Cassy's angry, calculating psychological attacks on Legree. Tom dies affirming the femininized virtues of Christianity while Cassy impersonates a demon, the madwoman, in her bid for freedom: none the less they mark extremes on the same spectrum. When Legree demands of the beaten Tom "'An't yer mine now, body and soul?'" he answers on behalf of all slaves but particularly on behalf of slave women whose bodies were subject but whose souls they dared call their own, "'No! no! no! my soul an't yours, Mas'r. You haven't bought it – ye can't buy it! It's been bought and paid for, by one that is able to keep it'" (ibid. 508).

Cassy's alternative strategy is resistance and escape. Her assault on Legree's already-shaky sensibilities parodies "woman's influence" in the home, showing, as Stowe says rather sardonically, "the kind of influence that a strong impassioned woman can ever keep over the most brutal man" (ibid. 526). When she speaks French quietly to Legree he becomes demented, almost as if she is uttering a spell. She alone calls him by his first name, Simon, a "wifely" act, yet she does so in a voice stiff with contempt. She both feigns an antic disposition and occasionally breaks "out into raving insanity" (ibid. 526). Instead of behaving as that central Victorian figure for the feminine, the Angel in the House, Cassy tells Legree: "'be careful, for I've got the devil in me!'" (ibid. 525). Through her parodies and inversions of conventional roles, she subverts Legree's masculine power. Legree, like Lewis' Monk, finds the empire of control and gratification of his desires collapsing through the rage of a woman. Consumed with lust for Emmeline, planning to force himself on her, he is undone even on his way up the stairs as he hears her singing "'*there'll be mourning, at the judgment-seat of Christ!*'" (ibid. 530). He thinks he sees a ghost, "something white rising glimmering in the gloom before him" and fears it is "the form of his dead mother" or the lock of golden hair risen "'from the dead!'" (ibid. 530–31). Cassy is a terrorist of the mind, playing on Legree's guilt until his sense of reality begins to disintegrate.

Legree's power outside the house, while still enough to have slaves beaten to death, is disabled by Tom's Christian challenge to his mastery; Legree's role inside the house is in ruins. Openly defiant, Cassy terrifies Legree, "who had that superstitious horror of insane persons which is common to coarse and uninstructed minds" (ibid. 526). Like the slave-owner Sarah Grimké tells of, haunted by a woman he abused, Legree is shadowed by the feminine. He dreams of his mother's (or is it Little Eva's?) hair twisting like a vice around his fingers, the "veiled form" of his mother's spirit, and Cassy laughing and pushing him into a "frightful abyss . . . down, down, down, amid a confused noise of shrieks, and groans, and shouts of demon laughter" (ibid. 535–36). The slaveholder in Grimké's story sees "black imps" on his deathbed; Legree sees demons in his sleep. Both scenes evoke the gothic vocabulary of sin, guilt and retribution.

Though most critics of *Uncle Tom's Cabin* read Tom's martyrdom as the central Christian act of black sacrifice, dwarfing all other episodes in its moral grandeur, Cassy and Emmeline's escape, and George and Eliza's flight, provide a powerful counter-narrative. In the end, Cassy and Emmeline's story, too, turns away from the gothic to embrace Christian resolution. But this does not diminish their rebellion: hiding out in the attic, traditional home of the discarded, of servants, ghosts and female maniacs, making a "tiny domestic circle drawn in the darkness" of the house where Cassy is "magically transformed back into a mother" (Halttunen 122). Cassy and Emmeline both impersonate the dead *and* constitute a living family. To Legree, Cassy is his own mother's ghost, symbol of his crimes against women, "the spectral presence of a dead-undead mother, archaic and all-encompassing, a ghost signifying the problematics of femininity" (Kahane 335–36).

It is true that Cassy and Emmeline, however transformed, must still make their "home" in a "corner of a house owned by a white man and in a religion controlled by white men" (Askeland 788). Yet the power of their rebellion is real. I disagree with Eric Sundquist when he says that, for Stowe, "black resistance could be imagined only as heroic pacifism (as in the case of Uncle Tom), or as the upshot of white blood (as in the case of George Harris), or as a species of insanity (as in the case of her maroon rebel Dred)." (Sundquist, *To Wake the Nations* 79). Sundquist misreads Tom's "heroic pacifism:" it is redemptive and resurrective and, to the militant Christian Stowe, the most profound revolutionary act. Moreover, Cassy, while seeming at times to be mentally unstable, mounts her resistance more from rage than insanity. Her resistance, too, is effective. It is not a national slave uprising: it is local and individual. But she gains her freedom and becomes an exemplar of a *woman's* struggle against the degradations of slavery.

Stowe is sophisticated in her use of the psychological gothic as a female strategy for resistance; Cassy as ghost drives Legree to drink excessively, depriving him of sleep, pushing him towards mental and physical collapse: "What a fool is he who locks his door to keep out spirits, who has in his own bosom a spirit he dare not meet alone, – whose voice, smothered far down, and piled over with mountains of earthliness, is yet like the forewarning trumpet of doom!" (Stowe, *Uncle Tom's Cabin* 595–96).

Wearing the sheet in which she "plays ghost," the black Cassy forces Legree to confront his white mother. At this crucial moment, Stowe backs off the gothic to parody it. She tells of the slaves whispering about the "footsteps in the dead of night" and speculates about the ghost's form:

> Authorities were somewhat divided, as to the outward form of the spirit, owing to a custom quite prevalent among negroes, – and, for aught we know, among whites, too, – of invariably shutting the eyes. . . . Of course, as everybody knows, when the bodily eyes are thus out of the lists, the spiritual eyes are uncommonly vivacious and perspicacious; and, therefore, there were an abundance of full-length portraits of the ghost, abundantly sworn and testified to, which, as is often the case

with portraits, agreed with each other in no particular, except the common family peculiarity of the ghost tribe, – the wearing of a *white sheet*.

(ibid. 594)

Here Stowe denies the reality of the supernatural to give further strength to Cassy's agency: she moves in and out of gothic discourse, evoking and parodying it to stress Cassy's central role in Legree's growing madness.[26] Cassy herself becomes a walking oxymoron; her "black blood," mark of her enslavement and status as a "fallen woman," covered in a near-white skin, is more opaquely masked in the white sheet she wears. She covers her "true identity" in a shroud – a sign of death – as her blackness is shrouded in her fair skin.

The sheet is a veil, that which obscures the sexuality of the heroine, the nun and the fallen woman in the gothic novel, yet which always threatens to come off, "revealing" the secret. Black women who "pass" as white none the less often appear veiled like Mme de Thoux, *two* in her blackness and whiteness. The veil signifies the doubleness of the mulatta, always of two races, "veiled" in one or the other: "the properties of figured flesh and the figured surface are contagious the same way as those of the veil" (Sedgwick, "The Character of the Veil" 260). The veil is prominent in both gothic and orientalist discourses; in the oriental tale, the veil signifies the ownership of the woman by one man. The woman is covered and *marked* by her status as property. The flesh of the slave woman in a slave society is marked by sexuality and pollution; the veil, intended to shield a woman from the sexual gaze of men, becomes, in gothic and in orientalist fictions, also an invitation. Cassy's sheet is revolutionary: it neither covers her sexuality nor constitutes a seductive lure, but allows her to act as Legree's mother's spirit, signifying the beginning of her return to religion, womanhood and society as a *mother*. The collapsing of the "opposites" the South hysterically tried to keep separate and defined, is volatile; Cassy subverts the binary in being both white and black, both dead and alive, both sane and mad, both mistress and mother. Finally the Christian story of redemption takes over from the orientalist and gothic stories of disordered sexuality and revenge. But even the calming of Cassy's monumental rage does not diminish its subversive power. The gothic heroines Eliza, Cassy and Emmeline escape the disintegrating Castle of Slavery into a free country, while the gothic victims Tom and Eva go to the Christian heaven. The good churchwoman Stowe places the languages of the oriental tale and the gothic novel at the service of a Christian narrative, showing how the instruments, or at least the fiction, of the devil can lead the nation to righteousness.

2

"INSTIGATED BY THE DEVIL"
The South and Harriet Beecher Stowe

*In the midst of political turmoil, Mrs. Harriet Beecher Stowe has
determined to put her finger in the pot, and has, it would seem,
made quite a successful dip. . . . Ten thousand dollars (the
amount, it is said, of the sales of her work) was, we presume, in
the lady's opinion, worth risking a little scalding for. We wish her
joy of her ten thousand thus easily gained, but would be loath to
take with it the foul imagination which could invent such scenes,
and the malignant bitterness (we had almost said ferocity) which,
under the veil of Christian charity, could find the conscience to
publish them.*

Louisa McCord, Review of *Uncle Tom's Cabin*
in the *Southern Quarterly Review*, 23 January 1853

After 1852, white women entered the debate over slavery in ever
larger numbers. They argued in women's magazines, in novels
and (often anonymously) in learned journals. Of course, white
men, black men and black women were still, as they had been all
along, thrashing out the issue in Congress, in state houses, in
pamphlets, in newspapers, in town halls, on college campuses,
from pulpits and in the streets.[1] But the frantic success of *Uncle
Tom's Cabin* and the fame (or notoriety) of its author opened up
the discussion for genres associated with women, particularly
fiction.[2]

Pro-slavery women, both Southern and Northern, publicly
criticized Stowe's book as a vicious, unfair and immoral attack on
the orderly, Bible-sanctioned, divinely ordained institution of
slavery; they damned Stowe herself for being unladylike, violating
the feminine sphere and addressing a political (therefore masculine) issue. Privately, they sometimes agreed with her.[3] Pro-
slavery women felt it their duty to defend the Southern way of life,
even if they had to do something so distasteful as enter into a public

debate. Stowe challenged the South's race, class and gender decorum. She must be refuted. As the *Southern Literary Messenger* warned:

> The success of *Uncle Tom's Cabin* is an evidence of the manner in which our enemies are employing literature for our overthrow. Is that effusion, in which a woman, instigated by the devil, sows the seeds of future strife between the two sections of her country, likely to be the last? No.
>
> (23 October 1856, 243)

The anonymous writer demonizes Stowe, seeing *Uncle Tom's Cabin* as literally subversive, a dangerous book with the power to destroy Southern society. The most effective counter-measure would be another book, the *Southern Literary Messenger* insists:

> As literature has been the most powerful weapon which the enemies of African slavery have used in their attacks, so, also, to literature must we look for maintenance of our position and our justification before the world. Let Southern authors, men who see and know slavery as it is, make it their duty to deluge all the realms of literature with a flood of light upon the subject.
>
> (ibid. 242)

It was largely *women* who claimed to "see and know slavery as it is" and who went to work to justify the ways of the South to the world. Responses to *Uncle Tom* and published assaults on Stowe flourished between 1852 and 1860, though many Southern writers answered and "corrected" Stowe for years after the Civil War. Mrs M. F. Surghnor's novel *Uncle Tom of the Old South*, published in 1896, answers Stowe from the belated perspective of the post-Reconstruction South, and as late as 1938, Margaret Mitchell wrote: "It makes me very happy to know that *Gone With the Wind* is helping to refute the impression of the South which people abroad gained from Mrs. Stowe's book" (Harwell 217).

Stowe and her bestseller, referred to by Grace King as "that black, hideous, dragonlike book," were the objects of an ideological and literary war that began nine years before South Carolina seceded. The attacks were various, the attackers came from all quarters. But in general, responses to *Uncle Tom's Cabin* employed a three-part strategy. First, they attacked Stowe *ad feminam*, impugning her Christianity, motherhood, wifehood, ladyhood, even gender. Then, they called sensationalist her construction of the South as a gothic realm, haunted by abused slaves, cursed by racial injustice, and dismissed it.[4] Finally, they offered a counter-vision of the South as the tidiest of paradises, presented as the "truth," negating Stowe's gothic version. Slavery reflected divine order; slaves were not tragic heroes and heroines but "lower" beings happily redeemed from barbarity and heathenism.

The pro-Southern responses to Stowe were highly conservative and sought to reinscribe the most traditional vision of the patriarchal household with the white master at the top and the slave at the bottom. Without doubt, the ideal of the plantation was difficult to attain, as many Southern writers themselves acknowledged. In the period 1820–60, the South was not without self-examination and internal criticism. Periodicals like the *Southern Literary Messenger* and Caroline Gilman's magazines for women and children, *The Magnolia, The Rose Bud, The Southern Rose* and *The Southern Rose Bud*, chastised, sometimes discreetly, sometimes more overtly, white men and women of the South for not living up to their own paternalistic, Christian standards. Yet when faced with what they saw as a broad attack on their most cherished institutions, generated from "outside" and recipient of international attention, Southern writers were united in their anger.[5] Stowe as transgressing woman, and her novel as disruptive fiction, were savaged as "unnatural" or even satanic. The literary battle over slavery was actually a battle over bodies – black bodies and women's bodies – and who had the right to control them. Attacking Stowe and her book formed part of the culture's policing of women and blacks: both sides knew the future shape (and colouring) of the United States was at stake.

Representation lies at the centre of controlling the black body and controlling the female body. As Peter Stallybrass remarks: "To examine the body's formation is to trace the connections between politeness and politics. But because the connections are never simply given, the body can itself become a site of conflict" (Stallybrass 123). Certainly the body's borders prove debatable in fiction and non-fiction both for and against slavery. Significant questions include the place of white women in the moral and social scheme of American culture, the "ownership" of black women's (and men's) sexuality and the restraints (or lack of them) placed on the bodies of white men. These questions outline the geography of gender and race relations in antebellum America: "bodily definitions were as important in the mapping out of gender as of class" (ibid. 125).

57

And race. The assumption that black women are "naturally" sexual while white women are "naturally" asexual, sets up a violent binary of bodily use. Opposites – black/white, polluted/pure, male/female, upper class/lower class – become the mode of definition, as we see in Stowe's conservative opponents. Mrs Henry Schoolcraft's novel *The Black Gauntlet* (1860) declares "God has placed a mark on the Negro, as distinctive as that on Cain;" God has also marked women in that he "ordered Adam, in consequence of his superiority, to rule over Eve" (Schoolcraft, vii, vi). Schoolcraft argues overtly in favour of the complete separateness of black and white: "I believe a refined Anglo-Saxon lady would sooner be burnt at the stake than married to one of these black descendants of Ham" (Schoolcraft, vii). For her, as for most of the polemicists, reviewers and novelists answering Stowe, sexuality is subject to a clear hierarchy of separation and submission. The slave South emerges as the most moral of societies (especially compared to the egalitarian North, home of abolition, "free love" and divorce) because it imposes the most defined order on the bodies of its women and its blacks. Violating that order, transgressing its well-signed frontiers, assaults the nation within a nation that built itself on difference. If the black and the female, the "marked," demand the place of the unmarked, chaos follows; the pure becomes polluted.

"THE MAN HARRIET"

Pro-slavery writers successfully linked abolitionism, feminism and socialism as catastrophic forces poised to destroy "Anglo-Saxon civilization." Criticism of slavery was identified with criticism of the church, the family and the institution of marriage. A writer in the *Southern Literary Messenger* asserted "Slavery is as essential a social institution in Virginia, as is marriage" (November 1856, 389). Pro-slavery writers feared abolitionism might unleash sexual anarchy, undermine class distinctions and destroy gender roles. *Uncle Tom's Cabin*, with its compendium of sexual sins charged to the South, and its class and gender transgressions, was clearly a powerful weapon in the abolitionists' arsenal.

For pro-slavery writers, Harriet Beecher Stowe's brand of abolitionism, moderate though it was compared to William Lloyd Garrison or Lydia Maria Child, bore the contaminated weight of all the "Yankee notions" defined as dangerous: race-mixing, feminism, Fourierism, free love, egalitarianism and property reform.[6] Harriet

Martineau, the British author of *Society in America* (1837), and even more strongly Frances Wright, the trouser-wearing radical opponent of marriage and feminist who tried to run a Utopian plantation in the 1830s, had been the chief female targets of Southern traditionalists.[7] However, after the publication of *Uncle Tom's Cabin*, Stowe took over as the symbol of New England perversity for conservatives everywhere. Forming his view from *Uncle Tom's Cabin* and its frontispiece portrait of Stowe, Matthew Arnold wrote to A. H. Clough calling her "a Gorgon" as well as "a Strong Dissenter – religious middle-class person – she will never go far, I think" (21 March 1853, Milford 133). Opinion on Stowe's side of the Atlantic was even more acid: William Gilmore Simms echoed Arnold's insult, calling her sarcastically "our fair author – whose daguerreotype, by the way, is such as to damage the reputation of any female writer under the sun" (Simms, "Stowe's *Key*" 221). George Frederick Holmes labelled Stowe "an obscure Yankee schoolmistress, eaten up with fanaticism, festering with the malignant virus of abolitionism, self-sanctified by the virtues of a Pharisaic religion, devoted to the assertion of women's rights" (Holmes 321). The *New Orleans Crescent* was still less delicate: "There never before was anything so detestable or so monstrous among women as this" (Gossett 190).

Stowe was tainted with the "unnaturalness" and "perversity" which her opponents saw as products of the poisoned politics of the North. Attacks focused on her person: she was a Gorgon, a female monster who was, at the same time, *not* female. Holmes described her as eaten up with political cancers, "festering with the malignant virus of abolitionism." Her foes called her "unwomanly;" in some critical assaults she even took on a grotesque masculinity. The woman writer intervening in the public, *male* realm of political discourse, even in a sentimental novel, an acceptable *female* form, slipped dangerously close to gender-switching in the eyes of conservative commentators. Holmes connected her with "mannish" women like Frances Wright and George Sand in a feminism which "unsexed in great measure the female mind and shattered the temple of feminine delicacy and moral graces" (ibid. 322). The feminist-abolitionist was neither quite a man nor any longer a woman. Her body was no longer a sacred "temple" but something distorted and dirty: "the mental aberrations of woman ... excite at once pity and disgust, like those revolting physical deformities which the eye turns from with involuntary loathing" (McCord, "Enfranchisement of Women" 325).

In a culture which valued categorization and the defining opposites which lent it order, *Uncle Tom's Cabin* – with its white women who turn out to be black, slaves who gain freedom, plantation owners from the North, women disguised as men, boys disguised as girls, and "ghosts" who aren't dead – wreaks havoc on the absolute status the white South tried to assign to race, gender and class. The novel operates on inversions. Stowe herself inverted the proper womanly role, acting as a man: a sort of transvestite endangering the edifices of white over black and male over female which the white South insisted were inviolable. Marjorie Garber reads this systematic violation of boundaries as "a failure of definitional distinction, a borderline that becomes permeable" (Garber 16).[8] Transgression points to a culture's weak points: "one of the most consistent and effective functions of the transvestite in culture is to indicate the place of what I call 'category crisis,' disrupting and calling attention to cultural, social or aesthetic dissonances" (ibid. 16). Stowe, deemed the most spectacular of gender traitors by pro-slavery writers, forfeited her claims to "ladyhood" with *Uncle Tom's Cabin*, as a number of hostile reviewers point out.[9] Some pro-slavery women saw writing as cross-dressing: Caroline Gilman recalled her unauthorized first publication with shame, saying "I wept bitterly, and was as alarmed as if I had been detected in man's apparel" (quoted in Fox-Genovese 246).

Pro-slavery readers detected no shame in the gender-bending author Stowe. One woman, writing to the *New Orleans Picayune*, simply refers to "the man Harriet," marking Stowe as contrary to what God intended: unnatural, perverse, a freak (Gossett 191).[10] By speaking out on a political (masculine) subject, Stowe ceases to be a woman, a privileged body, protected and enclosed by the "chaste" silence appropriate to her gender, becoming instead a monster, a literary cross-dresser. Furthermore, she suggests subversive possibilities outside the limits placed on whites, blacks, men and women.

Mary H. Eastman's *Aunt Phillis' Cabin* (1852), perhaps the most accomplished of the fictional responses to *Uncle Tom's Cabin*, fractures Stowe into three characters encountered by the heroine at a Washington party, each testifying to her freakishness. The first is a "Mrs. S.," who makes "a great exhibition of herself" waltzing over-energetically (Eastman 228). Dancing so excessively, she cannot be a lady; moreover, the waltz is a "fast" or sexually suggestive dance. Ellen Graham, a young lady from a Virginia plantation, is not allowed to waltz. Stowe's second aspect is "a lady writer," a pathetic creature with faded finery and artificial flowers, while the third is *"a she Abolitionist"* who "wants Frederick Douglass to be the next President and advocates amalgamation" (ibid. 229).

In the eyes of these critics, Stowe was guilty of gender transgression, of unsexing herself and making of herself something that could not fit into their recognized order of being.[11] For some, her monstrousness began with her daring to speak – that is, to write – on the subject of slavery at all. George Frederick Holmes quoted the First Epistle to Timothy: "But I suffer not a woman to teach, nor to usurp authority over the man, but to be in silence" (*Southern Literary Messenger* 18 October 1852, 631). Louisa McCord, on the other hand, saw nothing wrong with a woman teaching as long as she taught *womanly virtues*: for her, Stowe, like all feminist-abolitionists, abdicated her gender to drift like a lost soul in a desert of deformed, sexually-undefined bodies. For others, Stowe had not masculinized herself so much as become a *fallen* woman: by speaking/writing in public, she displayed herself like a prostitute. Critics maligned her chastity and assaulted her in print: "where a writer of the softer sex manifests, in her productions, a shameless disregard of truth and of those amenities which so peculiarly belong to her sphere of life, we hold that she has forfeited the claim to be considered a lady" (ibid. 630).

Use of a word like "shameless" connects Stowe not just with philosophical offenders but sexual offenders. Ellen in *Aunt Phillis' Cabin* suggests that the "she Abolitionist" might like to marry an old slave on her plantation, Uncle Bacchus, then satirically decides "I do not think she is stylish enough for him" (Eastman 229). William Gilmore Simms insinuates that the runaway slave George Harris' "good looks and locks" in *Uncle Tom* excited Stowe ("Simms," Stowe's *Key*" 221). An erotic connection between a white woman and a black man was the most appalling perversion in a slave South convinced of the need for subordination of "the African."[12] Despite the large number of slaveholding men with mixed-race children by slave women, officially amalgamation was a vice that only the truly depraved could support. A white woman showing sexual interest in a black man, even an imaginary, light-skinned black man, revealed herself as a monster or a whore: this is what Simms (who wrote his own fictional response to *Uncle Tom's Cabin*, *The Sword and the Distaff*) is really saying. Ellen in *Aunt Phillis' Cabin*

61

declares "'when a woman approves of amalgamation, she is so lost to every sense of propriety that it makes no difference to her whether a man is married or not'" (Eastman 229–30).

Elsewhere in that *Southern Quarterly Review* piece, Simms characterizes Stowe's authorship: "the petticoat lifts of itself, and we see the hoof of the beast under the table" (Simms, "Stowe's *Key*" 226). Here the cross-dressed author becomes a devil disguised in women's clothing. The image of the petticoat lifting "of itself" is supernatural and demonic, insisting that despite Stowe's claims that God wrote *Uncle Tom's Cabin*, her inspiration actually came from below.[13] However, something else reveals itself when the petticoat of the female author rises; the "hoof of the beast," the "mark" of the devil, also signifies the "mark" of the female, that is: the genitals. The woman who speaks or writes "in public," who makes herself a "display" like a prostitute, in effect flaunts her genitals. She shows what no lady even admits to having; she unveils what her culture covers in layers of skirts and mystifies in language. As well as violating the conventions of her gender, according to her critics, Stowe violates the definition of the body assigned her class and race. Underscoring her perceived distance from the lady's classical body with its smooth, orificeless surface, lonely and elevated as a statue on the pedestal, Simms and others are determined to connect Stowe to the grotesque body, a polluted, low body.

I see this in what her detractors ostentatiously decry as her "disgusting" imagination, her "profanity" and the "horrors" of her fiction. Mary H. Eastman calls Stowe's descriptions of Legree's plantation "scenes that a woman's pen should never describe" (Eastman 267). In particular, Stowe's rendering of Cassy, the much-violated mulatta, "appalls" in a novel by a woman. Cassy is "a most infamous creature" whose only character trait is "vileness" (ibid. 269). Eastman dismisses Cassy for unchastity; and condemns Stowe for having the temerity to write sympathetically of an unwed, mixed-race mother who had been the mistress of a number of vicious white men. By addressing sexual matters, Stowe exposes herself as "unclean" and therefore not to be listened to by "decent" people, especially women. Holmes says that Stowe is "coarse" and knows more of "corruption" than men in the South. Moreover, he hopes that Southern women will not read *Uncle Tom's Cabin* – as if it were a work of pornography which would "violate" their innocence.[14]

Indeed, it is as pornography that *Uncle Tom*'s harshest critic, the South Carolina essayist and dramatist Louisa McCord, responds to it.[15] In an 1853 review-essay in the *Southern Quarterly Review*, McCord links class with pornography, charging Stowe with catering not only to "second-rate literary taste" but to a "diseased taste" (McCord,"Review of *Uncle Tom's Cabin* 83). According to the aristocrat McCord, Stowe is, as Matthew Arnold pointed out, hopelessly middle class – *lower* middle class, even. McCord constantly ridicules one of Stowe's sources for her Louisiana episodes, her brother who had served as a clerk in New Orleans, calling him "Mrs. Stowe's store-clerk brother" (ibid. 89). She is also given to saying things like: "Mrs. Stowe has associated much, it would appear, with negroes, mulattoes and abolitionists;" and she sneers at Stowe for writing a scene showing a slave-trader sitting in a planter gentleman's parlour (ibid. 93). McCord feels Stowe is incapable of realistically presenting the Southern upper classes, as demonstrated when she makes Marie St Clare utter the word "sweat." McCord calls Stowe a liar and a purveyor of smut, castigating her severely for depicting scenes "most revolting at once to decency, truth and probability" as well as "nauseating," displaying the sexual use of slave women in the South.

In her "Enfranchisement of Women," McCord tidily equates abolitionism, feminism and atheism: "*Justicia*, shouts Cuffee, means that I am a sun-burned white man. *Justicia*, responds Harriet Martineau, means that I may discard decency and my petticoats at my own convenience; and, *Justicia*, echo her Worcester Convention sisters, means extinction to all laws, human and divine" (McCord, "Enfranchisement of Women" 323). To question slavery is to question divine authority, the law of nature that ordains subservient places for women and Africans. Underneath McCord's anger at the attempts of abolitionist-feminists like Harriet Martineau and Frances Wright to argue for women's rights and against slavery lurks fear of "amalgamation":

> Madness becomes, sometimes, contagious; and to judge from the symptoms, society labours, at present, under a high state of brain-fever. . . . Communism and abolitionism have been dancing their antics through its bewildered brain; and now behold the *chef d'oeuvre* of folly! Mounted on Cuffee's shoulders, in rides the lady!
>
> (ibid. 327)

The woman and the black man touch in a scandalous manner and society runs amok; the terror of cross-racial sexuality emblematized in the white woman riding the shoulders of the black man. Amalgamation, or hybridization, is, as Stallybrass and White see it, part of the grotesque, the disorderly, the "intense interfusion of incompatibles which was such anathema to classical reason with its predilection for a rhetoric of clean antithesis" (Stallybrass and White 47–48). McCord is certainly a classical reasoner, a believer in hierarchies and irreconcilable opposites: white and black, male and female. Still, McCord locates this particular breakdown of decorum in the North. Below the Mason–Dixon line "our modest Southern sisters have held aloof from the defiling pitch, and Worcester Conventions are entirely a Yankee notion" (McCord, "Enfranchisement of Women" 326). Below the Mason–Dixon line, she insists, antitheses are still "clean," no matter what messy inversions and confusions trouble the North.

McCord attacks still more pungently when she raises the spectre of amalgamation as a companion to woman suffrage, essentially saying that gender equality would lead to racial equality and the pollution of ladyhood. She pictures women and blacks competing for political attention:

> Imagine the lovely Miss Caroline, the fascinating Miss Martha, elbowing Sambo for the stump! All being equals, and no respect for persons to be expected, the natural conclusion is, that Miss Caroline or Martha, being indisputably (even the Worcester conventionalists will allow that) corporeally weaker than Sambo, would be thrust into the mud.
>
> (ibid. 332)

Slavery, to McCord, is the glue that binds western civilization together, and race the most obvious distinction between persons who are, of course, ordained as *unequal*.[16] Without slavery, all social institutions will collapse:

> Negro emancipation would be inevitably the death-blow of our civilization. By *ours*, we meant not ours of Georgia, Alabama, Mississippi or Carolina – nay, nor of these Southern United States – nay, nor of this whole great empire, this young giant, whose infant strength startles its European forefathers with its newborn might; but *ours* – our civilization of this world of the nineteenth century, *must fall* with negro emancipation.
>
> (McCord, "Negro and White Slavery" 129)

64

"NAUSEOUS DIET": SOUTHERNERS ON STOWE'S GOTHIC

Louisa McCord names and ridicules the gothic in *Uncle Tom's Cabin* while appropriating gothic discourse and turning it against Stowe and, by extension, against abolitionism, feminism and egalitarianism. In her 1851 essay-review "Negro and White Slavery," McCord gothicizes all political progressivism: "Communism and Socialism, in their various forms and divers masks, now show themselves in bald and fiendlike horrible indecency, with their bold cry of 'no property,' 'no family'" (McCord, "Negro and White Slavery" 120). Abolitionism and its still more evil twin, feminism, are also "monstrous" and unnatural, a perversion of the "correct" order exhibited on the paternalistic plantation. Clearly McCord's understanding of liberalism as something both "horrible" and pornographic ("indecent") dates from well before she was confronted with *Uncle Tom's Cabin*. Her suspicions about the North are merely confirmed: it harbours philosophies that would turn America into a "nightmare."

McCord's review of *Uncle Tom's Cabin* cleverly juxtaposes Stowe's novel with gothic fiction, attempting to undermine it as a "Christian" tale of virtue. She plays on the moralists' suspicion of the novel genre as a suitable form for ethical discussion, placing *Uncle Tom* in the category of fiction "spiced too high" along with Eugène Sue's sensational *The Mysteries of Paris* (1842–43) and *The Wandering Jew* (1844–45), pandering to the "diseased taste of the reader who has long subsisted on such fare, sick, sick and palled as it is with the nauseous diet, still, with a constant craving, like that of the diseased palate of the opium eater" (McCord, Review of *Uncle Tom's Cabin* 83). McCord taunts Stowe for disguising her gothic intent in supposed reality, particularly in the character of Simon Legree:

> If the lowest vices of the lowest men, – if the darkest crimes of the darkest villains, – actions which the vilest of mankind, only in their moments of blackest passion, can perpetrate, – are to be culled out with care, and piled upon each other, to form a monster disgusting to humanity, let the creator of so unnatural a conception give to his Frankenstein the name as well as the character of the monsters of fable.

(ibid. 88)

McCord seems torn between satisfaction that the worst villain in *Uncle Tom's Cabin* is a New Englander and anger that Stowe presents such a "devil" as a human being. McCord may also be insulted on behalf of an aristocratic South Carolina family, the Legarés, whose name is pronounced "Legree": she insists that Stowe give her villain a name befitting "some ghoul or afrite." It is most interesting that McCord connects *Uncle Tom* with *Frankenstein*; not only does she undermine Stowe again with the "taint" of the gothic novel, questioning the legitimacy and veracity of *Uncle Tom* by placing it in the same category as a horrifying "fable," but she indirectly invokes Mary Shelley, another female writer attacked for her "irregular" private life, her feminism and her involvement in radical politics.

As if it is not enough to equate Stowe with sexually and politically suspect gothic writers, McCord goes on to say "Mrs. Stowe has a fertile imagination, and has got up quite a respectable collection of 'tales of wonder,' which would rival in horrors those of Monk Lewis" (ibid. 109). By comparing *Uncle Tom* to the lurid excesses of *The Monk*, with its satanic abbot, incest, drugs, rape and murder, McCord dismisses Stowe as a pure sensationalizer. McCord then turns around and aims Stowe's gothic back at her, saying that however Stowe might terrify the reader with her slave-state atrocities, her fiction is inadequate to describe the *real* horrors that would result from the abolition of slavery:

> "though she should go on, and on, and on, till even *her* thought should quail, and even *her* heart sink at the fearful picture, yet will she not have touched, yet can she not have began [sic] to imagine, the fearful penalties which indignant nature would attach to her so outraged laws."

> (ibid. 109)

As we have seen, pro-slavery writers argue that the destruction of the slave South would mean a gothic catalogue of catastrophes far more fearful than any found in a novel. McCord employs the anti-abolitionists' favourite example, Haiti, to describe the murder and rapine that would be visited on whites by outraged and vengeful black "barbarians." She scoffs at what she sees as Stowe's weak threats of "a second Hayti" if slavery is not abolished. Again she turns the rhetoric around, insisting that the atrocities of Haiti would be visited a hundredfold upon America if the decorum of slavery is violated. Slavery is equated with paternal order and divine hierarchy: to abolish slavery is to flout nature, to pervert God's law and to unleash sexual and social anarchy on the nation, destroying the family. While McCord's images of white female virtue menaced are more implied than stated, unlike pro-slavery novels, she operates out of the same background, stressing that "barbarism" is Africans' natural state, and only slavery keeps them from fulfilling their "natural" destiny as murderers and rapists.

Stowe and McCord charge each other with endangering the family; but they have different definitions of the family. For Stowe, as we have seen, the family ideally operates as a liberal democratic structure, a system of kinship and shared work. McCord's sense of the family, however, follows paternalistic lines, a household hierarchy rather than a companionate system, including not just kin but slaves. Stowe and McCord also charge each other's political camps with sexual transgression: to an abolitionist, slavery was institutionalized rape and sanctioned adultery; to a slaveholder, abolitionism was a threat to the chastity of white women.

In her preface to *The Planter's Northern Bride* (1854), Caroline Lee Hentz critiques *Uncle Tom's Cabin* as both gothic and pornographic, outraged at "the dark and horrible pictures drawn of slavery and exhibited to a gazing world" by Stowe (Hentz, *Northern Bride* I iv). Later, Hentz asserts her own veracity in describing the amenities of plantation life and its moral beneficence for both black and white: "We have not gone groping in dark by-lanes and foul dens for tales of horror, which might gratify a morbid and perverted taste." (ibid. II 280). She implies that *Uncle Tom's Cabin*, in displaying a gothic South full of "tales of horror," undermines its credibility and destroys its respectability as a novel: it is both untrue and unhealthy, dark pornographic stuff feeding the depraved tastes of the South's enemies, the "fanatics" (abolitionists) determined to destroy the Edenic plantation. The gaze of the North demands a grotesque South, but the South defines itself as pure and elevated, like the body of the lady herself. Hentz implies there is something "improper" in the examination, just as it is improper for men to see women unclothed. The plantation elite of the South extended their imagery of the sacrosanct white lady with her closed, veiled body to the land itself. A favourite representation of the plantation drew it as a walled garden, a *hortus conclusus* hidden from the profane eyes of the rest of the world. To open it up is to violate it. Various critics, most notably Annette Kolodny, have shown how the Southern land is typically figured as a female body.[17] Scrutiny, here in the form of Stowe's fiction, is a form of invasion or *penetration* which Southern authors like Hentz find as shocking as rape.

Pro-Southern writers answered the call of the *Southern Literary Messenger* and the *Southern Quarterly Review* for corrective fictions parading the "true," healthy picture of a divinely ordered society. An America in the hands of the abolitionists would be gothic, *not* the slave South. If the abolitionists got their way "the reign of animal passion and power" (*Southern Literary Messenger* June 1853, 213) would take over and America would become a physical and ethical wilderness:

> "should the burning lava of anarchy and servile war roll over the plains of the South, and bury, under its fiery waves, its social and domestic institutions, it will not suffer alone. The North and the South are branches of the same parent tree, and the lightning bolt that shivers the one, must scorch and wither the other."
>
> (Hentz, *Northern Bride* II 281)

For Hentz, the true gothic threat lies in the possibility of freed slaves running amok, sexually assaulting white women, "amalgamating" with "the white race." Despite Stowe's insistence that white men sexually exploit slave women, Hentz's hero insists that a "'white woman who marries a negro, makes herself an outcast, a scorn and a byword. The white man who marries a negress forfeits his position as a gentleman'" (ibid. I 203). Even an abolitionist cannot possibly be serious when he advocates race-mixing: "'in his heart, he recoils from it in horror. He would sooner see a son or a daughter perish beneath the stroke of the assassin than wedded to the African'" (ibid. I 203).

The "horror" of miscegenation becomes, for pro-slavery writers, the gothic consequence of abolitionism. The sexual anarchy Stowe (and other abolitionists) identify as the location of the Southern gothic is turned around: again, the pro-slavery argument holds that sexuality is controlled *in* slavery. In *The Planter's Northern Bride*, Hentz's South is idyllic: terrors come from outside: abolitionists, foreigners, Yankees. Eulalia, the New England-bred wife of a Southern planter, converts to slavery almost instantly; her Garrisonian father, however, represents the horrors that may lurk in the bosom of every Northern home. He aids a runaway slave, not only inviting the man to eat with his family but giving him the best bedroom as well. The implied sexual danger of a free black man in a house with young white women, treated as a guest, allowed in the private (female) spaces of the home, inspires Eulalia's suitor, Moreland, to swiftly remove his bride to the plantation, where contact between white women and black men is highly circumscribed. He need not worry over her politics, sexual or social: she falls ill the minute the ex-slave is in the house, signifying the danger that a free black man poses to a white female body as well as the danger abolition poses to the national body.

Not that the plantation is entirely free of perils for the upper middle-class white family, however. The occasional visits of Moreland's wicked first wife, Claudia, whom he divorced, hints at the threat of race-mixing. There is no overt suggestion she is part black (she is described as a sort of Italian gypsy) but the terms in which Hentz condemns her insinuate miscegenation: the dark-haired, dark-eyed, sexually-charged Claudia (her appearance has much in common with conventional fictional representations of mulattas) bears a "taint" in her blood. The notion of a genetic curse is also common to tragic mulatta novels (ibid. II 79).[18] The menacing presence and eventual vanquishing in the novel of tainted "foreign" women and subversive abolitionists demonstrates a symbolic need to purge America of elements threatening racial decorum. In the end, Claudia dies repentant, Eulalia's father converts to the Southern cause, and a foolish runaway slave named Crissy repudiates the abolitionists who "seduced" her and comes back to the plantation.[19] Hentz answers Stowe with a positive vision of an Arcadian South while promising a scorched earth policy for the North if the South should have to go to war to protect her "civilisation." Instead of a site of gothic atrocities, the South is seen as the bulwark against them.

The North, not the South, is constructed as one large torture chamber in many pro-slavery novels.[20] Caroline Rush's *The North and the South, or Slavery and Its Contrasts* (1852) rehearses the familiar argument that black Southern slaves fared better than white Northern workers. What little Rush shows of the South – a model plantation – is a vision of perfect aristocratic order with loyal slaves, chivalric men and a madonna-like mistress who acts as mother to all. The North is, of course, the opposite: delicately-raised white children work from dawn to dusk and are regularly beaten, young ladies are threatened by rape and violence, ruined fathers turn to alcohol and middle-class white families find themselves neighbours to "uncivilised" free blacks in Philadelphia who live in "sin and debauchery" (Rush 15).

In *Ellen; or the Fanatic's Daughter* (1860) by Mrs V. G. Cowdin, abolitionists as well as free blacks pose a sexual threat to pure white women. Mary, raised a lady on a Louisiana plantation, unwisely marries a Northerner under the influence of his evil "fanatic" brother-in-law, Parson Blake. Her life becomes a series of indignities as she is forced to work as a servant and live with free blacks. Parson Blake is a sexual danger first to Mary – "the cold leaden eyes of Parson Blake . . . seemed to emit fiery serpents that darted their fatal thrusts at the heart of Mary" – then to her daughter Ellen. Ellen is further harassed by a married abolitionist who looks to score political points by making this impoverished daughter of Southern gentry his mistress (Cowdin 9, 116). The evil of abolitionism works even after death on the privileged person of the white woman. After she dies, Mary's pathetic corpse is taken away to be dissected in a medical school class. The implication in both Rush and Cowdin is clear: abolitionism attacks the body of the white woman; the end of slavery will mean sexual anarchy and a destruction of the hierarchy that makes the lady sacred.

Eastman, Hentz, Rush, Cowdin and numerous others appropriate gothic modes for their counter-fictions. The haunted house symbolizes the North, abolitionists are lechers hell-bent on destroying the chastity of white women, while back in the sunny South, kindly masters battle to hold back the "dark flood" of liberal thinking assailing the institutions of slavery, marriage and motherhood. Fictional critiques of *Uncle Tom's Cabin*, conventional and sentimental though they may appear, answer its radicalism point for point. These novelists correctly read Stowe's vision of the central threat of slavery as its assault on the family and set out to refute it, substituting the body of the white woman for the body of the slave mother as the privileged focus. Abolitionists (and feminists) are depicted as ugly, disappointed women, or misguided men who need only come South to see the error of their ways, or else lustful hypocrites preying on white (and occasionally black) women. Pro-slavery writers insist that even the most virulent abolitionists cannot seriously believe in race-mixing: in Robert Criswell's *"Uncle Tom's Cabin" Contrasted With Buckingham Hall* (1852), the abolitionist Dr Tennyson says he finds the way Little Eva *touches* Uncle Tom most distasteful (Criswell 139). In the same novel, a story is told of an abolitionist in the South who, despite his liberal racial politics, could not bear to be touched by a black person or eat food cooked by a black hand. He unwittingly marries a mulatta slave and when he realizes who and what she is, he runs away from her in horror (ibid. 60–61).

Sexual disgust and sexual paranoia drive political positions in anti-*Tom* novels. Over and over again, anti-*Tom* novels deny Stowe's assertion of the South's sexual crisis. Instead, they hold up the South as a place of ideal sexual order. To Stowe's critics, the North fosters sexual anarchy, swarming as it is with free blacks and free-love abolitionists. They warn constantly that if slavery collapses, the sexual decorum of America will explode: the morality that places the sacrosanct body of the white woman at the spiritual peak of the nation will fragment. Emancipation could turn America into "Hayti" or, as Thomas R. Dew warns in *The Pro-Slavery Argument* (1853), into Guatemala where murder is commonplace, men are drunk and women are whores (Dew 445).

The Pro-Slavery Argument, a non-fiction collection of responses to Stowe, is, like the anti-*Tom* novels, much concerned with slavery's contribution to the high moral tone of the South (as opposed to the North, Britain, or anywhere else, for that matter). In the first essay, Chancellor Harper argues that even sexual transgression in the slave South occurs in a more orderly fashion than anywhere else. "Fallen" black women are tolerated in the South in a way that fallen white women are not in the North. Opinion held it to be, after all, "natural" for slave women to behave promiscuously: "The colored prostitute is, in fact, a far less contaminated and degraded being" (ibid. 43).[21] More importantly, white men who sleep with black women are not so culpable as if they sinned with white women because the liaisons are automatically "casual" (ibid. 44–45). And, most importantly, this division of sexual labour "elevates the [white] female character" (ibid. 66). Dew agrees, declaring that slavery has even lifted black women out of total savagery and has revealed white women as angelic beings. Only slavery keeps a necessary class hierarchy functioning; only slavery keeps sexual anarchy at bay.

COUNTER-FICTIONS

According to Eric Sundquist, the South "performs" its story of racial order and harmony before a Northern audience (Sundquist, *To Wake the Nations* 273). Pro-slavery writers elaborate on a preexisting "other" South, appropriating the criticism of anti-slavery writers and turning it to their own use – making an insult into a proud virtue. This is evident in the ways pro-slavery writers pirate the gothic "curse" which abolitionists located in the South, although they see it as a different curse, emanating from a mythic time. Apologists for slavery trace the curse, historically and theologically, to "Bible days," arguing that it is not the yoke of slavery but the taint of race itself: the "Mark of Cain," the "Mark of Ham" or the "Mark of Ishmael," that dooms Africans. The South acts as a sort of glamorous purgatory (for slaves, not masters) in which these lesser beings learn from "the highest type of Christian civilization on earth." Slavery becomes not a series of tortures out of Monk Lewis but a manifestation of divine order.

Louisa McCord's writings ring with the language of *order* – "God's and Nature's laws." As we have seen, the aims of abolitionism are, for her, equivalent to the aims of feminism and egalitarianism, all of which she rejects. In reasoning against feminism, McCord dismisses the argument of the Worcester Convention of 1850 that "distinctions of sex and colour are accidental and irrelevant to all questions of government" as "illogical" (McCord, "Enfranchisement of Women" 329).

For McCord, and other pro-slavery writers, abolitionism, like feminism, sins against the divinely-sanctioned regime of the plantation South, and *Uncle Tom's Cabin*, in particular, commits calumny against what she calls "the God-established system of slavery, which our Southern states are beautifully developing to perfection" (McCord, Review of *Uncle Tom's Cabin* 109). McCord vehemently denies any veracity to one of Stowe's central devices in *Uncle Tom*: that is, the romance of the tragic mulatta. For Stowe, the elision of black and white demonstrates the hypocrisy and arbitrary cruelty of slavery. The torment of slaves like Cassy, George, Eliza and Madame de Thoux, who could not only "pass" for white, but who had "white" sensitivity, refinement, cultivation and all those other delicate attributes even abolitionists thought more "natural" to whites than to blacks, is of vital political use. Readers sympathized more easily with characters "like" themselves. McCord, of course, denies any likeness of even mulattoes to whites. She dismisses the scene where Cassy and Madame de Thoux travel as French and Spanish ladies as "impossible within the law of nature." Mulattas are inevitably "woolly-headed and yellow-skinned" – any Southerner would recognize them (ibid. 114). McCord's racial ideology holds that the "mark" of blackness, however small, must be evident in the form of the bearer. Anything else would flout God's law.

Attacking on a related front, McCord says (with some justice) that Stowe seems much more interested in the "slightly black" mulatto than the "true negro." McCord notes with satisfaction that Stowe, perhaps unwittingly, shows how "well suited" most slaves are for their position. Moreover, Stowe exhibits some "natural" sense of decency about deeply black slaves: "even she would not have a pretty little Quakeress liberator snatching up a negro bantling and covering it with kisses, and putting the mother into her own bed. . . as she does by the white mulattoes she introduces" (ibid. 117). McCord cannot quite make up her mind about "negroes" and "mulattoes;" sometimes she draws firm distinctions between mulattoes and blacks, at other times she places them as qualitatively just about the same for the purpose of showing how utterly alien and loathsome the black body is to whites.

None the less, McCord insists the mulatta is a monster, a freak of "no class and no caste" (ibid. 117). She does so to undermine Stowe's charge (and that of many other abolitionist writers) that the South was full of these displaced white slaves, children of plantation masters and overseers. Indeed, McCord borrows (as she does with Stowe's gothic imagery) a central abolitionist contention that slavery includes in its catalogue of immoralities enforced concubinage, then turns the argument around, calling the mulatto or mulatta an "unhappy being [who] must occasionally exist, wherever the two peoples are brought in contact." However, she concludes triumphantly, race-mixing appears "more frequently where abolition license prevails, than under the rules and restraints of slavery" (ibid. 118).

McCord and other pro-slavery writers, especially novelists, present a counter-story to Stowe's infernal South, even as they attempt to challenge her point for point. For them, the plantation South seems an earthly Eden. In J. Thornton Randolph's *The Cabin and the Parlor; or Slaves and Masters* (1852), money-grubbing Yankees force the young lady of the plantation out of her home: "Yet as the mansions disappeared behind them in the shadows of night, she felt like Eve when our first mother left Paradise forever" (Randolph 49). Isabel Courtenay differs from Eve in being evidently without sin.[22] The integrity of the plantation intersects with the integrity of the lady's body in the pro-slavery mind. Stallybrass reminds us that the body of an idealized virgin (specifically Elizabeth I) approximates Eden: "her enclosed body *was* that paradise (a word derived from the Persian *pairidaeza*, meaning a royal enclosure)"

(Stallybrass 130). The *closedness*, the lack of opening, or sexuality, in the white woman's body emblematizes the closed plantation world, figured in fiction by William Gilmore Simms, Caroline Lee Hentz, Caroline Gilman and others as the *hortus conclusus*. In defining their world as Eden, pro-slavery writers insist on the elevation of the classical (white) body, asserting its opposition to, and its distance from, the tainted Other: the grotesque (black) body. Their system demands, as always, absolute racial definition.

The South as paradise counters Stowe's haunted house. In Hentz's *The Planter's Northern Bride*, the flowers and warmth of the South are constantly contrasted to the cold barrenness of New England, as they are in Cowdin's *Ellen; or the Fanatic's Daughter*, in which the South is seen as a heaven-like reward for the sufferings of Ellen Layton in the North (Cowdin 152ff.). At the Bellamy plantation, in Hentz's *Marcus Warland* (1852), the families of slaves are never separated, the master is kindly and the mistress angelic. The place even resurrects itself: when the plantation house burns it is soon rebuilt, more beautiful than before. Freed, the slaves refuse to leave.[23] In *Aunt Phillis' Cabin*, the slave Susan also recognizes the proper order of things (even if she *is* black) when she returns from a mistaken stay with Northern abolitionists (Eastman 58). Susan finds the North anarchic, dangerous and perpetually snow-covered. In obvious contrast, Exeter Plantation in Virginia is overloaded with flowers (ibid. 26). Aunt Phillis (saintly, long-suffering counterpart to Stowe's Uncle Tom) inhabits a cabin positively dripping in roses – and no weeds (ibid. 112). The master offers Aunt Phillis her freedom, but she prefers to die a slave. She is represented, like Uncle Tom, as an exemplary Christian. However, Eastman draws a radically different conclusion from Stowe; instead of seeing slavery as a state such paragons of righteousness should be liberated from, Eastman declares it a condition of Christianity for the African. Still, Uncle Tom is altogether too good to be true, according to Eastman's sardonic "Concluding Remarks:" "One would have thought his master. . . would have kept him until he died and then have sold him bone after bone to the Roman Catholics" (ibid. 266).

The binaries placing the black body on the bottom of the social structure in the South carry an implicit anxiety about that body, a fear that disorder lies in wait if the vigilance of absolute opposites is not maintained. We see this manifested in some of the more eccentric episodes in anti-*Tom* novels: for example, in Towsend's

The Brother Clerks (1857), Minny, the mostly white half-sister to the heroine Della, can be read both as a pathetic victim of slavery and a threat of what might happen if slavery were abolished. She has been illegally married to the man Della loves, she is abused by their father (who refuses to acknowledge her) and is finally shot by her sister's – her own former – husband. In J. Thornton Randolph's *The Cabin and the Parlor* (1852), the mulatta Cora, a "well-treated" favourite of the heroine, foolishly runs away to the North where rioting whites and "trashy" free blacks threaten her with violence and rape. Away from the plantation, she meets with nothing but chaos. Another mulatta Cora, in *Marcus Warland*, is so beloved of the plantation mistress that the mistress gives her one of her fine white gowns for a wedding dress which promptly catches fire during the ceremony.[24] Cora dies of her burns and haunts the house dressed as a bride.

The burned bride, her marriage never consummated, is an emblem of the anxiety over black sexuality that the white South felt but rarely expressed openly. The fire destroys the black woman but also signifies her "hot" flesh; Mary Chesnut calls black women "Animals – tout et simple – cordifiamma – no – *corpi*fiamma" (Woodward 243). Chesnut underlines *body* not *heart*, placing the "flame" she fears and dislikes not in the spirit but in the sexuality marking black women, a mark white women took care to distance themselves from. In a way, the very presence of the black body undercuts the Edenic, orderly South, so successful at repressing sexual passion. As characters, these Minnys and Coras are nearly-absent, ghosts or shadows, subsumed in a conventional narrative where the plantation runs correctly and proper race and gender relations are always restored. Still, they testify to a masked fear that Stowe's gothic pronouncements might come true and the whole fragile edifice of caste and colour might collapse into a romantic ruin. Eden, by its very nature, must be lost. The white South is caught in a contradiction of its own making: slavery frames the hierarchy of white over black, lady over whore, spirit over flesh, through which the South represented its women, and, at the same time, endangers it. The constant proximity of slaves, the touch of black hands on white property and white skin, cleaning, feeding, dressing, at once asserted difference and threatened barriers. The white South drew ever-heavier boundaries only to see them erased on all sides. The paradise of their plantation gardens and the "royal enclosure" of their women's bodies were bound to be symbolically violated by anti-slavery ideas – *Uncle Tom's Cabin* proved hard to ban – and by "invading" Union troops, imposing a new bodily order.

3

MISS WRIGHT, MRS TROLLOPE AND MISS MARTINEAU
or, Three British women look at American slavery

[women will be glad] to see their houses in flames, to hear the com-
ing tornado, to feel the threatening earthquake, if these be indeed
the messengers who must open their prison doors and give their
heaven-born spirits the range of the universe. . . man does that
which he would not have woman hear of. He puts genius out of
sight and deprecates calamity. He has not, however, calculated all
the forces in nature. If he had, he would hardly venture to hold
either negroes or women as property.
　　　　　　　　　　　　Harriet Martineau, *Society in America*

Early nineteenth-century America looked like a country in a per-
manent state of revolution – social, if not military. The United States
in the first eighty years of its independence was animated by
violent dissent and debate. Newspapers, journals and books re-
sounded with searing self-examinations and outside assessments
by visiting foreigners, betraying enormous anxiety over what being
American meant, what politics that identity implied, what pieties
it demanded.[1]

Race was then, as it is now, a flashpoint of righteous anger and
earnest moralizing for competing social critics coming both from
within and without. Twenty years before Harriet Beecher Stowe
became the popularly-designated galvanizer of the nation on the issue
of slavery, a number of women writers and political activists caused
riots, incurred threats of violence and inspired vitriolic exchanges in
the press. Particularly offensive to insular Americans were the British
women who published journals or commentaries on American subjects: they were often reviled, even by those who agreed with salient
points of their racial critiques, as representatives of the wicked aristocratic culture whose chains (white) Americans had thrown off a
generation before, returning to snipe at the vigorous young nation.

Britain abolished the slave trade in 1807 and slavery in its colonies in 1833. Therefore the British women attacking American slavery in print did so from what appeared to be a moral high ground, though pro-Southern writers were quick to counter that British "wage-slavery," urban poverty, class immobility and other social ills tarnished their diadem of ethical superiority. Still, as in the United States, British abolition societies flourished and, beginning in the 1840s and 1850s, ex-slaves like William Wells Brown and William and Ellen Craft toured England and Scotland, lecturing on the evils of American slavery.[2] The women discussed in this chapter – Frances Wright, Frances Trollope and Harriet Martineau – were all, in their different ways, abolitionists. While a few British women apologists for slavery (such as Janet Schaw, author of *Narrative of a Journey from Scotland to the West Indies, North Carolina, and Portugal in the Years 1774 to 1776* and Sarah Jones, author of *Life in the South* (1863) published conservative accounts, most of the women who ventured to Jacksonian America were involved in social reform, Utopian projects and feminism. America, with its promise of democracy and its practice of slavery, displayed contradictions ripe for exposure and interesting to readers on both sides of the Atlantic.

While Britain solidified colonial control of India and substantial portions of Africa in the first sixty years of the nineteenth century, the image of the "coloured" person, Asian, Arab or black, acquired great social currency. Edward Said points out that this period is when the "orientalizing" of the Orient by western writers became strong.[3] The empire provided all manner of exotics for the national fantasy life and its literature; highbrow poets like Shelley and Byron appropriated images and characters from Islamic and eastern cultures, while middlebrows like Thomas Moore played on "the Orient's" erotic associations in *Lalla Rookh*. The West Indies were also important as a location of disordered passions and mysterious dark-skinned people: it is no accident that Bertha Mason, *Jane Eyre*'s madwoman in the attic, is a West Indian, possibly, like Cora Munro in *The Last of the Mohicans*, a mulatta.

The American exotic, particularly the black slave, fascinated British culture.[4] From the 1830s onward, freeborn blacks and refugee slaves crossed from the United States to Britain to teach, lecture and raise money for the anti-slavery cause. At churches and halls in London and Glasgow, Edinburgh and Liverpool, British audiences became familiar with American blacks. Beginning in 1850,

Henry "Box" Brown and William Wells Brown travelled the country with "panoramas" depicting "Scenes in the Life of an American Slave, from his Birth in Slavery to his Death or his Escape to his First Home of Freedom on British Soil" (Ripley I 190). The panorama presented a slave biography, including the separation of a child from his mother, which properly shocked British audiences. The Description says tersely: "You readily recognise two Slaves as being nearly white" (ibid. 194). Other scenes show slaves in prison, slaves getting sold or beaten, slaves trying to escape and slaves being killed.

Ten or fifteen years before the largest wave of American blacks lectured all over Britain, familiarizing a great many Britons with the abuses of the slave body in the United States, books and essays by Frances Wright, Frances Trollope and Harriet Martineau helped to make the plight of blacks central to the British understanding of America.[5] Writing before Stowe, they too employ the discourses of the oriental and the gothic to indict a society where the slave body, particularly the female slave body, is subject to criminal sexual assaults, pain and death at the hands of white "Christian" men. Their fictional and sociological accounts of slavery, and their representations of blacks, shape their various reform projects. Wright and Martineau worked for egalitarianism and rights for women; Trollope was less of a political activist but she, too, had interests in Utopian communities and education reform. All three write to imperil the hierarchies of British and American society that place male over female and white over black.

Wright, Trollope and Martineau are important in their own right: their polemics, fiction and commentaries constitute a British feminist intervention in American slavery paralleling and often amplifying the work of the Grimké sisters, Maria Chapman, Lydia Maria Child and other abolitionists. They are also significant as part of the intellectual and social background to Stowe (and to Frances Kemble: see Chapter 4). Wright pioneered the female radical in America, pushing at the boundaries of acceptable speech and expanding women's political interests; at the same time, her behaviour helped create the image of the "immoral" gender-bending activist against which later women abolitionists had to struggle. The ways Trollope and Martineau represent blacks, particularly black women, in the 1830s, expanded the preliminary vocabulary for the sexual abuses of slavery in the "New World." Their accounts of the lives of white and black women forced to live as chattel, white women "confined" in the unequal though sanctified institution of marriage, and black women oppressed in slavery, perpetuate the connection of women's circumscribed lives with the circumscribed lives of blacks that Aphra Behn made in 1688 and that British women reformers had been pushing ever since. Moira Ferguson critiques this move:

> [White] women mediated their own needs and desires, their unconscious sense of social invalidation, through repre-sentations of the colonial other, who in the process became more severely objectified and marginalized – a silent or silenced individual in need of protection and pity who must always remain "under control."

(4)

I question how unconscious Behn's or Martineau's or Trollope's or certainly Wright's sense of "social invalidation" could have been: in their activism these women seem highly aware of the ideological links, however imperfect, they ask readers to forge between whites and blacks, free women and slaves, abolitionism and feminism. Certainly Ferguson has a point in identifying the ways white British women often clung to a damaging sense of African otherness or else refused to recognize crucial differences of race and class. But the writings of Wright, Trollope and Martineau, while very differ-ent from each other, all attempt a fundamental realignment of binarist thinking about race and the body. Their priorities and their solutions, are various, but all three struggle with the categorization of bodies into the familiar high/low, white/black hierarchies on which slavery was built. Though none of them had the audience, the fame or the influence Stowe gained in her writings about race in America, each contributed to the climate that fostered *Uncle Tom's Cabin*.

FRANCES WRIGHT THE REVOLUTIONARY

For pro-slavery apologists, anti-feminist polemicists, American clergy and ordinary citizens as well, the name of Fanny Wright became a synonym for the most radical social progressivism. Anti-abolitionists called William Lloyd Garrison "bad and dangerous," "an infidel – a sabbath-breaker" and, worst of all, a "Fanny Wright man," stained by the doctrine of "free love" with which she was particularly associated (Chapman 51).

As discussed in the previous chapter, conservatives in the 1830s, 1840s and 1850s noted with displeasure alliances between feminist and abolitionist groups, reporting with horror that women attended abolitionist meetings and could, in some cases, vote. Male and female abolitionists were seen as sexual rebels, advocating marriage reform and a place for women in politics. Antebellum conservatives heard calls for racial and gender equality as assaults on Christianity and the patriarchal family in the same way that the contemporary American religious right claims that the Equal Rights Amendment would lead to unisex public lavatories and enforced homosexuality in primary schools. Sexual transgression of all kinds fired traditionalists' fears in the 1830s, but interracial "congress" was their greatest terror. They warned that the real aim of the anti-slavery movement was amalgamation: "negro beasts" marrying the white daughters of America. George Fitzhugh in *Cannibals All!* (1857) charged that abolitionists wanted to set up "free love villages" (Fitzhugh 194).

Frances Wright was a Scot, born in 1795 in Dundee, a feminist and a free-thinker with her own fortune who often wore trousers and was philosophically opposed to marriage. In the 1820s, she bought land and slaves in southwestern Tennessee to found the Nashoba Community, a "model" plantation inspired by Robert Owen's Utopian community at New Harmony, Indiana.[6] Wright's slaves were to be freed after they had "given" a certain amount of work; however, Nashoba failed almost from the beginning, though Wright eventually manumitted most of her slaves and sent them to Haiti in 1829.

Wright was a disruptive presence in the counterrevolutionary America of the 1820s and 1830s, scandalously crossing the boundaries set out for her class, her race and her gender. The public on both sides of the Atlantic ridiculed her for her attachment to General de La Fayette, the hero of the American revolution and moderator of the French (Wright and her sister Camilla stayed with the La Fayette family in France and tried to persuade the General to adopt them). Later, during La Fayette's tour of the United States in 1824–25, the sisters followed him around, always arriving one day behind so as to avoid open scandal. But the implications were not lost on the popular press who castigated Wright for her forwardness and lack of a chaperon.[7] When she wasn't being branded a harlot, she was accused of being masculine, or at least not feminine. The *New York Courier* called her "Miss Epicene Wright," underlining her threatening lack of gender definition. An account of a Wright lecture from the *Allegheny Democrat* of 1829 combines conventional language about feminine appearance and morality with accusations of a clear breach of gender decorum: "Her fame and misapplied talents attracted crowded audiences. . . .The dogmas inculcated by this fallen and degraded fair one, if acted upon by the community, would produce the destruction of religion, morals, law and equity, and result in savage anarchy and confusion" (Lerner 95). Catharine Beecher (Harriet Beecher Stowe's elder sister), a resident of Cincinnati in the late 1820s when Wright lectured there, was appalled by her:

> who can look without disgust and abhorrence upon such a one as Fanny Wright, with her great masculine person, her loud voice, her untasteful attire, going about unprotected, and feeling no need for protection, mingling with men in stormy debate, and standing up with bare-faced impudence to lecture a public assembly ... with brazen front and brawny arms, attacking the safeguards of all that is venerable and sacred in religion, all that is safe and wise in law, all that is pure and lovely in domestic virtue.
>
> (Beecher 23)

In response both to her writings and her public appearances, other commentators called Wright "a female monster" and "a voluptuous preacher of licentiousness" as well as a "bold lady-man" (Perkins 233; Eckhardt 224).

Like Stowe, Wright appears both male and female in the minds of her conservative critics, slipping vertiginously from implied sexual looseness to gender role violation. Wright is at once "voluptuous" and "brawny," she crosses genders as she cross-dresses; as she violates gender decorum by addressing "promiscuous" audiences (of men *and* women), she herself is seen as promiscuous: "Women who crossdressed were less often accused of sexual perversion than of sexual incontinence, of being whores." Like a prostitute, who frequents public places alone, Fanny Wright is "unprotected" by a male authority and therefore a "masterless" woman: "this threatened overthrow of hierarchy was discursively read as the eruption of uncontrolled sexuality" (Howard 424).

The Nashoba scandal in 1827 underlined the public perception that Wright encouraged sexual licence. The plantation log kept during one of her absences by James Richardson, a Nashoba trustee, records a series of shocking events. First, a woman slave complained of a man slave's attempts to rape her in her room at night. The woman was refused a lock for her door on the theory that everyone must regulate his or her own sexuality and that the man involved must be persuaded, not forced, to respect the bodies of women: "we consider the proper basis of sexual intercourse to be the unconstrained and unrestrained choice of both parties" (Eckhardt 142–43; Trollope, *Domestic Manners* 17ff.). The 24 May entry reads (Richardson writes of himself in the third person), "Two women slaves were tied up and flogged by James Richardson" and the 17 June entry announces "James Richardson informed [the slaves] that, last night, Mamselle Josephine [a quadroon] and he began to live together; and he took this occasion of repeating to them our views on color, and on the sexual relation" (Eckhardt 143).

The Genius of Universal Emancipation, an abolitionist newspaper, published the log to howls of outrage across the political spectrum. Nashoba, supposedly dedicated to reforming the patriarchal plantation where women slaves were at risk of violence and rape, had replicated the plantation's worst abuses. Abolitionists, working very hard in the 1820s and 1830s to charge *pro-slavery* forces with promoting sexual anarchy, decried Nashoba as "one great brothel" (Eckhardt 143). Pro-slavery commentators in papers such as the Cincinnati *Evening Chronicle* seized on Wright's acceptance of miscegenation as "inimical to sound morals [and] repugnant to the delicacy and purity of a virtuous female," (ibid. 177). Nashoba failed because it was economically unfeasible; it also failed because Wright did not understand the absolute division of genders, races and acceptable behaviours on which American society sustained itself. She *transgressed*, breaking

loose from the restraints of decorum, which draw a circle round the life of women; and with a contemptuous disregard for the rule of society, she has leaped over the boundary of feminine modesty, and laid hold upon the avocations of man, claiming a participation in them for herself and her sex.

Miss Wright stands condemned of a violation of the unalterable laws of nature, which have created a barrier between the man and the woman.

(*Louisville Focus*, quoted in Waterman 162)

Frances Wright was a gender outlaw, appropriating men's clothes and activities for herself, acknowledged a "lady" (by birth and by fortune) yet consorting with people of all classes, declaring marriage a perversion of passion, and, if not precisely advocating miscegenation, at least asserting its inevitability. In later life she would recant some of her more "extreme" positions, but no one listened: Fanny Wright had created herself as the radical monster America could not tolerate.[8] Her very life imperiled the names by which the nation understood itself, creating what Marjorie Garber calls a "category crisis," that "permits of border crossings from one (apparently distinct) category to another: black/white, Jew/Christian, noble/bourgeois, master/servant, master/slave" (Garber 16). With such "border crossings," it is easy to see how conservatives conflated abolitionism, atheism, feminism, dress reform and Jacobinism: all these came together in the eccentric form of Frances Wright. The failed but none the less alarming slave conspiracies of Gabriel Prosser in 1800 and Denmark Vesey in 1822, as well as the Haitian revolution in 1801, frightened not just Southern slaveholders but white Americans all over the country. The threat of "a Toussaint or a Spartacus" amongst the slaves loomed large in their minds. In 1822, Charleston editor Edwin Holland called blacks "the Jacobins of the country" (quoted in Sundquist, *To Wake the Nations* 33). The discourses of the French Revolution survived in the South beyond Reconstruction with Confederate women like Rose O'Neal Greenhow, Virginia Clay and Mary Chesnut comparing themselves to the beleaguered aristocrats of 1789.[9] To a wary America, negotiating the discontents of Nullifiers, Jacksonians, expansionists and abolitionists, Frances Wright looked like a loose cannon.

In the end, Wright's commitment to racial equality remains unfocused. Her *Views of Society and Manners in America* (1821) ends with the triumphant "the day is not yet far distant where a slave will not be found in America!," yet never directly addresses the sexual exploitation of women slaves, the problem of slave marriages unprotected by law, or the precipitous position of the mulatta (Wright 523). Her successors in the feminist–abolitionist camp, Trollope, Martineau, the Grimkés, Kemble and Stowe, took up these problems in their work. Later activists, condemning the sexual lawlessness of slavery, argue a Victorian bourgeois Christian ideal of chastity and fidelity, outside and inside marriage, the sanctity of motherhood and the "purity" of the female body. Wright was a Wollstonecraft radical informed by the "blissful dawn" of the Jacobins for whom the equality of persons transcended gender. Her kind of progressivism was suppressed in America though her notoriety persisted. Sylva d'Arusmont, Wright's daughter by Phiquepal d'Arusmont, rejected her mother's radical politics, becoming a conservative Christian who dismissed Wright's ideas as "infidel trash" (Eckhardt 290). When, in 1874, she testified against extending the vote to women before a congressional committee, she said, sounding like her mother's old critics:

> As the daughter of Frances Wright, whom the Female Suffragists are pleased to consider as having *opened* the door to their pretensions, [I ask you] to *shut* it forever, from the strongest convictions that they can only bring misery and degradation upon the whole sex and thereby wreck human happiness in America!
>
> (*Memorial on Suffrage*, 3 February 1874)

None the less, Frances Wright opened a door to the United States for a procession of British women who came to study Americans and their "peculiar institution" first hand.

FRANCES TROLLOPE AND THE INFERNAL SOUTH

It was Wright who, back in England, persuaded Frances Trollope, wife of a sedate, vague and financially-inept canon, to come and make her fortune, and educate her younger children cheaply, in the United States. In 1827, Frances, Emilia, Cecelia and Henry Trollope (Anthony Trollope stayed at school at Winchester) sailed from England and made their way to Nashoba where the great democratic dream was supposed to become a reality. However, Frances Trollope did not have Frances Wright's faith, patience or money. The primitiveness of Nashoba horrified her; she did not fancy sleeping in a roofless hut or committing her son Henry to an as-yet-unbuilt school, however theoretically progressive. Nor was she convinced by Nashoba notions of racial liberalism. As Trollope saw it, slavery was still slavery, even if the slaves had a fixed term with emancipation guaranteed at the end. Moreover, Wright's ideas of sexual self-determination seemed ill-conceived, even dangerous. Trollope records the story of the harassed slave woman who wanted a lock for her door with more than a little distress.

Like Maud Gonne, Frances Wright was her own best work of political art; Frances Trollope was a less likely revolutionary, channelling her abolitionism and feminism into her books. Unlike

Wright, whose radicalism took the form of a kind of transgressive theatre, standing trousered in front of audiences exhorting them to liberate their sexual selves, Trollope understood the interaction between slavery, violence and the oppression of women. Her famous *Domestic Manners of the Americans* (1832) deals mainly with the iniquities of tobacco-spitting men and useless servants in Cincinnati, but in so far as the book addresses slavery, it criticizes the sexual exploitation of black women. Where *Uncle Tom's Cabin* and Frances Kemble's Georgia *Journal* move us from North to South, from the head to the loins of the national body, Frances Trollope begins at the bottom. She represents the South not as the body but as the underworld. She enters at the mouth of the Mississippi and pushes deeper in and further *down*, ascribing all sorts of hellish qualities to the South. She calls the Delta country "another Bolgia," comparing it to the circle of Dante's Inferno reserved for seducers, politicians and thieves: a pointed comment on the power structure of the plantation South (Trollope, *Domestic Manners* 2). In her novel about the South, *The Life and Adventures of Jonathan Jefferson Whitlaw* (1836), she describes the landscape as an infernal wasteland of ruined plantations and rocky ground: the fertility of the South, like the bodies of its black women, misused and exploited.

In New Orleans, on her way to Nashoba in 1827, Trollope became intrigued by the quadroon *demi-monde*, as were most visitors to the centre of trade in "fancy women." Her descriptions of *plaçage* are fairly standard. She notes the careful upbringing of quadroon girls, many of them convent-educated, most of them as "accomplished" as middle-class white women, as light in complexion, too, yet legally prohibited from marrying the white men with whom they lived, by whom they were supported, and whose children – slaves themselves, though "whiter" still than their mothers – they bore (Trollope, *Domestic Manners* 15–16).

Trollope confines herself to a cool description of the quadroon's status in New Orleans, then, a page later, comments that, (whatever the reality of the place) at Nashoba, Frances Wright is determined "to show that nature had made no difference between blacks and whites, excepting in complexion" (ibid. 17). Trollope's juxtaposing an explication of quadroon culture and the powerlessness of the *placée* with the breezily-defiant statement of the Nashoba mission that discrimination is based on superficial, not innate, qualities which education can "correct," is potentially explosive. In their very persons, the mulattas of New Orleans refute the rhetoric of colour (and therefore intrinsic) difference which is the foundation of slavery. If blacks and whites must be opposed, unassimilable, two ends of a hierarchy of high (white) and low (black), rational and irrational, intellectual and physical, what do we do with all those educated, pious, "ladylike," fair-skinned mulattas who are none the less slaves?

Aside from her repeatedly-expressed horror at the general bad manners she felt American "democracy" endorsed, it was the matter-of-fact exposure of such hypocrisies that got Trollope's *Domestic Manners* into such trouble with American readers of the 1830s: they could not abide attacks on their institutions, whether chewing tobacco or slavery, by a toffee-nosed Englishwoman. The book inspired so many vitriolic reviews that in 1833 a volume was brought out in London called *American Criticisms of Mrs. Trollope's Domestic Manners of the Americans*. The *American Quarterly* tars Trollope with the "free love" brush, attacking the coalition between sexual liberation and abolitionism, sneering at her friendship with Frances Wright: "both these ladies appear to regard moralities with some dislike" (*American Criticisms* 2). While many of the reviews try to answer Trollope's charges of provinciality, philistinism and vulgarity, the inflammable combination of women's rights and slaves' rights provided the best insult ammunition. A New England journal plays slyly with the author's name (Trollope by name, trollop by nature, and therefore dismissable on *sexual grounds*: a common attack on female writers), while another sniffs that women in the United States are far more chaste than the décolletéed hussies of Europe. As for slavery, Trollope's account is simply "full of errors" (ibid. 20).

Trollope implicates American slavery in lawless sexuality while destabilizing the white/black hierarchy most overtly and powerfully in her novel *The Life and Adventures of Jonathan Jefferson Whitlaw*, (1836). An astonishingly dark piece of fiction, it prefigures (and outstrips) *Uncle Tom's Cabin* in its sensational elision of slavery and rape. Though his middle name might imply otherwise, Jonathan Jefferson Whitlaw is no revolutionary fighting for the self-evident truth that "all men are created equal;" he is Simon Legree's unacknowledged father: sadistic, greedy and lascivious.[10] An overseer, he represents the "white law" of the South that says a black man is subject to death if he rebels (thus the prefix to later editions of the novel, "Lynch Law") and that a black woman is subject to rape. While the novel exhibits as much confidence as *Uncle Tom's Cabin* (but sixteen years earlier) that slavery is destined to collapse, Trollope provides fewer family reunions, earthly rewards or heavenly assurances than Stowe. Unlike Uncle Tom or Little Eva, Edward Bligh, Trollope's martyr to slavery, does not die a transcendent death, but is lynched unceremoniously by a pro-slavery mob. Nor are her mulattas transformed into exemplary Christians by meeting their long-lost mothers or children; instead, they are killed or driven to vengeful murder. Trollope sees no promised land in Canada or Liberia, just violence and anarchy in a South where the "white law" inscribes itself on the bodies of the powerless – clergy, women and slaves.

Like her *Domestic Manners*, Trollope's *Jonathan Jefferson Whitlaw* begins in the "mournful" Mississippi river country, not overtly a region of Dante's hell yet none the less a place of ruin and desolation. Gothic representations of the postbellum South, with their ruined houses and blasted lands, are practically a cliché, but abolitionist writers like Trollope, and later Stowe, show a decayed South at the height of its historical prosperity.[11] The Whitlaw family farm is ominously called "Mt Etna," encompassing both an infernal image and an apocalyptic prophecy. At the other end of the metaphorical arc, the plantation Jonathan Jefferson Whitlaw oversees is called "Paradise," an unsubtle and ironic name implying that, for slaves, it is just the opposite. These Miltonic extremes, constructing the South as a hell of slavery rather than the Eden of order and grace insisted upon by Southern apologists, reinforce the North–South, head–loins, reason–passion pairings which Trollope evokes in the novel's dedication: "To Those States of the American Union in which Slavery has been abolished or never permitted these volumes are respectfully dedicated."

Trollope speaks to the morally elevated, but her subject is the *low*. By writing the South as an underworld, corresponding to the unspeakable regions of the body, Trollope insists on the threat of slavery as sexual, though in several guises. Her spectrum of metaphors represents the South as infernal but also fecund: "luxuriant orange-trees sent their fragrance through the large windows and the flocks of green birds ... looked like the brightest emeralds in Aladdin's enchanted garden" (I 118). This orientalist description of Paradise Plantation sounds so like Stowe's description of the St Clare place that one is tempted to see direct influence.

Trollope's orientalism operates not just in the service of romance; like Stowe, she uses it to make a political point, to inject unease in the mind of the British or American reader. After all, as Said reminds us, "the Orient seemed to have offended sexual propriety. . . exuded dangerous sex, threatened hygiene and domestic seemliness" among other things (Said, *Orientalism* 162). The same could be – and was – said of the American South. Of course, the sexual impropriety of the South became its most important signifier. As, according to Said, Flaubert in his Egyptian writings makes "an almost uniform association between the Orient and sex," abolitionists make an almost uniform association between the slave South and sex. Trollope's use of orientalist imagery also introduces the erotic, conjuring up the most important sexual irregularity of the South, its *harems*. We have seen how Stowe employs shadows and implications of the harem in *Uncle Tom*, both seductively and indignantly. Trollope, simultaneously committed to her political mission and to an enticing fictive exploration of territory that was, for her British readers, as exotic as the East itself, raises the issue of illicit sexuality as well. British women found this aspect of slavery outrageous and irresistible. Harriet Martineau remarks:

> Every man who resides on his plantation may have his harem and has every inducement of custom and pecuniary gain to tempt him to the common practise. Those who, not withstanding, keep their women undefiled may be considered as of uncorruptible purity.
>
> (Martineau, *Society in America* II 112)

The eroticization of the American landscape, particularly what would become the slave societies of the Atlantic colonies and the Caribbean, pervades early European commentaries. Sir Walter Ralegh wrote, "Guiana is a countrey that hath yet her maydenhead" (Montrose 1). Philip Amadas and Arthur Barlowe, two English sea captains, found themselves in 1584 off the coast of what would become North Carolina, surrounded by "so sweet and strong a smell as if we had been in the midst of some delicate garden abounding with all kinds of odiferous flowers" (Kolodny 10). We see the equation of female body and colonized landscape work the other way in Donne's famous "Elegy XIX: To His Mistress Going to Bed" where the lover is "my America! my new-found-land" to be claimed, penetrated and conquered.[12] Later, the Swedish writer Frederika Bremer brings together orientalism and the representation of the South as a pliant (though weak) female body in her *Homes of the New World*:

I see a feeble Southern beauty reposing upon a luxurious bed of flowers in a nectarine grove, surrounded by willing slaves, who at her nod bring her the most precious fruits and ornaments in the world. But all her beauty, the splendour of her eye, the delicate crimson of her cheek, the pomp which surrounds her couch, cannot conceal the want of health and vigour, the worm which devours her vitals. This weak, luxurious beauty is *South Carolina*.

(Bremer I 274–75)

Annette Kolodny argues that fiction by upholders of the plantation ideology, such as John Pendleton Kennedy, Caroline Gilman and William Gilmore Simms, recasts the Southern land from virgin/sexual partner to mother: slavery, patriarchy, the class system depend upon the maternal image of the fertile garden:

As a psychological phenomenon, the plantation recapitulated infantile gratifications and predicted the inevitability of the South's resistance to abolition; for, even though slavery was fast becoming economically unfeasible, it was nevertheless the very bedrock on which pastoral ease was supported.

(Kolodny 131)

For Southern apologists, the plantation is the revered mother; the sexuality of the feminized landscape defused and decentred in virtuous motherhood. For abolitionist writers and critics of the plantation system, the South acts not as mother but as seductress or rape victim. The Southern landscape is not a formal garden but an oriental site of disordered passions manifested in the bodies of slaves (seductive, sexually-exploited) as well as in the lushness of the vegetation and the eclectic architecture.

In Trollope's South, men can and do act on erotic impulses towards slave women. The first victim of Jonathan Jefferson Whitlaw's desire is Phebe, a young girl remarkably similar to Eliza in *Uncle Tom's Cabin*: intelligent, pious, chaste and engaged to an equally-worthy young slave, Caesar. Like Eliza, Phebe was brought up on an "enlightened" plantation in Kentucky and educated by her saintly owners, Lucy and Edward Bligh. The traumatic selling of favourite (and "superior") slaves, the disastrous movement from the upper South, nearer the "head" and "heart" of the rational, pure, free North, to the lower South, the region associated with hell (the "deeper" South a slave travels, the worse his or her life is seen to be), the concentration on the sexual dangers to women slaves as the action moves closer and closer to New Orleans (where the largest market for slaves sold as sexual goods was), and the use of a "Tragic Mulatta" plot, suggest that a reading in comparison with *Uncle Tom's Cabin* will cast some telling light on strategies of abolitionist discourse in fiction.

Uncle Tom himself has no exact equivalent in Trollope's novel: *Jonathan Jefferson Whitlaw* puts forth a less glorious view of Christian martyrdom than *Uncle Tom's Cabin*. Trollope concerns herself more with the sexual violence of slavery and with the assaults on women's bodies for which there is no reparation, heavenly or otherwise. Her precursor to Stowe's outraged Cassy is Juno, a kind of up-market mulatta conjure woman whose horrendous story anticipates Cassy's. In *Jonathan Jefferson Whitlaw*, Juno was the possession and mistress of an Englishman by whom she had a daughter. He sold her to another white man as "fancy goods," then took the daughter to Europe. Meanwhile, she had eight children by the second owner/lover, all of whom were sold away from her; he sold her to yet another man, until she ended up finally on Paradise Plantation. It is a shocking story, intended to outrage, yet no more than a parallel to so many slave narratives of the 1830s, 1840s and 1850s.

For all Juno's brutal treatment at the hands of white men, she is a powerful figure. Whitlaw is terrified of her, as Legree is of Cassy, because of her supposed magical powers. A leader amongst the slaves, she can create or halt an uprising and engineer the deaths of her white enemies. She is obsessed with finding her elder daughter or her daughter's descendants which, of course, she does, as Cassy stumbles onto her daughter Eliza. However, as Trollope realizes, recognition equals pain for the mulatta. Forcing the granddaughter Selina Craft, raised to believe she was white, to acknowledge her "black blood" subjects her to possible rape and drives her to suicide.

When everyone thinks Selina the beautiful heiress of a rich English merchant, Jonathan Whitlaw courts her as a potential wife; but when word gets out that "'Miss Craft's mother come of a nigger,'" her status plummets from lady to "fancy girl" (Trollope, *Jonathan Jefferson Whitlaw* II 316). Louisiana law defines her as an object, not a person, so Whitlaw offers to buy her as his concubine, no longer paying the elaborate compliments appropriate in a white man–white woman "romance." Instead he makes the lewd advances, practically molesting her, perfectly acceptable in a white man–black woman transaction. Like fictional mulattas before and after her – Fenimore Cooper's Cora Munro, Lydia Maria Child's Rosalie, Charles Chesnutt's Rena, Robert Penn Warren's Amantha Starr – Selina Craft feels "dirty" and "tainted" by her slave blood.[13] She is forced to face the unvarnished, unsweetened truth about the imbalance of power between men and women in a sexual relationship, unmitigated by bourgeois social conventions: as a "black" woman, she is merely a body to be exploited, a candidate for legal rape. Confronted with unbearable truth, she takes an overdose of laudanum: "'Oh, God! – I have killed her!' shrieked Juno in bitter agony; 'she saw me, she knew me, and she died!'" (ibid. III 28).

Recognizing her femaleness, her powerlessness, her blackness, acknowledging her true family, destroys Selina Craft. The apparent hierarchy of white and black collapses in her body; she is both sacrosanct "white" flesh and available "black" flesh, both pure and "tainted." The suicide note she left says she killed herself so "the curse will not cling to us forever!" – the paradox of being both white and black, both free and slave, is unbearable. The mulatta heroine dies, or else suffers terrible abuse: no decent space exists for her in an America under slavery. If the nation legally and socially defines itself through the violent hierarchies of white and black, high and low, the mulatta is at best a mix of intolerables, a volatile hybrid. A Bakhtinian analysis speaks of "the seductive power of the hybrid," of the uncomfortable commingling of high and low (in this case, white and black) which, in occupying the unacknowledged territory between, imperils both (Stallybrass and White 31). Trollope, like so many abolitionist writers after her, sees the mulatta as a useful fictional device to challenge the racial categories on which slavery was erected. She realizes (as did her fellow Britons Harriet Martineau and Frances Kemble and the American Lydia Maria Child) that the mulatta was the most powerful Other which defined what the white world "believes to be not itself" and a *mirror* of the white world's failure to effectively "differentiate itself" (Said, *The World, the Text and the Critic* 12).

The mulatta also challenges the oppositional categorizing of women as "lady" and "prostitute." In death, they dress Selina as a bride wreathed in orange-blossom, an insistence on her virginity. Yet the mulatta, as we see from Jonathan Jefferson Whitlaw's *volte-face* when he learns that Selina is part black, is assumed to be sexually available to all white men. Put in terms of Bakhtin's classical and grotesque bodies, where the classical body is represented by the white lady and the grotesque body is represented by the black "wench," Selina descends from the pedestal to the pit. The pedestal is traditionally the preferred location for white Southern women (as described by white Southern men from William Gilmore Simms to Wilbur J. Cash) and a good home for a statue-like classical body, too, its orifices closed, "entirely finished, completed, strictly limited" (Bakhtin 320). The classical body is "impenetrable" while the grotesque body is "open to the outside world" (ibid. 320, 26). As a white lady in the South, Selina cannot be touched; as a black woman, her destiny is to be a sexual object. Where in England she could have been legally married to a rich man of the upper classes, in the South she can only become a *placée*, reliving Juno's sad life with white man after white man, used and sold. Her suicide forces a confrontation between her white self and her black self. Trollope insists (as Stowe does with Eliza and Emmeline in *Uncle Tom's Cabin*) on the mulatta's capacity for purity by displaying Selina's legally "black" and "open" body in the trappings of virginity: the wedding dress, the orange-blossom, the absolute closure of death itself.

Unlike Stowe, Trollope does not place her abolitionist hopes in a Christian renovation of the world but affords her abused slave women revenge on the body of the white man who tortured them. Juno gets four slaves to beat Whitlaw to death, echoing the humiliating and painful death died by so many blacks in America, worse even than lynching (the death died by the young white abolitionist Edward Bligh). While Cassy cedes her full vengeance to heaven in *Uncle Tom's Cabin*, Juno claims a small bitter triumph over the white man who can with impunity buy and sell female flesh and who has destroyed her life and Selina's. The bloody end Trollope's anti-hero meets is a warning to the slave states of judgement to come: a just nation cannot long tolerate such outrages on the bodies of women, whatever category, lady or "wench," white or black, they inhabit.

HARRIET MARTINEAU'S FEMINIST CRITIQUE OF SLAVERY

When the social critic Harriet Martineau took ship for America in 1834, she was already notorious in pro-slavery circles for "Demerara," a story in *Illustrations of Political Economy* (1832–34) dramatically arguing that slavery is both economically unsound and morally reprehensible. By the time she got through with Southern slavery in *Society in America* (1837) and published her abolitionist romance about Toussaint L'Ouverture, *The Hour and the Man* (1841), she could write contentedly in her 1877 Autobiography:

> I am pleased to find, however, within the last few days, that in the South I am still reviled, as I was twenty years ago, and held up, in the good company of Mrs Chapman and Mrs Stowe, to the abhorrence of the South.
>
> (Martineau, The Hour and the Man II 40)

Angry planters threatened her with violence in the South; pro-slavery newspapers issued mock invitations to her to come back to where they would be pleased to cut out her tongue or hang her (Wheatley 156). Even in Boston, Brahmin society ostracized her as a "foreign incendiary" (Pope-Hennessy 291). The American public never castigated Martineau for her *Society in America* as they did Frances Trollope for her *Domestic Manners*, nor considered her a shameless menace to "Christian" family life like Frances Wright. Still, Martineau was another dangerous foreign female reformer, unnaturally freed from the domestic sphere by fame and an independent income to stab at the heart of American institutions: another unchaperoned, "masterless" woman on the loose.[14] If anything, Martineau proved more difficult to dismiss than other female radicals because her life was, in high Victorian terms, "exemplary," and her writing, even her fiction, was closely-observed and intellectual rather than sensational: the original title of *Society in America* was *Theory and Practise of Society in America*. Martineau relentlessly took the moral high ground, focusing on what she called the "positive licentiousness" of the slave South (Martineau, *Society in America* II 116). Pro-slavery writers, in turn, focused on attacking Martineau, branding her, as they had Wright, a promoter of miscegenation. Martineau records in her autobiography that an American lady asked her if she would "interfere" in the marriage of a white friend and a "negro." Martineau said she would not and the lady "cried out in horror, 'Then you *are* an Amalgamationist!'" Martineau goes on to say sardonically "I was not then aware of the extent to which all but virtuous relations are found possible between the whites and blacks" (Martineau, *Autobiography* II 14–15).

The perversion and degradation of sexuality in slavery parallels, in Martineau's writings, the cooler analysis of its inadequacy as an economic system. As in *Uncle Tom's Cabin* and *Jonathan Jefferson Whitlaw*, in "Demerara" the orientalized Guianan landscape implies lawless sexuality and disordered passions. Paradise Plantation (possibly the inspiration for the estate in *Jonathan Jefferson Whitlaw*) is run by an evil overseer; the "good" plantation owned by the Bruce family is none the less in bad repair with half-naked servants and an indolent mistress (as neurasthenic as Marie St Clare) who lies about all day in a ball dress. The ways slavery warps women's lives particularly concern Martineau; white women find themselves reduced to useless ornaments, not given the opportunity to perform useful work, while black women are physically brutalized. As the slave Will points out in "Demerara," a white woman accepts rule by her husband within the framework of Christian marriage; a slave woman is denied legitimate marriage and must primarily obey the white master who has the power to beat or rape her with impunity (60–61). This attack on the integrity of the body and the liberty of the spirit creates such rage amongst black men that they might try to revenge themselves on plantation owners by raping white women. As Mr Mitchelson of Paradise Plantation says, "'Alfred, I had rather you and I had to battle with wild beasts than women with slaves'" (ibid. 85). Slavery endangers the lofty ideals on which Victorian womanhood rested as well as the physical well-being of women whom "civilization" was supposed at all times to protect.

Martineau depicts slave owners and slaves each living in a constant state of anxiety about the other's sexuality, black women subject to assault by white men, white women threatened with rape by rebellious slaves. Martineau saw that the treatment of slave women by whites (and sometimes by black drivers) and the fear that a reciprocal fate would be meted out to white women should slaves get the opportunity, depended on slave-owning culture's insistence on a violent hierarchy of white femininity opposed to (and above) black femininity.[15] White women were held to be fundamentally "pure," thus, in terms of the perceived binary, black women had to be fundamentally *impure*, polluted by their race. However, "disgust bears the impress of desire": the white woman's body was designated *asexual* but the black woman was a *sexual* being, or so white men told themselves (Stallybrass and White 77). Moreover, the white/black opposition is unstable: the "purity" of whiteness teetered perpetually on the brink of collapse into the "impurity" of blackness, a danger made manifest, as we have seen, in the body of the mulatta. Though the goal of white discourses (defined always as normative) was "to understand and confine non-whites in their status as non-whites, in order to make the notion of whiteness cleaner, purer and stronger," as in Trollope's Selina Craft, the strands get hopelessly tangled in the figure of the mulatta – or in the body of any white woman "reduced" to the sexual (Said, *The World, the Text and the Critic* 224).

But Martineau backs off from this form of subversion. Rather than insisting on the right of white women to sexual expression (as Frances Wright did), writers of the abolition romance undermined the perceived polarity of white and black, appropriating "white" chastity and morality for "black" slave women. In *The Hour and the Man*, Martineau emphasizes that Haitian society celebrates Toussaint L'Ouverture's wife and daughters for their refinement, delicacy and purity: the qualities essential to "white ladyhood." The ex-slave Thérèse, once a white man's concubine (another ancestress of Cassy's), finds her voice and her sense of bodily integrity only in legitimate marriage: "'And I was sinful but no one told me so. I was ignorant, and weak, and a slave. Now I am a woman and a wife. No more whites, no more sin, no more misery!'" (Martineau, *The Hour and the Man* II 184–85). The juxtaposition of *white* with *sin* and *misery* rattles the edifice slave society built to sustain itself: that sin, sexuality and impurity belong at the *bottom*, that is, amongst the slaves, even while it bolsters the high Victorian celebration of sacred wife-and-motherhood.

Society in America is Martineau's most comprehensive attack on the dishonest binary of white women's and black women's sexuality. In it she tenaciously hammers away at the official foundation of pro-slavery that the subjugation of Africans (and women) is physically, morally, religiously and economically essential. In the section "Political Non-Existence of Women," she quotes Caroline Gilman, author of the pro-slavery novel *Recollections of a Southern Matron* (1838) and fellow member, with Harriet Beecher Stowe, of the Cincinnatti literary society the Semi-Colon Club: "'it is so right that the one race should be subservient to the other!'" (Martineau, *Society in America* I 153). Gilman's statement appears slightly differently in Martineau's autobiography: "One race must ever be subordinate to the other, and that if the black should ever have the upper hand, she should not object to standing on that table and being sold to the highest bidder" (Martineau, *Autobiography* I 34). Thus did pro-slavery women participate in their own orientalization, their own "non-existence," as Martineau put it.

Martineau identifies this hierarchical rigidity as the defining sensibility of a slave society: white over black, men over women, rich over poor. It allows the abuses of black *and* white women, the most serious manifestation of Southern decadence:

> A lady of Mobile was opening her true and noble heart to me on the horrors and vices of the system under which she and her family were suffering in mind, body and estate ... the trouble caused by the licentiousness of the whites among the negro women.
>
> (Martineau, *Society in America* I 373–74)

Again, this sexual criminality triggers violence in reaction: Martineau tells of a young white girl raped and murdered and two white women threatened with assault in revenge for the brutalization of black women. The slaves involved were caught and lynched in Mobile, "burned alive there, in a slow fire, in the open air, in the presence of the gentlemen of the city" (ibid. I 373). These vicious attacks on female and black bodies, used as a means of control, ruinously involve all: violated woman, violent man. Martineau demonstrates how the whole society, despite its protests of refinement and chivalry, is implicated in its perverse assignments of lasciviousness to blacks and chastity to whites. She argues for a re-alignment, a re-vision of moral designations. Recounting the story of the slave repeatedly raped by her master's son, producing two mulatto children about which she refused to tell her (sold away) husband, Martineau asks, "if this be not chastity, what is? where are all the fairest natural affections, if not in these women?" (ibid. I 384). Just as the refugee slave Harriet Jacobs erases her sexuality in Christian motherhood, or Stowe's Cassy becomes a "pure woman" despite her many liaisons, or Thérèse in *The Hour and the Man* achieves true womanhood in marriage, Martineau reclaims chastity for "fallen" (owing simply to their colour) slave women.[16] Moreover, she disables the class-and-colour-bound rhetoric of ladyhood in using the word "fairest" in connection to black women; suddenly black appropriates white and achieves moral stature equal to, perhaps greater than, the pale Angel in the House.

Like the Grimkés, Trollope, Stowe and every woman abolitionist after her, Martineau is intensely concerned with the white male slave-owner's legally-sanctioned ability to run a harem on the plantation, or to keep a mulatta *placée*. Despite protestations that the white lady was "above" the dirt of the slave quarters, the violence of black "animal" passion and the "helpless lusts" of their husbands, Martineau pitilessly implicates upper-class white women in this diseased culture: the "degradation of the [white] women is so obvious a consequence of the evils disclosed above" (Martineau, *Society in America* II 125). Slavery besieges the family, the central unit through which individuals defined themselves in relation to the world. Martineau indignantly recounts incident upon incident of viciousness, charging that white women collude in their own degradation as well as that of their slaves, and that marriage is made a mockery of. Martineau grimly recounts one instance of a white woman selling a slave girl to a white man who desired her obsessively because the white woman "'pitied the poor young man'" (ibid. II 123).

Martineau, like Trollope, reports that in New Orleans this moral inversion is commonplace, victimizing both slave and free women, especially the fabled quadroons, the centre of the erotic fantasy life of the city. She recounts a now-familiar story of near-white girls educated in French convents, taught all the accomplishments of white ladyhood, yet whose only possibility in life is to be the sexual slave of some white man. Martineau reiterates the popular "romantic" myth that when the quadroon's white lover made a legitimate marriage or died, rather than find a new man she committed suicide or died of a broken heart. Martineau reads this as a celebration of true womanly chastity and feminine fidelity; elsewhere, however, she realizes that men kept mulatta mistresses even after their marriages, or abandoned them, or sold them from man to man, as Trollope shows. The slavishly loyal mulatta, described by a white, upper-class Southern man in Faulkner's *Absalom, Absalom!* is

> trained to fulfill a woman's sole end and purpose: to love, to be beautiful and to divert. . . . Sometimes I believe that they are the only true chaste women, not to say virgins, in America, and they remain true and faithful to that man not merely until he dies or frees them, but until they die. And where will you find whore or lady either whom you can count on to do that?
>
> (117)

Yet however seductive the romance of the *placée*, Martineau recognizes the double tragedy in this exploitative system: "Every Quadroon woman believes her partner will prove an exception to the rule of desertion. Every white lady believes her husband has been an exception to the rule of seduction" (Martineau, *Society in America* II 117). There is evidence that slaveholding women were not, despite the rosy picture painted in anti-*Tom* novels and public denials, unaware of their husbands' transgressions. While Sarah Gayle Gorgas and Mary Chesnut tell of slave–master liaisons on other plantations, at least one woman, Ella Clanton Thomas, struggled to speak of adultery in her own household. Nell Irvin Painter suggests that some obscure, difficult and obviously tormented entries in her journal actually refer to her husband Jefferson Thomas' "sexual relations with a slave" (Burr 59). Ella Thomas writes on 2 January 1859,

> I know that this is a view of the subject that it is thought best for women to ignore but when we see so many cases of mulattoes commanding higher prices, advertised as "Fancy Girls," oh is it not enough to make us shudder for the standard of morality in *our* Southern homes.
>
> (ibid. 168)

And, angrily, near the end of the war in 1865:

> The time will come when Southern women will be avenged – let this war cease with the abolition of slavery and I wish for the women of the North no worse fate than will befall them. Their husbands already prepare for them the bitter cup of humiliation which they will be compelled to drink to the dregs.
>
> (ibid. 252)

In the system of *plaçage*, women – white or black – are exchanged as sexual commodities, valued according to colour and birth. The *placée* herself is a figure of sexual wish-fulfillment: the appearance and accomplishments of the white lady without the legal or moral obligations of "Christian" companionate marriage. Despite embroidered accounts of duels fought over quadroons and men shunned by New Orleans society if caught abusing their mistresses, the *placée* had no real power. Her family could exert no pressure on a white man; her mother's family were slaves or statusless free blacks and her white father probably did not acknowledge her. She brought only her body and her education, her amusing conversation, singing, harp-playing, and elegant clothes to the liaison. For dynastic connections, political advantage, enlargement of estates and legitimate children, the white man had to acquire a certified white wife. For a submissive yet exciting sexual partner, the quadroon was a dream come true: a beautiful woman wholly in the man's power, outside church and society. Martineau identifies this masculine-controlled subculture of female bodies as an attack on marriage and the individual conscience:

> What security for domestic purity and peace there can be when every man has had two connexions, one of which must be concealed, and two families, whose existence must not be known to each other, where the conjugal relation begins in treachery and must be carried on with a heavy secret in the husband's breast, no words are needed to explain.
>
> (Martineau, *Society in America* II 117)

Martineau's language constructs an underworld, a "low" and secret region, *sub rosa*. Once again the official is built on top of the illicit, the elevated implicated in the debased. The South's "lower" geographical position with regard to the rest of the United States translates into metaphor by association with "lower" regions of the body, "base" passions, hell. Slavery creates clandestine relationships outside the rules of church and state. Worse still, it becomes the governing structure of *all* relationships. As Martineau sees it, white men own both black and white women. As one planter's wife says, she is merely "the chief slave of the harem" (ibid. II 118).

The harem, the hermetic, concealed space occupied by women but controlled by men, is a dominant image for Martineau as it is for Trollope and Stowe. The harem expresses the "veiled" world of sexual dissembling in the male rule of the female, as well as the female body itself: the hidden spaces of women are regulated and exploited by men. Martineau quotes a man, horrified that some women in the North (he means *white* women, of course) actually work, praising slavery for how it increases the *idleness* of women in the South (he means upper middle-class women, of course). The impetus of "Southern civilization," as he sees it, is toward simultaneously increasing the independence of land-owning men and the dependence of their women. The South, he declares, is "'always advancing toward orientalism'"(ibid. II 128). The harem – black and white – becomes a social aspiration; the low, the chaotically sexual, the "oriental" invades the high, the chaste, the "Christian." Self-determination pertains to white men only: women and slaves must be owned. Martineau's assessment of the "theory and practice" of American society bluntly distinguishes between ideal and real, between the self-construction of America as democratic and free and the fact of slavery. She works to *unveil* the Southern harem, and uncover the secret family relationships between white and black, demanding the North recognize its own complicity in slavery. Martineau's detailed attention to the low-Other of the South at once stresses its place as the American underworld and pleads for reform. As she reveals the misery of black slaves for free whites, she insists on a connection between the two, an attempt to debilitate the opposition white American society so adamantly set up between the originary (themselves) and the alien (slaves). Apparent racial oppositions slide toward each other creating dangerous moments in various guises: the South is a site of struggle over slavery, but so is the North. Focused mainly on the body of the black woman – but also on the white – Martineau demands self-determination for both.

In her millennialist vision of the end of slavery, Martineau juxtaposes the black and the feminine, calling up sacrificial and apocalyptic images of "houses in flames," and "tornadoes." Emancipation will be a New Heaven and a New Earth, "prison doors" will be opened and the meek shall inherit, all at the agency of women (ibid. II 127). Martineau suggests that the white mothers of the South might band together to overthrow slavery, but certainly that wronged women, robbed of their own bodies, will rise up. She tells of three "white" girls discovered to be mulattas and sold "for the vilest of purposes" to settle their uncle's estate. But when women unite to defeat slavery, these violated innocents "will rise to the light in the day of retribution" (ibid. II 115). Martineau saw the God of the Old Testament "tramping out the vintage where the grapes of wrath are stored" well before Julia Ward Howe wrote her anthem to the mystical union. A true Father could not allow the bodies of his daughters to be defiled forever: those trapped in the harem would be liberated in the dawn of equality and the lower regions of the South cleansed.

4

THE STRANGE CAREER OF FANNY KEMBLE

> *Beat, beat, the crumbling banks and sliding shores, wild waves of the Atlantic and the Altamaha! Sweep down and carry hence this evil earth and these homes of tyranny, and roll above the soil of slavery, and wash my soul and the souls of those I love clean from the blood of our kind!*
>
> Frances Anne Kemble, *Journal of a Residence on a Georgian Plantation,* 3 March 1839

In 1835 the actress and diarist Frances Kemble, member of the famous British theatrical family, wrote to her friend Mrs George Combe on the evils of slavery, saying that

> the demoralisation and degradation which exists wherever they [slaves] exist ... extends from the souls of men downward to their intellect, their body, and the very soil they cultivate. The white population of the slave states are, I should think, the most depraved of their species.
>
> (Wister 53–54)

Piling on words like "degradation," "depraved," and "demoralization" in the older sense of *corrupting morals,* Frances Kemble represents the South as polluted. The slave states are the "low-Other" where the prescriptions of middle-class Victorianism, what Bakhtin calls the "new bodily canon" – decorum, rationality, chastity, cleanliness and order – are attacked by a dangerous, chaotic tangle of passions: violence, rage, filth and lust. The South incorporates moral and metaphysical dirt; in Kemble's writings the geographical space corresponds to the grotesque body: "The essential principle of grotesque realism is degradation, that is, the lowering of all that is high, spiritual, ideal, abstract; it is a transfer to the material level, to the sphere of earth and body in their indissoluble unity" (Bakhtin 19–20).

102

Kemble writes of the slave South as a descent into the bowels, the filth, the mud of human depravity where the spiritual incompletely challenges the physical. For Kemble, slavery is ethically and literally diseased, a social abomination to be examined and cured. In this way, her writing intersects with other nineteenth-century projects: "In Chadwick, in Mayhew, in countless Victorian reformers, the slum, the labouring poor, the prostitute, the sewer, were recreated for the bourgeois study and drawing room" (Stallybrass and White 125). *The slave* must be added to the list, especially the female slave (who overlaps with the prostitute). In detailing the degradations of Southern life, Kemble exhibits the "fascinated gaze" which the high turns upon the low: filth is certainly seductive (ibid. 139). But she, like Stowe, Trollope and Martineau, also shows a focused and structured determination to accuse slavery of sins against the sanctity of marriage, the decorum of the family and the integrity of women's bodies, both white and black.[1]

At the time Kemble wrote that letter to Mrs Combe, she had been retired from the stage and married to Pierce Butler of Philadelphia for less than eighteen months. Some time after the wedding she discovered that the Butler family wealth came from plantations in Georgia:

> when I married Mr. [Butler] I knew nothing of these dreadful possessions of his, and even if I had I should have been much puzzled to have formed any idea of the state of things in which I now find myself plunged, together with those whose well-doing is as vital to me almost as my own.
>
> (Kemble 138)

Though she had married a substantial slaveholder, Kemble saw no reason to alter her commitment to abolitionism; later her politics exacerbated the acrimonious disintegration of her marriage. She had already defied her husband in publishing her *Journal* of 1835, an irreverent look at American manners and customs which produced (on a smaller scale) the same howls of outraged patriotism and misogynist reviews that Frances Trollope's *Domestic Manners of the Americans* provoked three years earlier.[2] Edgar Allen Poe, in the *Southern Literary Messenger*, attacked her diction and said "For a female to speak thus confidently is indelicate," and another reviewer, evoking Lady Macbeth, one of Kemble's famous roles, charged "the authoress has unsexed herself" (Pope-Hennessy 181, Wister 146). Had the original epilogue, a denunciation of American slavery, not been destroyed by Pierce Butler, the scandal would have undoubtedly been still more ferocious.

It was 1838 before Kemble actually went to Georgia and confronted the "degradations" of blacks in white society, but she never altered the terms for the South she used in her letter; in her *Journal* (published in 1863), going South is no less than a visit to the underworld of the spirit *and* the body. Slavery corrupts *downward*, from the soul to the mind to the body to the earth itself. "Down there" refers not only to the Southern states but to the unspeakable lower half of the body, the bowels, the genitals, associated with the "dirtiness" of digestion, urination, defecation and sexuality. Kemble's travels from North to South, upper to lower regions, is not just a negotiation of geographical space, allowing her to create the South as a sinful landscape, but a journey through the body itself. Kemble and her family move from upper middle-class propriety in controlled, cold Philadelphia with its republican heritage, to a wilderness world in the warm, earthy, feudal, tropical excess of Butler Island, Georgia. While Philadelphia had its turbulent side – Pierce Butler told his wife that he feared a pro-slavery mob would burn down their house if she published the abolitionist epilogue to her American *Journal* – Kemble knew it as a place of stifling propriety. The Butler family valued their lineage and status: they were cool, distant, alarmed at Pierce's marrying an *actress* (little better than a prostitute to conventional Americans in those days) and discreet. Their tainted riches came from far away, down South in the veiled Orient of America, the dirty secret of the democracy, hidden from view like the troublesome parts of the body. Yet it is "down there," the scandalous region of America, that Kemble became intimate with a range of behaviours unacknowledged, repressed or forbidden to someone of her gender, her race and her class. She wrote explicitly of sexuality and violence on her husband's estates, transgressing the role of mistress of the plantation whose function was, in Mary Chesnut's words, to "play the ostrich-game" (Woodward 54).

Frances Kemble's engagement with the lower regions both of actual and symbolic geography, and her attempts to expose and control the chaos confronting her, encourage a reading of her Georgia *Journal* as at once reportage on Southern slavery at its historical height and a sort of political *Bildungsroman*. In confronting race, Kemble also confronts questions of gender and class that troubled her, and troubled many white women of her time. Not published until 1863, when it was also read out in the House of Commons, supposedly dampening the pro-Confederacy lobby in Britain, the Georgia *Journal* is the most explicit white text on slavery as institutionalized rape. A pamphlet of 1863, extracting the juicy bits, proclaims "a woman tells the world what the black women of the South have so long endured," while an advertisement on the back cover declares:

> not Mrs Stowe's most vivid and thrilling pictures can compare with the true horrors set out in Fanny Kemble's volume. Even *Uncle Tom's Cabin* is only founded upon fact. The journal of Mrs Kemble is fact itself.
>
> ("The Views of Judge Woodward")

Much speculation has been devoted to whether the *Journal* might have outstripped *Uncle Tom's Cabin* as the abolition block-buster had it been published in the 1840s or 1850s; perhaps Frances Kemble might have been invited to the White House as the "little woman" who started the Civil War.

THE MATERIAL SLAVE BODY

Like Harriet Martineau, Kemble's abolitionism concentrates on women; the back-cover advertisement on the "Judge Woodward" pamphlet goes on to read:

> Her sex brought her specially in contact with the slave *women*. A man, unless he had been a physician, would have known nothing of most of the sorrows and sufferings which were confided to her without scruple. As we read we wonder how the women of the South could endure a system which brought such shame and such pain and worse than pain, on so many of their sisters. We wonder how the wives of slaveholders could bear to see and to know what was passing about them, or by what art they managed to shut eyes and ears and heart.
>
> ("The Views of Judge Woodward")

This language places Kemble in the privileged position normally occupied by a (male) doctor, privy to secrets of the female body and the *slave* body which she then confides to the public, speaking the body in a way most of her society found inappropriate for a man but almost criminal in a woman. Still, for abolitionists, representing the slave body was an important political strategy. Women abolitionists, in particular, were determined to discuss slavery in concrete, physical, not abstract, terms.

The pamphlet, coming after the Emancipation Proclamation and the bloody Southern defeat at Antietam (following an initial run of Confederate victories) must have been preaching mainly to the converted. A woman had already "told the world" about the horrors of slavery in *Uncle Tom's Cabin*, dressing her novel in the discourses of the gothic. In the United States, Kemble's *Journal* was surprising only in the degree and authentication of the atrocities it details, an energizing text for Unionists to rally around. In Britain, however, an independent South had a hold on the imaginations of many in the government and members of the aristocracy (who thought they recognized in the South a land-owning elite comparable to themselves and preferable to the democratic tendencies of the North), as well as owners of Midland textile mills dependent on Southern cotton.[3] The pro-Confederate *Times* had scoffed at the Emancipation Proclamation and everywhere the British press seemed to accept the irrevocable breakdown of the American Union.[4] As John Anthony Scott, in the Introduction to the 1984 edition of the *Journal*, points out, Kemble's main concern was to produce a counterbalance to such opinions in an English edition, not an American one (Kemble xlix). However, Scott goes on to correct the notion that the *Journal* stopped the House of Commons from voting to recognize the Confederate government, pointing out that by May 1863 the passion for an independent slave republic had cooled; the *Journal*'s political influence was greatly exaggerated (ibid. l–liii).

By the middle of the Civil War, and probably well before, the South as a jungle of licentiousness, hypocrisy, violence and rape where white men kept harems and white women had to stop up "eyes and ears and heart" in order to maintain their vaunted "purity" was perfectly familiar to Northern (and British) readers. The infernal South of Legree's plantation, an underworld of misery and degradation, or else the luxurious, beflowered false Eden of "base" liaisons and unholy lusts, were the poles of possibility for the South seen from outside; abolitionist romances and, to some extent, even plantation novels, had done their work producing the idea of a culture where passions ran amok, freed from the usual controls of "decent" society. Beneath the official rhetoric of liberation, found in abolitionist romances dedicated to uplifting the downtrodden slaves and preserving the mystical union from a sacrilegious divorce, the war was being fought over flesh, over the control of the bodies of millions of slaves and over a conflict in the definition of sexual integrity. Publicly, Southern apologists insisted on the chaste and honourable behaviour of slaveholders toward their female slaves, going so far as to deny the possibility, ethical or biological, of "amalgamation." Privately, their wives damned slaveholding men, if not their own husbands and fathers, then the master or the overseer on the next plantation, for their licensed harems and slave children. As Mary Chesnut acidly remarks: "every lady tells you who is the father of all the mulatto children in everybody's household, but those in her own she seems to think drop from the clouds." (Woodward 29). Kemble's *Journal*, far more than *Uncle Tom's Cabin*, focuses attention on the disputed, simultaneously desired and despised body of the female slave and the false hierarchy of white over black that subjugates her.

The movement of the Butler family from North to South describes a displacement from purity to vice, from bourgeois gentility to feudal violence, from the upper body to the lower. Kemble's *Journal* is a full-scale attempt by one representing the "high" or "classical" to confront the "low" or "grotesque" in her determination to make clean, chaste and "rational" the dirty, promiscuous or sexually-exploited slaves of her husband's plantations. In short, she wants to uplift the race.

Kemble's Georgia *Journal* complicates Stowe's, Trollope's and Martineau's representations of the South as oriental, gothic and immoral. She incorporates these discourses into her rendering of the black female body as the chief signifier of the South, but delves most deeply into the material conditions of slavery. Her constant interaction with the "unclean" bodies of the slaves mounts a fundamental challenge to the separation between white lady and black servants, between the closed, individual classical body and the open, multiple grotesque body.

The plantation mistress paradoxically embodies the *disem*bodied classical – elevated, pure, closed, single. As many critics have said, she is the designated work of art of the Old South.[5] Of course, most white women hardly queened it like the rich, spoiled belles of plantation novels: only a tiny percentage lived on estates of more than fifty slaves. None the less, the plantation lady bears white ideals, white "honour," the expression of the aristocratic aspirations of the slaveholding gentry that regulated Southern culture. Wilbur J. Cash's famous "gynaeolatry" passage constructs the Southern lady as "the shield-bearing Athena gleaming whitely in the clouds, the standard for [the South's] rallying, the mystic symbol of its nationality in the face of the foe." (Cash 86). The mistress of the Big House occupies the position of the Virgin Mary in the mediaeval church: she is mediator, mother and saint:

> What she really was was known only to God. Her life was one long act of devotion – devotion to God, devotion to her husband, devotion to her children, devotion to her servants, to her friends, to the poor, to all humanity. Nothing happened within the range of her knowledge that her sympathy did not reach and her charity and wisdom did not ameliorate.
>
> (Page, *The Old South* 155)

The plantation master holds the actual legal and economic power on the plantation: he owns the land, the slaves *and*, to all intents and purposes, he owns the plantation mistress. But Southern chivalric convention dictates that the plantation mistress be deferred to, as long as she remains within her "sphere" of ladylike concerns. She is an emblem of the planter's wealth and class position. She is the guarantor of legitimate, white heirs, yet she is spirit, not flesh: her sexuality does not officially exist (slave women were designated sexual in contrast).[6] White women's bodies are untouchable, remote, idealized: "the 'classical body' denotes the inherent *form* of the high official culture and suggests that the shape and plasticity of the human body is indissociable from the shape and plasticity of discursive material and social norm in a collectivity" (Stallybrass and White 21). The human, specifically the female, body is the site of the South's most intense discursive battle. "Ladyhood" and slavery intertwine: official Southern culture's insistence on the elevation of the white woman means nothing without the corresponding debasement of the black woman. The white lady "playing statue," as Lillian Smith put it, is sexless, seamless and silent (*Killers* 141). She represents the smooth ideal preferred over the "protuberant," insistent body of the "black wench;" her form is the preferred utterance of the powerful group, here, the plantation class: "the classical statue is the radiant centre of a transcendent individualism, 'put on a pedestal,' raised above the viewer and the commonality, anticipating passive admiration from below. We *gaze up* at the figure and wonder" (Stallybrass and White 21). Wilbur Cash could not have put it better himself: the white lady is an icon, isolated, singular, literally and metaphorically raised up while her perceived opposites are multiple, on their hands and knees scrubbing the floor or bent over picking cotton. Where the badly-clothed, barely-covered bodies of slave women are revealed and exposed, especially on a rice plantation like the Butler Island estate where women would hike their skirts up to their hips to stand in the rice fields, the white lady's body is covered, unmentionable.[7] Where the perpetual pregnancies, breast-feeding and illnesses of slave women are displayed around the plantation, white women operate in a private sphere of child-bearing and rearing. In the classical body, "All orifices of the body are closed. The basis of the image is the individual, strictly limited mass, the impenetrable facade . . . prohibit[ing] all that is linked with fecundation, pregnancy, childbirth" (Bakhtin 320).

The plantation mistress as Virgin Mary, in Thomas Nelson Page's Virginia hagiography so high up the Great Chain of Being as to be "known only to God," the impervious, singular, spiritualized body, is the representation imposed on Frances Kemble when she comes to Georgia as the slaveholder's wife. The slaves petition her to intercede with the master (God the Father) on their behalf, to save them from a beating or to get a little extra sugar or flannel. They say they admire her for her fair skin: Kemble tells of one old slave woman exclaiming to Pierce Butler, "Oh massa, where you get this lilly alabaster baby!" (Kemble 66). Kemble reports that at first she thought the slave Rose was speaking of her child but then realized she was being admired, as she says, "for the fairness of *my skin*." The mistress is both marble statue and infant. Yet, as Kemble realizes, whiteness is also a function of power, for she goes on to say:

> I suppose that if I chose to walk arm in arm with the dingiest mulatto through the streets of Philadelphia, nobody could possibly tell by my complexion that I was not his sister, so that the mere quality of mistress must have had a most miraculous effect on my skin in the eyes of poor Rose.
>
> (ibid. 66)

By the rules of the society she had entered, Kemble should have accepted her *whiteness* and her *ladyhood* along with the title of mistress. Pierce Butler does not challenge his class, race and gender position. Kemble, however, does. She hates being called "missis," exclaiming to slaves "For God's sake do not call me that!" adding "though I was the wife of the man who pretends to own them, I was, in truth, no more their mistress than they were mine" (ibid. 60).

Kemble's trip South and stay in Georgia becomes an attack on her husband's world; she constantly transgresses, putting her "alabaster" body, her *classical* body in the way of those black bodies which are supposed to be anathema to her. These slave bodies are represented by the multiple, "animal," unclosed, "always conceiving" grotesque body (Bakhtin 27, 21). Helping to care for an ill slave woman, Kemble says "This woman is young, I suppose at the outside not thirty, and her sister informed me that she had ten children – ten children, E[lizabeth]!" (Kemble 76). Kemble repeats stories of pregnancy and labour, dropped wombs and backache, over and over again, as she reports the dirty conditions in which slaves lived, unhygienic medicine, overt bodily functions. All this was outside her sphere, yet she allows her "ladyhood" to be violated by smells, pain, filth and knowledge of a world of violence and sexuality officially forbidden to the plantation mistress. While it is true that the plantation ethic charges the mistress, as "mother" to the household, with nurture of everyone from her own children to slave babies, nursing of blacks was not allowed to pull the mistress off her pedestal. She dealt with ailing slaves, mostly house servants, when she had to. Fox-Genovese quotes Anna Matilda Page King recommending that her husband buy good meat "in order to let the Negroes keep well" so that she would not have to deal with ill slaves, and Mahala Roach complained that she had to do a sick slave's jobs as well as nurse her (Fox-Genovese 129). None of these women seemed to like the role of ministering angel. But Frances Kemble takes as her province slaves beyond the master's house (the old overseer's house the Butlers lived in was small and needed few servants) into the dirt and disease of the slaves' "low" world, pushing the limits – or, in a sense, fulfilling the idealized maternal image – of the mistress-role.

The plantation infirmary particularly interests Kemble: she tries to improve it single-handedly, nursing the sick herself, though she finds her genteel background an impediment: "How much I wished that, instead of music, and dancing, and such stuff, I had learned something of sickness and health, of the conditions and liabilities of the human body" (*Journal* 75). Exasperated, disgusted and fretting over conditions for women and children, Kemble writes of washing insect-infested slave babies and infected women:

> [I] found one side of her face and neck very much swollen, but so begrimed with filth that it was no very agreeable task to examine it. The first process, of course, was washing, which,

however, appeared to her so very unusual an operation, that
I had to perform it for her myself.

(ibid. 98)

Kemble's project is not only combative, it is reformist. She will tell
the truth about slavery and try to better it, especially for the women.
Anecdotes of her attempts (usually unsuccessful) to teach chastity,
hygiene, culture and religion to her husband's slaves, as well as her
horror and disgust at the casualness with which women are raped
or beaten, implicate her in the classical body/grotesque body hierarchy. In the beginning, she defines slaves as "low" and finds slave
bodies ugly and foul. Describing the Butler Island servants, she
says they "are perfectly filthy in their persons and clothes – their
faces, hands, and naked feet being literally encrusted with dirt –
their attendance at our meals is not, as you may suppose, particularly agreeable to me" (ibid. 60–61). Initially, Kemble also sees the
slaves as collective, a rather carnivalesque mob: "the crowd thronged
about us like a swarm of bees; we were seized, pulled, pushed, carried,
dragged, and all but lifted in the air by the clamorous multitude. I was
afraid my children would be smothered" (ibid. 50).

The Butler Island slaves look like "a cloud of dingy dependents"
without individuality until Kemble begins to hear their stories and
attempts to bring them around (or *up*) to her "classical" sense of
closed, clean, separate bodies. After a while, the slaves are not
"them," a multiple Other, but a series of characters. The *Journal*
entry for 28 February–2 March 1839 (Chapter 19) contains a list of
slave women and their troubles:

Fanny has had six children; all dead but one. She came to beg
to have her work in the field lightened.

Nanny has had three children; two of them are dead. She came
to implore that the rule of sending them into the field three
weeks after their confinement might be altered.

Leah, Caesar's wife, has had six children. Three are dead. . . .

Sally, Scipio's wife, has had two miscarriages and three children born, one of whom is dead. She came complaining of
incessant pain and weakness in her back. This woman was a
mulatto, daughter of a slave called Sophy by a white man of
the name of Walker who visited the plantation.

(ibid. 229–30)

111

These slave women now occupy another category for Kemble: they are *mothers* and within the web of pieties which Victorian culture created for motherhood. By *naming* them (the list includes five more women), and telling their stories, Kemble releases them from their designated location at the bottom of the white/black binary: she makes common cause with them as *women* and so puts at risk her own placement above them as the mistress. Toni Morrison suggests studying blackness (as Kemble, in her Georgia sojourn can surely be said to do) "will reveal the process by which it is made possible to explore and penetrate one's own body in the guise of the sexuality, vulnerability and anarchy of the other" (Morrison, *Playing in the Dark* 53). By touching blackness, in however limited a way, Kemble troubles the barrier between white lady and black "wench," entering, in a sense, into the experience of the slave. When she speaks of Pierce Butler as her "owner" and tells of her failure to persuade him to do good by his slaves, when she describes placing her hand on black skin or washing black bodies, she moves in the direction of identification with them. I agree with bell hooks that however oppressed white women were in marriage they still did not experience the "dehumanization of slavery," but Kemble is not simply "appropriating the horror of slave experience to enhance" her "own cause" (hooks 126). She pushes herself, and the reader, toward a sense of solidarity, however incomplete, with blacks under slavery by bringing slave women "up" to her standards of health and by moving herself "down" to deal with the filth of slavery.

Kemble's increasing engagement with the slaves, as it unfolds in the *Journal*, destabilizes the rigidity of the binary; her visits to slave homes, to the plantation hospital, getting her hands dirty, indeed, her very insistence on going South, defying Butler family wishes, going "down there" into the underworld, living in a crude house that was not only a far cry from the plantation of romance, with its white-columned house and its walled gardens, but removed from her own tidy cottage outside Philadelphia, is itself disruptive. In the *Journal*, the fixed division between black and white, high and low, is made precarious by Kemble's refusal to abide by the defining oppositions of Southern culture. She places her "sacred" self in the way of pollution, she tries to be the iconoclast who smashes her own "alabaster" image.

112

THE ODOUR OF SLAVERY

Kemble's account of her trip into the Heart of Darkness begins with the harsh, noisy journey from the daylight world of Philadelphia to the gothic underbelly of America, the South.[8] Like Frances Trollope before her, Kemble describes the arduous, dangerous excursion on which the expectations of a lady accustomed to a certain level of comfort – baths, warmth, food – were constantly denied her. Pierce Butler seems to have understood the perils of bringing his avowedly anti-slavery wife to a plantation; he and his family had resisted earlier attempts by Kemble to go South. In an 1836 letter to Mrs Follen, she comically complains:

> I am not to accompany my husband in his expedition. I am not to open his mind to the evils of slavery, I am not to ameliorate and enlighten the minds of those whose labour feeds me, nor am I to be *lynched*; alas! all of which I had so fondly anticipated.
>
> (Wister 155–56)

Kemble already felt some sense of mission, even (though expressed mockingly) of possible martyrdom, as it was a known fact that abolitionists in the South (and sometimes in the North) were subject to vigilante murder. Harriet Martineau describes the notices and handbills of Southern "committees of vigilance," "offering enormous rewards for the heads, or for the ears, of prominent abolitionists" (Martineau, *Society in America* I 134). She adds that "high official persons sat on these committees," forerunners of the Ku Klux Klan. So involvement with the sufferings of slaves or proximity to them in these volatile lower regions of America could result in a loss of bodily integrity – bits lopped off. It was unthinkable that the sacred object, the statue-lady, would put herself in the way of such desecration or dismantlement or even an intimacy with the dirt and odour of slavery. Yet Kemble was determined to risk it.

In the white mythology of race, odour is a mark of blackness. The grotesque body, because of its opened orifices and centrality of the genitals, stomach and bowels, is signified by smell. Racist discourse still employs notions of "the negro smell" (or, in other cultures, "the Paki smell," "the Arab smell," "the Chinese smell"). Even romantic racial moderates like Faulkner spoke of "the strong warm negro smell" in *Go Down, Moses* as if identifying some kind of biological

113

fact. Smell becomes "an agent of class differentiation. Disgust was inseparable from refinement: whilst it designated the 'depraved' domain of the poor, it simultaneously established the purified domain of the bourgeoisie" (Stallybrass and White 140).

Frances Kemble's early distress at how the Butler Island slaves smelled led her to violate class decorum (again) and do things for herself: "the consequence is that, among Mr. [Butler's] slaves, I wait upon myself more than I have ever done in my life" (Kemble 61). Yet, like her own imagined fairness of skin, Kemble analyses odour as a function of class and power (revealing her own prejudice):

> About this same personal offensiveness, the Southerners, you know, insist that it is inherent with the race, and it is one of their most cogent reasons for keeping them as slaves. . . . I am strongly inclined to believe that peculiar ignorance of the laws of health and the habits of decent cleanliness are the real and only causes of this disagreeable characteristic . . . if you have ever come into anything like neighbourly proximity with a low Irishman or woman, I think you will allow that the same causes produce very nearly the same effects.
>
> (ibid. 61)[9]

Kemble goes on to expose the hypocrisy of Southern insistence on an absolute division of white and black:

> But, as this very disagreeable peculiarity does not prevent Southern women from hanging their infants at the breasts of Negresses, nor almost every planter's wife and daughter having one or more little pet blacks sleeping like puppy dogs in their very bedchamber, nor almost every planter from admitting one or several of his female slaves to the still closer intimacy of his bed . . .
>
> (ibid. 61)

Kemble speaks the forbidden erotic truth of the South: black and white bodies are *not* carefully separate but in constant, unequal intercourse. She raises the oriental, writing of "several" slaves sharing the master's bed, underscoring the fact that slaveholding men had access to all the female bodies in the household. The *Journal* sets out to ridicule one of the keystones of Southern society and a chief justification of slavery: that the black body is naturally disgusting to whites, that the animal inferiority of blacks can only produce horror and revulsion in whites, and that the two races cannot interact in any meaningful way except as subjugated and subjugator. If the separation of races is so "natural," Kemble argues at the beginning of her *Journal*, why are laws needed to forbid the marriage of blacks and whites? The dirty is also the desirable.

Kemble writes her journey "down there" to the swampy, benighted, comfortless, hot circles of the Southern interior, as a means to confront and attack the culture of sexual exploitation: institutionalized rape being the most obvious (and, ironically, most veiled) evidence of the "oriental" intercourse between blacks and whites. Early on, she blasts *plaçage* in New Orleans, describing *placées* as "a class of unhappy females ... whose mingled blood does not prevent their being remarkable for their beauty, and with whom no man, no *gentleman*, in that city shrinks from associating" (ibid. 9–10). Here, Kemble's attack on slavery is in line with most of the women abolitionists, both British and American, of her generation from Angelina and Sarah Grimké to Harriet Beecher Stowe; the problem with building slavery on the theory that blacks are inexorably *other*, inferior and naturally *low*, is that plenty of "high" whites find them erotically acceptable, and the products of their various "minglings" transgress racial, and often class and gender borders, confusing slavery's sustaining definitions.

It will not do to read Kemble anachronistically as a modern liberal. She has her racialist prejudices: she finds black hair exceptionally ugly; she praises the looks of black children only up to a certain age: "I have seen many babies on this plantation who were quite as pretty as white children" (ibid. 78). While Kemble is not immune to thinking blacks less intelligent and less attractive than whites, she also turns the idea of black "ugliness" against whites to expose the instability of Southern absolutes: "yet it is notorious, that almost every Southern planter has a family more or less numerous of illegitimate coloured children" (ibid. 10). While this is doubtless something of an exaggeration, Kemble makes the same point as Chesnut, Thomas, Stowe, Trollope and Martineau: slaveholding men can command the bodies of slave women without social consequence. Kemble raises the possibility that this is done out of cynical economic interest since the more slaves a plantation produced, the richer it became (and mulattoes sold for more than so-called "pure" Africans), but she then dismisses it, preferring to see even in the wicked, exploitative connections between white men and black women evidence of desire which shows that blacks and whites are *not* inherently antagonistic.

The signal evil of black women's exploitation by white men lies in the devaluation of marriage. To Kemble, as to Stowe, Child, Martineau, Trollope, Chapman, Jacobs and other abolitionist writers, slavery destroys marriage as a moral, religious, social and sexual contract. In the infernal South, a world upside down, marriage, available only to whites, is a travesty:

> That such connections [between slave women and white men] exist commonly is a sufficient proof that they are not abhorrent to nature; but it seems, indeed, as if marriage (and not concubinage) was the horrible enormity which cannot be tolerated, and against which, moreover, it has been deemed expedient to enact laws . . . there is no law in the white man's nature that prevents him from making a coloured woman the mother of his children, but there is a law on his statute books forbidding him to make her his wife; and if we are to admit the theory that the mixing of the races is a monstrosity, it seems almost as curious that laws should be enacted to prevent men marrying women toward whom they have an invincible natural repugnance, as that education should by law be prohibited to creatures incapable of receiving it.

(ibid. 10–11)

Kemble's goal, as she makes plain with this display of inversions, is to establish the slaveholding South as an enemy to the family, the foundation of Christian society, and to *women*, both white and black. Despite the official Southern insistence on the elevation of women (the madonna mistress of the plantation) and the ennobling sanctity of the family, Kemble perceives that these institutions precariously cover an antithetical system that assaults women and the family from within. The image of the plantation as a benign patriarchy, with the master as a "father" to all, the mistress as mother, and the slaves as happy, naive primitives far more fortunate than the "wage slaves" of the North or Britain, was carefully cultivated by plantation novelists such as John Pendleton Kennedy, Caroline Gilman, Caroline Lee Hentz, Mary H. Eastman and William Gilmore Simms.[10] Kemble does not buy into the Southern self-construction; she lacks that essential commitment to "ladyhood." The over-elevated status of the white woman in the slave South, in her analysis, means nothing without slave concubines. White men assign sexuality to the subaltern group of women in order to exempt ladies from it. Kemble attempts to cross this

116

boundary and so sins against the pieties of the South, exposing the edifice of benevolent slavery, ladyhood and the false hierarchy of white over black, lady over slave, to be a corrupt, unstable social imposition.

Frances Kemble literally dirties her hands. She visits the slave houses and infirmary, reporting Spanish moss mattresses, filthy blankets, and open sewer ditches: so much for Aunt Phillis' charming cabin, or even Uncle Tom's rose-trellised one, for that matter (ibid. 67–68). Trying to impress the need for cleanliness on the people, she sweeps dirt floors and picks up wood for the fire, much to the evident shock of "old Rose" the midwife. She scrubs the infirmary: "I left this refuge for Mr. [Butler's] sick dependents with my clothes covered with dust and full of vermin." (ibid. 71). Later, she reports washing slave babies, nursing sick slave women and demonstrating hygiene to the bemused people (as she sees them) of the Butler estate. She never flinches from describing the most unappetizing medical conditions, such as the young girl "whose hands and feet were literally rotting away piecemeal" or the epileptic woman wrapped in excrement-covered rags (ibid. 76, 75).

Kemble insists that slavery, for women, means "improper treatment of the female frame," *improper* in the sense of "damaging" and *improper* in the sense of *sexual*. She recounts painful stories of slave women forced to go back to field work shortly after giving birth, or women who have had ten children by the age of thirty, or women who are whipped because they dare complain to her about their lives. She commits crimes against white bodily propriety in merely *touching* blacks. Once she kisses a slave baby,

> as beautiful a specimen of a sleeping infant as I ever saw. The caress excited the irrepressible delight of all the women present – poor creatures! who seemed to forget that I was a woman, and had children myself, and bore a woman's and a mother's heart toward them and theirs
>
> (ibid. 78)

Kemble's troubling of the waters of Southern decorum demonstrates the fragility of racial and class boundaries. Her touching and kissing, her dirty hands, force the white lady and the slave woman, the classical body and the grotesque body, into some communication. Writing of the law against teaching a slave to read, she turns the opposition between herself and Pierce Butler as mistress and master over the slaves of St Simons Island, into an opposition between Pierce as representative of patriarchal law and herself and the slaves as property.[11] She says "but teaching slaves to read is a finable offence, and I am *feme couverte*, and my fines must be paid by my legal owner" (ibid. 272). By speaking of Pierce as her owner, she appropriates the position of chattel for herself, once more crossing the colour line. She also conjures the oriental, placing herself most prominently in the "harem" of the master. Though Pierce Butler was not accused of sexually exploiting his slaves (according to what Kemble heard, the overseer's family was most active in that regard), Kemble still plays a dangerous game here. As we have seen, slaveholding women *did* wryly (in their *tableaux* of *Lalla Rookh*) or angrily (the mistress who told Harriet Martineau she felt like "the chief slave of the harem"), refer to the orientalism of the South. But for one to place herself discursively (and questionably, since no mistress ever lived as badly as a slave) is nevertheless a "lowering" intolerable in the public commitment to dividing the bodies of the South according to race, gender and class. When a woman of the plantation class imagines herself a slave, perhaps like Hiram Power's *Greek Slave*, fragile, chained and vulnerable, she both participates in an erotic image system of subjugated women and confuses the justifications of slavery.

Kemble's account of a society in which one woman kissing another's child could cause such a sensation reveals profound anxiety over the body. In the South's sustaining story, the black woman (defined as everything from very dark to the mulatta with one "drop of ink") is a natural prostitute, properly "oriental," a seductress without the inherent sense of morality ascribed to white women: "It was above all around the figure of the prostitute that the gaze and touch, the desires and contaminations, of the bourgeois male were articulated" (Stallybrass and White 137). Stallybrass and White are speaking of the nineteenth-century European, city-dwelling white man, but the idea works just as well for the nineteenth-century American, slave state-dwelling white man: black women were assumed to be sexually available to any white man while the sexuality of white women was circumscribed. In Faulkner's *Absalom, Absalom!*, Quentin Compson's father schematizes womanhood in the antebellum South: "ladies, women, females – the virgins whom gentlemen someday married, the courtesans to whom they went while on sabbaticals to the cities, and the slave girls and women upon whom that first caste rested and to whom in certain cases it doubtless owed the very fact of its virginity" (Faulkner, *Absalom, Absalom!* 109). The discourse of female sexuality surrounded the black woman because it could not be associated with the white woman. Black men are, of course, tame in slavery but potential rapists. White women must be constantly on guard against black men: Kemble rows home with some of her slave men, who say there was "not another planter's lady in all Georgia" who would be alone with black men. She, however, does not fear rape any more than she hesitates to identify herself and her position with the black women on her husband's plantation. But Kemble is always an outsider, a foreigner: "I *am* going prejudiced against slavery, for I am an Englishwoman, in whom the absence of such a prejudice would be disgraceful" (Kemble 11). And she is an *actress*, an outsider in the class systems of both Philadelphia and the plantation South. Perhaps that is why she is inclined to play roles, to play at being the Other, the slave – the actress in metaphorical blackface. She said no one could tell her from the sister of "the dingiest mulatto": in a sense, she takes on the part herself in order to challenge racial proscription.

Kemble sets out to dismantle the story of the seductive black woman. She does not romanticize New Orleans *placées*, nor does she subscribe to the idea of irresistible "beastly Negress beauties," as Mary Chesnut calls them. The women of the Butler Island and Hampton Island plantations are hardly seductresses; indeed, Kemble sees them unequivocally as victims, separated from their children, raped and impregnated against their will by slave drivers like Frank or even the overseers, Roswell King, Sr, and Roswell King, Jr, beaten for their "crimes" by the order of one of the Mrs Kings when she discovers her husband's liaison.

In Kemble's narrative, the equation of female chastity with goodness, with virtue, even with ladyhood itself, begins to slip, just as her chronicling of all those children by one King or another, looking nearly white, and various instances of amalgamation, such as the children Ben and Daphne, show the slippage of whiteness into blackness. Kemble records how her husband shows particular "interest in and pity for them, *because of their colour*" (ibid. 282). She goes on to say that she realizes it is unjust to the other slaves that she and Pierce Butler should be so sympathetic toward them but worries especially for Daphne and a life of "coarse labour." It does not comfort Kemble that if Daphne lived in a city she would be put on the market as a "fancy woman," or mulatta concubine. In any case, she says, death is preferable.

Kemble attacks the "chivalric" pretensions on which both the ideal of ladyhood and the practice of black concubinage rests. She says,

I think an improvement might be made upon that caricature published a short time ago, called the "Chivalry of the South." I think an elegant young Carolinian or Georgian gentleman, whip in hand, driving a gang of "lusty women" as they are called here, would be a pretty version of the "Chivalry of the South" – a little coarse, I am afraid you will say. Oh! quite horribly coarse, but then so true.

(ibid. 170)

She visits the Demere plantation on St Simons Island where, she says,

I was received by the sons as well as the lady of the house, and could not but admire the lordly rather than manly indifference with which these young gentlemen, in gay guard chains and fine attire, played the gallant to me, while filthy, barefooted, half-naked negro women brought in refreshments, and stood all the while fanning the cake and sweetmeats, and their young masters as if they had been all the same sort of stuff.

(ibid. 343)

Kemble critiques the elevation demanded of the white women; she utters the forbidden, and she "taints" the Marian plantation mistress with an indecorous knowledge of miscegenation and brutality when the lady of the Big House retained her status and value by her *lack* of intercourse with the low. The young men see the vulnerable "half-naked" bodies of slave women all the time: no wonder they view them as objects for their use. At the same time, they are taught to venerate the covered, forbidden bodies of white women, to act as "knights." Kemble, however, does not accept the fictions of the South. She endangers the lady on the pedestal merely by speaking out on a subject which was supposed to be *terra incognita* for her; the black body should have elicited only fear and disgust, not compassion, not engagement. Women who transgressed this rule, like the Grimké sisters and other female abolitionists, were damned from the lecterns and pulpits of both pro- and anti-slavery men, and accused of loose morals. As one minister in the 1830s raged:

The term Female Orator has a sound too nearly allied to another that may not be named. And all approaches to the

120

character of a female public speaker proportionally detract from the honor appropriate to females.

(Barnes 156)

Publication is another form of public speaking, as Harriet Beecher Stowe found out in the attacks declaring her "no lady" for addressing the black body in *Uncle Tom's Cabin*. The similarity of sound between the words "orator" and "whore," the "one which may not be named," equates the political, analytical woman with sexual sin. One is tempted to play further with these "allied" words and name the unnameable as "orifice," as well, the sign of the female (and black) body that stands against the closed, classical disembodiment of the ideal. Like a gynaecologist, Kemble speaks of orifices, as the sensationalist blurb writer for the *Journal* quoted above in the "Judge Woodward" pamphlet and an affronted reviewer for the *Saturday Review* understood: "The coolness with which she prints sundry details which few ladies would put on paper . . . is quite inimitable. We never met with such minutiae in print except in the pages of professedly medical publications" (13 June 1863, quoted in Lombard 338). By recognizing the position of the black woman in the slave economy, indeed, by recognizing her own position, falsely elevated as the white mistress but also the white man's property, Kemble intervenes in the separations which define Southern society. By speaking the forbidden, transgressing her role, doing things a white plantation lady is not supposed to do, Kemble forces the classical and grotesque bodies into some collusion: however limited in its actual benefit to the slave women she agonized over.

Her journey South, down to the realms of appetite, desire and violence, marked the beginning of the end of her marriage. Because she refused to accept her husband's "ownership" of her, as she refused to accept ownership of slaves, he drove her away. Their life together after the time spent in Georgia became increasingly tense and painful.[12] His 1845 "Conditions" for her continued presence in his house and communication with their children, are an attempt to silence her, to rewrite her story, forcing her to agree to never mention the past and to "submit her will" to his.[13] It was to no avail: the Court of Common Pleas of Pennsylvania decreed their divorce in 1849, giving Pierce Butler custody of their two daughters, Sarah and Fanny. His post-divorce "Statement," privately printed and distributed to his friends, contains the scandalous information that Mrs Butler "held that marriage should be a companionship on

121

equal terms" (Wister 177). Given this connection of marriage with slavery, which Kemble makes time and time again when she recognizes her powerlessness to ameliorate life for the Butler slaves – as Elizabeth Fox-Genovese points out, "missis" is not the same as "massa" – it is poignant that she suffered a fate similar to that of so many slave women she pitied; her children were taken from her by their (and her) legal owner.

REVISITING THE GEORGIA PLANTATION

In 1883, twenty years after the publication of *Journal of a Residence on a Georgian Plantation*, Frances Butler Leigh, younger daughter of Pierce Butler and Frances Kemble, answered her mother's book. *Ten Years on a Georgia Plantation Since the War* does not mention either Frances Kemble or her Georgia *Journal* directly, but both haunt the daughter's production like outrageous spirits.

Frances Butler Leigh takes issue with her mother's book beginning with the title: she holds "ten years" up against the four months her mother spent on the Butler estates, giving herself an authority she clearly felt her mother lacked. Like Kemble, Leigh begins promising to tell the unvarnished truth, unlike other accounts written "by travellers, who, with every desire to get at the truth, could but see things superficially, or by persons whose feelings were too strong either on one side or the other to be perfectly just in their representations" (Leigh 4). This is somewhat conciliatory language: talking back to her famous mother, but not too loudly. Indeed, concern for reconciliation runs alongside a need to "correct" what she saw as negative images of the Old South: *Ten Years* begins with a poem called "Brothers Again," and, like so many Lost Cause books published in the 1880s, stresses both re-union and the hope that "Southern" values would prevail in a chastened America.

Frances Butler, called "Fan" by the family, was born in 1838, the same year the Georgia *Journal* was begun, and taken South on her mother's original journey to the plantations. Where that trip, which she would not remember, being only a few months old, was dominated by the mother, this Reconstruction return is dominated by the father. While her elder sister Sarah took after their mother in her abolitionism and Northern sympathies, Fan sided with Pierce Butler and the South, erasing her mother and her mother's works from this attempt to renew the plantation. Though Pierce Butler died in August 1867, Fan Butler decided to stay: "I went down to the South to carry on his work, and to look after the negroes who loved him so dearly and to whom he was so much attached" (ibid. 72).[14]

This directly challenges her mother. Where Kemble begins by declaring her implacable opposition to slavery, Leigh coolly assesses the Reconstruction South's unwise encouragement of "the negroes in all their foolish and extravagant ideas of freedom" (ibid. 2). Later she says: "I felt sure then, and still think, the pure negro incapable of advancement to any degree that would enable him to cope with the white race, intellectually, morally, or even physically" (ibid. 93).

It is almost uncanny how *Ten Years on a Georgia Plantation* follows the movement of *Journal of a Residence*. Like her mother thirty years before, Butler moves from relative order in the North to what she describes as "CHAOS" in the South. Just as her mother did, she had to make the still-primitive house more comfortable (she hangs up a picture of General Lee) and teach the servants (many ex-slaves of the old estate) to do the things she wanted: "I generally found that if I wanted a thing done I first had to tell the negroes how to do it, then show them how, and finally do it myself" (ibid. 57). She sounds eerily like her mother when complaining of a housemaid who uses her toothbrush to clean the bath: "needless to say, I presented her with that one, and locked my new one up" (ibid. 38). Yet Leigh, unlike her mother, refuses to analyse the "stupidity" and "childishness" of blacks in terms of powerlessness. There is no acknowledgement of the abuses of slavery, but a positive nostalgia for the old days which denies everything Kemble said without mentioning her. Instead of Pierce Butler's aloofness from and general distaste for blacks, his daughter insists on their mutual admiration. The ex-slaves' "love for and belief in my father was beyond expression.... They never spoke of him without some touching and affectionate expression" (ibid. 77). Historically underlining the Butler family love for their slaves, she tells of her great-grandfather rewarding his favourite slave Morris with an offer of freedom. Naturally, the devoted slave refused, and in gratitude, Major Butler had a silver cup engraved for him (ibid. 184–85). Leigh perceives no ridiculousness in presenting a slave, who probably did not get enough to eat and slept on an insect-infested moss mattress, with a silver cup. Moreover, she cites an 1827 letter from the plantation overseer (probably Roswell King, Sr) to her great-uncle, telling how he killed twenty-eight beef cattle for "the people's Christmas dinner. I can do more with them in this way than if all the hides of the cattle were made into lashes!" (ibid. 233).

A Southern apologist, Leigh, like so many writers of the 1880s and 1890s – Thomas Nelson Page, Marion Harland, Joel Chandler Harris and so on – subscribes to the antebellum Eden, the orderly, decorous, gentle world utterly wrecked by the war, emancipation and Reconstruction. Claiming to tell the real truth about the South, she compares its former glory and happiness to its current ruin and confusion. But her most pointed attack is on her mother's book. She says she tells stories to "refute" abolitionists; we can guess whom she has uppermost in mind. Where Frances Kemble decides that "ownership" of human beings is a sin, Frances Butler reports the servants coming to her, practically begging to be re-enslaved: "'We your people, missus,'" (ibid. 235). Instead of being cold and hungry much of the time, Leigh insists that in slavery the people were clothed in the best English wool and had thick blankets (ibid. 231). Instead of a lecher who produces (but does not acknowledge) half-white children, Roswell King, Sr is a generous man who throws a grand feast at Christmas. Instead of rape victims, black women are seductresses. They were always "inclined to be immoral [but] they have now thrown all semblance of chastity to the winds" (ibid. 237). Finally she says, defensively, "If slavery made a Legree, it also made an Uncle Tom." In other words, slavery might have made blacks suffer, but it also produced a black Christ, an exemplary sufferer. In a sense, though, it is as if Leigh does not realize what she has just said; Legree's wickedness stems not only from his beating slaves like Uncle Tom, but his sexual abuse of women slaves like Cassy and Emmeline. Leigh means to restore all she saw her mother (and those like her) destroying. Like Frances Wright's daughter Sylva d'Arusmont, Leigh reacts to her mother's "left-wing" politics by asserting her conservatism. She was not brought up a plantation lady of the spoiled, flower-like kind described in pro-slavery romances. Her actual history included a broken home, scandalous parents, financial insecurity and a certain loss of class status. In her book she rewrites history, claiming for herself a place amongst the Southern aristocracy and effacing her mother's radical bid to undermine paradise.

It is, of course, impossible to tell if Kemble's *Journal* or Leigh's account is the more "accurate:" both are products of historical and ideological moments. But *Ten Years on a Georgia Plantation* has often been used by Southern scholars to "correct" *Journal of a Residence on a Georgian Plantation*. In Ulrich B. Phillips' classic *Life and Labor in the Old South* (1929) he attacks *Journal of a Residence* as "a monotonous view of the seamy side" and claims Leigh's *Ten Years* "refutes her mother's argument and poses experience against theory as to Negro quality, white responsibility, Pierce M. Butler's character, and the regime on Butler Island" (Phillips 261, 267). As late as 1960, Southern historians attacked Kemble in terms of Leigh: Margaret Davis Cate speaks of the "overdrawn picture of life" in *Journal of a Residence*, charging Kemble with constant errors because her dating of a notorious duel was inaccurate and because her version of the silver cup story does not match her daughter's. Cate says Kemble's original manuscript was "dull" so she exaggerated to arouse "public indignation" (Cate 5). If Leigh's intention really was to take on her mother's book and subvert its argument, she succeeded beyond her wildest dreams with some Southerners; Cate ends with: "every statement in the *Journal* is open to suspicion. Can anyone know *fact* from *fiction* in Mrs. Kemble's *Journal*?" (ibid. 17).

The continuation of this covert debate nearly one hundred years beyond the Civil War speaks to the continued guilt and volatility of opinion over race and gender in the South. The subtext to what Phillips, Cate and others say of Kemble is that she was no lady, no *Southern* lady, the way her daughter was. Where Kemble refuses the iconography (though not the role) of plantation mistress, Leigh takes it up with relish. Where Kemble reveals white Southern men's sexual exploitation of black women, Leigh denies it, insisting on the traditional (white, upper-class, chivalric) view of slavery as a benign institution. Kemble speaks the unspeakable, exposing the tangle of sexuality and race, "down there"; her daughter insists on the South's innocence – there are no orifices in the regional body.

Frances Kemble's radical stripping away of the veils of slavery to enlighten Britain and America, and Frances Leigh's revisionist re-draping of the institution to ward off the gaze of the curious, illustrates more than a private family quarrel. In their texts, mother and daughter play out the national narrative of the South; before the Civil War, books on the abuses of slavery (amplified by *Uncle Tom's Cabin*) ignited feelings and sold hugely, but in the decades following Reconstruction, the Lost Cause recaptured the national imagination the way the defeated, but romantic, Jacobite rebellions gave Sir Walter Scott his greatest fictional subject. If *Journal of a Residence on a Georgian Plantation* belongs in the liberalizing context of reform created by *Uncle Tom's Cabin*, then *Ten Years on a Georgia Plantation* comes in at the beginning of reactionary romances such as Thomas Nelson Page's "Ole Virginia" stories, Harris' Uncle Remus, and Thomas Dixon, Jr's Ku Klux Klan bestsellers. Just as Kemble's book was produced out of the abolitionism of the 1830s, Leigh's proceeds from Lost Cause rhetoric. After Reconstruction and the withdrawal of Union troops from the South in 1877 (called "Redemption" by white Southerners), the Old South became the hottest subject in publishing, just as minstrel shows and black music and dance from small-time outfits touring rural America to elaborate Broadway productions (like the 1913 *Darktown Follies*) were changing popular entertainment. There was an important economic aspect to re-representing the South as a plantation performance: the South needed investment and the North a stable region to build industry in. As Eric Sundquist points out, the spirituals and scenes from plantation life (as well as Booker T. Washington's "compromise" speech) at the 1895 Cotton States International Exposition in Atlanta "demonstrated that the South had economic as well as cultural reasons to promote the plantation mythology of kind masters and contented slaves – or, in the modern guise, benevolent white employers and happy, subservient black laborers" (Sundquist, *To Wake the Nations* 73). The North won the military conflict; the white Southern elite won the nostalgia war.

The struggle over black and white bodies was not resolved by the Emancipation Proclamation or the surrender at Appomattox or the first Civil Rights Act. Where Stowe, Martineau, Trollope and Kemble had represented a South of gothic horrors and oriental sexual transgression, Lost Cause writers battled back with a Golden Age dream of order. Once "redeemed" from occupying federal troops, Southern legislatures began to create the Jim Crow laws which would further separate and define white over black. Informally, white Southerners began campaigns of terror and lynching that enforced their definitions with violence. White ladies were still sacred spirits; black women were still exploitable flesh. A war had been fought, but the binary ideology of the body still reigned.

5

OLLA PODRIDA AMERICA
Lydia Maria Child and radical miscegenation

I am well aware that many will accuse me of indecorum for presenting these pages to the public. . . . This peculiar phase of Slavery has generally been kept veiled; but the public ought to be made acquainted with its monstrous features, and I willingly take the responsibility of presenting them with the veil withdrawn. I do this for the sake of my sisters in bondage.

Lydia Maria Child, editor's Introduction to
Harriet Jacobs' *Incidents in the Life of a Slave Girl*

What is an American? Who can claim Americanness? Until the social protests and civil rights legislation of the 1950s and 1960s, "American" meant European-American, *northern* European-American – Greeks, Italians, Hispanics and certainly Latin Americans, Asians, Jews, Arabs and blacks were "ethnic." Even today the Ku Klux Klan and organizations like Aryan Nation base their white supremacist platforms on the argument that "Americans" are threatened by "brown" people who breed like rabbits, who do not speak English, and who "smell." Ex-Klan Wizard and perennial candidate David Duke's standard campaign stump speech asserts the superiority of "white" culture in the United States; and in September 1993, Patrick Buchanan, another perennial candidate, declared to a meeting of the Christian Coalition in Washington that "European Christian" civilization is superior to all others. The "Culture War" was declared in the Reagan–Thatcher eighties with academics like Allan Bloom, William Bennett and Dinesh D'Souza writing that the west was about to be overwhelmed by multiculturalism – a kind of educational miscegenation.

Despite the Right's nostalgia for past days of cultural cohesion, quarrels over social, literary and cultural "race-mixing" date from the early days of the nation. Lydia Maria Child was fighting these battles over national definition and national privilege in the nineteenth century. Her *An Appeal in Favor of that Class of Americans Called Africans* (1833) calls for immediate emancipation for all slaves, and integration of those of African descent into mainstream American society. She demands of her "fellow Americans" that "In order to decide what is our duty concerning the Africans and their descendants, we must first clearly make up our own minds whether they are, or are not, human beings" (Child, *Appeal* 148). Child, of course, had already decided – the title of her book renames these "Africans" Americans.

Child's writings, whether fiction, history or polemic, insist on the inclusion of blacks in American society. She wants emancipation, then she wants integration. She sees one way to accomplish this, through miscegenation and the creation of a people with both "white" and slave ancestry. After abolition, mulattoes, emblems of white slaveholders' sexual exploitation of female slaves, will help redraw the racial map of a truly free nation.

Race-mixing, or "amalgamation," as antebellum Americans liked to call it, created intense anxiety for abolitionists and their pro-slavery opponents. Both sides claimed concern with purity of the body, with integrity of race. The black body – both male and female – and the white female body were the objects of conflict: the disposition of these bodies determined the shape of America, and the colour of its republic.

Each side charged the other with gross sexual misconduct. Abolitionists declared "the Southern States are one great Sodom" where "that wretched, and shameful, and polluted intercourse between the whites and the blacks" happened with distressing regularity (the *Liberator*, 10 May 1834, comments on address by James A. Thome; Elijah Lovejoy in the *Emancipator*, 14 September 1833). Pro-slavery writers characterized Northern society as sexual bedlam, full of divorce and prostitution, not to mention abolitionists who promoted illicit relationships between black men and white women. They feared that if slavery was abolished "the reign of animal passion and power" would take over, making America a moral wilderness (Hentz, *Northern Bride* 213).

Some abolitionists used miscegenation in the slave South as evidence that slavery was wicked and that the sinful practice would cease once the slaves were emancipated: the progressive Garrisonian minority went further, seeing miscegenation as a possible solution for America's racial polarization. William Lloyd Garrison asserted that "inter-marriage is neither unnatural nor repugnant to nature, but obviously proper and salutary; it being designed to unite people of different tribes and nations" (the *Liberator*, 7 May 1831). His associate, Lydia Maria Child, concurred: "As for the possibility of social intercourse between the different colored races, *I* have not the slightest objection to it, provided they were equally virtuous and equally intelligent." She goes on to argue for the repeal of the Massachusetts anti-miscegenation law saying: "the government ought not to be invested with the power to control the affections, any more than the consciences of citizens. A man has at least as good a right to choose his wife, as he has to choose his religion" (Child, *Appeal* 132, 196). Intermarriage becomes both a metaphor and a prescription for the vigour of a mixed America: Child facilitates the breaking down of what she sees as the false (and damaging) binary of white over black through the creation of a generation of Americans who will incorporate both the black and white bodies.

Child's career can be called a conversation between missions. As a Garrisonian she moved in the most revolutionary circles of the abolition movement, and she was also famous as a writer of house-keeping manuals and children's books and editor of *The Juvenile Miscellany*, a children's magazine. Her position as a sort of guru of domesticity and housewifery merged with her commitment to ending slavery. Her handbooks, like her sentimental fiction, "show that literary reformers and abolitionists consciously used matriarchal plottings and emblems to exercise moral suasion" (Mills 266). In her *Correspondence Between Lydia Maria Child and Governor Wise and Mrs Mason of Virginia* (1860), Child debates with Margaretta Mason, wife of a senator from Virginia, over the merits of nursing the imprisoned John Brown and whether pro-slavery or abolitionist women perform better "womanly duties" (Karcher, "Lydia Maria Child and John Brown" 30–33). She had begun a promising fiction career at the age of 22 with her novel *Hobomok* (1824), but her attention in the 1830s to the anti-slavery cause irritated the public who wanted stories and not rabble-rousing tracts. Indeed, Jean Fagan Yellin suggests Child's *Appeal in Favor of that Class of Americans Called Africans* wrecked her chances of becoming a popular novelist; Child had both the research on slavery and the political credentials Harriet Beecher Stowe lacked.[1] Like Stowe, Child employed the domesticity which formed women's culture in the nineteenth century, using the models of home and family to subvert slavery. Unlike Stowe, however, Child took far greater risks in her writing, foregrounding the Tragic Mulatta and, instead of killing or converting her every time, put her forward as the mother of the new nation.[2] In *A Romance of the Republic* (1867), simultaneously her most revolutionary work in that it promotes miscegenation, and her most conventional in that becoming the Angel in the House is prescribed for women, Child's mulattas do not die but live to people the United States with children whose heritage is both European and African. Child reimagines the nation as an *olla podrida*, a Spanish stew, a spicy combination of incongruous ingredients.[3] Child fearlessly disrupted the fictional and non-fictional genres in which she published: as she rewrites the script for the Tragic Mulatta, she also rewrites the Bible in *The Freedmen's Book* (1865) and church doctrine in *The Anti-Slavery Catechism* (1836), and she rewrites patriarchal history in her *A Brief History of the Condition of Women in Various Ages and Nations* (1835).

The Phoenix America Child sees rising from the ashes of the Civil War looks like a multicultural (for want of a better term), bourgeois, liberal state dedicated to uplifting ex-slaves and re-educating prejudiced whites. The important movement is *mixing*: in *A Romance of the Republic*, the two ex-slave heroines marry two European American men and produce families who cherish their various ancestries. Rosa and Flora are part African, Spanish, French and Anglo; Franz Blumenthal (Flora's husband) is German; Alfred King (Rosa's husband) is Anglo-Saxon, his name conjuring up visions of English nobility and a romantic evocation of the Common Law.[4] The novel teems with German, French, Spanish and Italian: "'Do hear them calling Alfred *Mein lieber bruder*,' said Flora to her husband, 'while Rosa and I are sprinkling them all with pet names in French and Spanish. What a polyglot family we are! as *cher Papa* used to say'" (Child, *Romance* 431–32). When the state, in the form of planter Gerald Fitzgerald and their father's creditors, imposes its will on the bodies of the two sisters, language becomes circumscribed. Flora complains "'We don't hear Mamita's Spanish and papa's English any more. We have nobody to talk *olla podrida* to now. It's all French with Madame and all Italian with the Signor'" (ibid. 64).

Child's work frames Stowe's: *Uncle Tom's Cabin* and *Dred* were informed by the anti-slavery fiction and non-fiction which must have been part of the Beecher family's intellectual diet during the 1830s, and *A Romance of the Republic* grew, in some ways, out of *Uncle Tom's Cabin*. But Child's work makes still more complex

Stowe's attempts to show that the body – colour, gender – is a shifting sign of identity and status. For Stowe, miscegenation took place in the past (for Mme de Thoux, Susan, George and Eliza's parents, or Cassy) or else is a present threat (for Eliza or Emmeline). In *Uncle Tom* liberation and Liberia will reinscribe racial boundaries. For Child, miscegenation is a political strategy to create an America where race is complicated, multiplied and therefore defused in volatile assimilations rather than confined in separations. Mixed-race people carry with them a host of invisible markers: "If the body is an inescapable sign of identity, it is also an insecure and often illegible sign" (Sanchez-Eppler 29). In the classic Tragic Mulatta narrative, the heroine "reads" her body as "white" until her society unveils her as "black." Then she is read not just differently but *as opposite*. In Child's fictions, the mixed-race character achieves (usually tragic) dignity when she gains control over how she is read. In other words, Child's mulattas *can* "pass" but do not. They accept the consequences of their "polyglot" heritage and, in *A Romance of the Republic,* triumph over a racist society. However, revolutionary as the idea of programmatic race-mixing might seem, Child draws back from its full implications; her colour-matching is in line with Stowe's, unable to face in fiction the visible sign of "original" miscegenation – the very dark African paired with the very light European – and there is no pairing of a black man with a white woman. Child concerns herself with the second, third and fourth generations of this mixing. In giving her slaves fair skin, she dilutes the shock to the sensibility of her times – she waters the strong flavours of her American stew.

I do not mean to lessen Child's achievement. While her work generally belongs, as Carolyn Karcher has pointed out, to the genteel tradition of nineteenth-century American women's fiction, it also attempts to sabotage prevailing attitudes towards race and sexuality.[5] Child moves to reclaim the black body from its primary erotic association and, in a sense, to redefine chastity more significantly even than Stowe, who left nothing but born-again virginity and repentance for her "fallen" mulattas. Though incompletely, Child re-envisions America's sense of its racial self, creating spaces for middle-class blacks, women who have been victims of slavery and "promiscuous" blood – a mixed race that combines the best features of a potpourri of cultures and ethnic backgrounds. Child boldly advocates an amalgamated nation which, despite her endorsement of conventional gender roles and her insistence on the primacy of the patriarchal family, is none the less more defiant than most of her colleagues in the feminist abolitionist movement.[6] But then, Child believed in continuing revolution. As she wrote to her brother Convers Francis in 1835: "A principle of despotism was admitted in the very foundation of our government. . . . I believe the world will be brought into a state of order through manifold revolutions" (Child, *Letters* 38–39). Child hoped that her writing, her recasting of race in America, would contribute to the process of correcting and refining the republic.

DESIRE IN THE NEW WORLD

Child's first effort to stretch the limits of racial and sexual decorum comes at the very beginning of her career in *Hobomok* (1824), a novel written when she was twenty-two.[7] Mary Conant, the aristocratic heroine living in frontier New England, not only rejects her father's rigid Puritanism to love an Anglican Royalist but eventually runs away with an Indian, marries him and has a son by him. In the end, her original lover (thought dead) reappears, and the noble Hobomok divorces Mary so she can marry him. High church rebellion, mixed marriage, divorce, a half-caste child – it is no wonder the *North American Review* called the novel "in very bad taste," and said it offended "every feeling of delicacy in man or woman" (19 July 1824). None the less, Child became a literary celebrity in Boston. The august Athenaeum, a gentleman's club-library, extended her a membership (revoked when she published *An Appeal in Favor of that Class of Americans Called Africans* in 1833) and *Hobomok* sold well.

Racial distinctions are crucially blurred in *Hobomok*. Mary has a "secret desire to enjoy both" Hobomok and Charles, as Karcher points out, a desire which is fulfilled. Karcher goes on to show that in Child's fantasy of integration, the Indian Hobomok is made more like the English Charles and Charles more like Hobomok. In the beginning, Hobomok is associated with the wilderness, and thus with "savagery," while Charles is associated with the white settlement and the ultrasophistication of court circles in England's "'antique grandeur and cultivated beauty'" (Child, *Hobomok* 73). But by the last few chapters, Hobomok, as Mary's friend Sally Oldham says, "'seems almost like an Englishman'" while Charles has learned so much woodcraft that he can surprise the great hunter Hobomok in the forest (ibid. 137–38).

Believed drowned, Charles has been shipwrecked and held

prisoner on the coast of Africa: once merely a representative of the
elegant and sensual in contrast to the deprivations of the Puritan
world, he now incorporates an element of the Other, of the dark,
into his whiteness. He can negotiate the wilderness like a native;
he has been in Africa with blacks (some of whom would soon be
sent to the West Indies, Virginia, Maryland and Carolina colonies
as slaves), experiencing "the lot of the peoples the English have
been colonizing" (ibid. xxxi). Meanwhile, Hobomok has become a
sort of exemplary Christian, making the ultimate sacrifice in giving
up his wife and child: "'Ask Mary to pray for me – that when I die,
I may go to the Englishman's God, where I may hunt beaver with
little Hobomok, and count my beavers for Mary'" (ibid. 140).

By marrying Mary and "adopting" Charles Hobomok Conant,
Charles Brown becomes an "integrated" person, a model American
who will understand the experience of the European, the Indian,
even (Child projects) the African. Mary Conant's body facilitates
the movement toward integration in the narrative. Karcher links
this to another manifestation of female authority, Mary's "witchcraft," pointing out that to the Puritan patriarchs, "both Episcopa-
lians and Indians are minions of the Devil, the 'Black Man'" (ibid.
xxviii). Mary bridges these alternative spiritual possibilities and
mounts a specifically female challenge to the colony's religious
orthodoxy. The ritual she performs in the woods mediates between
Christian and pagan magical worlds, as it mediates between New
England and old England. *Hobomok* is an erotic fantasy about
miscegenation and a hopeful fiction where assimilation of different
races is an alternative to "genocide, race war and white male
supremacy as modes of resolving the contradictions" racking
American society (ibid. xvii). One of the alternatives the novel
posits is female authority rather than male authority as a way to
order society: the rule of the father subverted by female desire.

Women transgress in all sorts of ways in Child's Puritan New
England, bringing on themselves the censure of men. Yet they tend
to get their way. Dame Willets is criticized for wearing a "red
cardinal" cloak:

"I marvel that you should think it decent to call a Christian
garment by a name that appertains to the scarlet woman of
Babylon," said Mr. Oldham.

"It's no name of my making, Goodman; nor did I know that
evil was signified thereby," answered the widow.

(ibid. 45)

Men are constantly suspicious of women on sexual grounds ("scarlet woman of Babylon") while women take their lives into their own hands. Sally Oldham rejects a pious and exceedingly correct suitor to propose herself to his friend (ibid. 26–27). With the help of Dame Willets, Mary Conant defies her severe Puritan father's orders not to see Charles Brown the Anglican. Though Mary's mother, Lady Mary says, "'It is the duty of woman to love and obey her husband,'" she also allows an unofficial engagement between her daughter and the forbidden suitor and as good as welcomes him into her family (ibid. 74). Lady Mary disobeyed *her* father, the Earl of Rivers, to marry Roger Conant and move to the New World. In church, Mary Conant gazes at Charles Brown's "manly elegance" instead of attending to the interminable sermon. Finally, and most significantly, Mary disposes of her own body, instead of allowing her father to do so, first to Hobomok, then to Charles; she defies Roger Conant by living with a non-white man, then with an Anglican. In the end, her father is forced to acquiesce in all her choices. It seems that, for Child, rebellion amongst the women of New England is to be celebrated as quintessentially *American*, a foreshadowing of the revolution (Child would hope for *revolutions*) to come.

It is surely no accident that Child sets *Hobomok* in Naumkeak – a village later called Salem. The disobedient women in *Hobomok* prefigure Salem's most famous disobedient women, the "witches" who, a generation after, would make the village notorious.[8] Playfully underscoring the connection, Child shows Mary Conant working her own witchcraft (ibid. 12–14). On a moonlit night in the woods, Mary draws a "magic ring" on the ground, similar to the fairy circles in Britain and Ireland, she writes something in her own blood on a piece of cloth, and speaks a "spell" to see her future husband: "'Whoe'er my bridegroom is to be,/Step in the circle after me'" (ibid. 13). The belief that rituals performed on certain nights (like St Agnes' Eve and Midsummer Eve) would grant women a vision of husbands-to-be is very old in British folklore. Like the much-disparaged maypole at Merrymount (around which the English had danced with Indians in a miscegenous moment), Mary's subversive ritual signifies the pagan baggage the Puritans tried to eradicate from their "virgin land." Mary's "spell" places her, and the other women of Naumkeak, in a continuum with the transgressing women of Salem and later transgressing women in America, including Child herself. The Salem witches challenged

Puritan definitions of women's proper sphere, the definition of chastity and the lineaments of religion: Child makes a similar critique of male-defined roles for women in her novel.

The most rebellious act Mary Conant performs is to remove herself from the patriarchal Puritan economy in giving herself to two interdict men. It is true that in their meeting in the woods, Hobomok and Charles decide, without asking her, which should get her and the child. But she has already chosen to be involved first with one, then the other. And she is not punished for her scandalous intercourse with a dark man (conflated, in the minds of her father and his coreligionists with the "Black Man" or devil). "Indian romances" published a little after *Hobomok* (possibly in response to it) such as Catharine Maria Sedgwick's *Hope Leslie* (1827) and James Fenimore Cooper's *Last of the Mohicans* (1826) and *The Wept of Wish-ton-Wish* (1829) focus on the impossibility of miscegenation in expansionist America by showing mixed marriages as childless, sinful or simply impossible. In *Yamoyden*, Child's source, Nora, the heroine who has married Yamoyden, dies, though their mixed-race child is allowed to live.[9] Mary Conant is barely made to feel "degraded:" though she falls at Charles' feet, begging forgiveness for her "sin," and though her father expresses the wish that she had died rather than "'lie in the bosom of a savage,'" everyone seems to get over the shock remarkably swiftly. Mary's first marriage effectively disappears since the chief reminder of her transgression, Hobomok himself, disappears. Child does not entirely overturn conventional literary resolutions of miscegenation, but she does, at least, suggest mitigating alternatives to erasing all those who commit it.

Mary Conant, Charles Brown and Charles Hobomok Conant Brown, the child, remain in New England, becoming an exemplary "American" family. Child expresses ambivalence over the obviously Indian, "black-eyed," "swarthy" Little Hobomok: he is educated at Harvard and in England and "by degrees his Indian appellation was silently omitted" (ibid. 150). He is assimilated into white America. But, Child insists, Hobomok himself is not forgotten. And the promise of tolerance is contained in the way the dark Little Hobomok plays happily with the fair little girl Mary Collier. The nation itself is credited to the nobility of Hobomok: "the tender slip which he protected, has since become a mighty tree, and the nations of the earth seek refuge beneath its branches" (ibid. 150). Mary becomes a mother of the nation, a symbol of mixed American culture, having experienced both its native and European aspects, even though the Indian must fade away for the new nation to prosper.

SLIPPING THE VEIL: REDEFINING CHASTITY

The central problem of men's abolitionist writing is rebellion; the central problem of women's abolitionist writing is desire. Like most other women, black and white, involved in the abolitionist movement, Child defines slavery as a crime against the family and an assault on women's freedom to dispose of their bodies as they wish: "The negro woman is unprotected either by law or public opinion. She is the property of her master and her daughters are his property" (Child, *Appeal* 23).

Like Stowe, Martineau, the Grimkés, Frances Kemble and Frances Trollope, Child sets out to disrupt the misleading divisions of women into white and black, lady and prostitute, free and slave. But unlike some of her more conservative comrades, Child does not insist that women who lived outside of sanctioned, legal "Christian" marriage should be somehow cleansed to be accepted, as Stowe does with Cassy. Nor does she naively assert that chastity (strictly interpreted) should be the standard to which slave women are held. Child works to wrest control of the definition of a "good" woman from the old order and rethink it for a slave society: she makes chastity available to black women which they, by the very tint of their skins and the web of sexual associations which accompany that tint, had long been denied.

Child pushes sexuality to the foreground in her early "Tragic Mulatta" fiction, the stories "The Quadroons" (1842) and "Slavery's Pleasant Homes" (1843).[10] Here she focuses on slave women who do not have the edifice of white ladyhood to protect their bodies or give them at least a chance of self-determination. Mary Conant can decide to give herself to Hobomok: Rosalie in "The Quadroons" belongs to the white Southerner Edward. Though she loves him (and he claims to love her) the emotional circumstances prove inconsequential – what governs the relationship between them is her legal status as slave, his legal status as owner. Rosalie is forced to confront this when she discovers that Edward has married a white woman, a pale, blonde creature from a politically powerful family. Edward, of course, expects to have his cake and eat it, too, as owner of two women, his *placée* and his wife. He creates for himself a harem.

We have seen how the harem as slavery's attack on companionate marriage became an issue for Stowe, Kemble, Trollope and Martineau; it was, as well, covertly and bitterly evoked by slaveholding women such as Mary Chesnut and the plantation lady who told Martineau that the mistress was "the chief slave of the harem." For Child, the harem represents women's absolute powerlessness in a slave society – black *and* white women. Rosalie the slave dies of a broken heart; Charlotte the wife has her faith in her husband shattered. Xarifa, Rosalie and Edward's daughter (her Moorish name also evokes the harem), is sold, raped, goes insane and kills herself. All of this results from women's inability under slavery to protect their bodies.

Southern society allows the harem but Child argues that white women (the majority of her audience) can intervene: she insists that the white woman and the black woman make common cause instead of allowing themselves to be divided by the oppositions that delineate slave culture. Rosalie and Charlotte both suffer from Edward's betrayal and his sexual and economic exploitation of them. In "Slavery's Pleasant Homes" (obviously a sarcastic title), the doubling, rather than the opposition, of white and black women appears in the white bride Marion and her "foster-sister" the slave Rosa. When Marion marries Frederic Dalcho, Rosa (like Marion) becomes *his* property; and he wastes little time in attempting to assault her.

As in "The Quadroons," where the wife is conventionally described as very pale while the quadroon mistress is dark (though certainly not black), Marion is likened to a "white petunia" while Rosa (whose name is a variant of Rosalie) is a "dark velvet carnation." Though this light/dark binary would seem to signify the conventional division of women into virginal and sexual (like Alice and Cora Munro in *The Last of the Mohicans* or Hilda and Miriam in *The Marble Faun*), Child actually undercuts it by making clear, as she does in "The Quadroons," just what the women have in common. She implicates both in the harem; Marion "the bride had been nurtured in seclusion, almost as deep as that of the oriental harem," and both come from New Orleans, linking them to the *plaçage* system, as Karcher notes (Child, *Slavery's Pleasant Homes* 148; Karcher, "Rape, Murder and Revenge" 327). Rosa is not the only powerless, voiceless sexual object: Marion becomes aware that her husband habitually makes advances towards Rosa – "Poor young wife, what a bitter hour was that!" – yet she is also, eventually, able to sympathize with her. When Rosa cries, "'Oh mistress, I am not to blame. Indeed, indeed, I am very wretched,'" Marion and Rosa weep in each other's arms, though neither "sought any further to learn the other's secrets" (Child, *Slavery's Pleasant Homes* 153). Marion, especially, does not want to know details of Rosa's sexual life: Rosa is pregnant either by Frederic or perhaps by her lover George, Frederic's slave and also his brother.

Carolyn Karcher points out that, in the beating of Rosa, causing a miscarriage, Child "succeeds in evoking a scene whose every element is unmentionable in polite society: a husband's rape of his wife's foster-sister; a gentleman's sadistic flogging of a 'tenderly-nurtured' woman; a pregnancy resulting from illicit sex; a miscarriage induced by violence" (Karcher, "Rape, Murder and Revenge" 329). Not only does Child foist these unspeakable elements on her middle-class audience, she forces them to confront the clichés surrounding women. Identifying Marion with Rosa emphasizes Child's point that the white slave mistress is at once debilitated by the harem and obligated to combat slavery and its moral pollution.

"Are not women the greatest sufferers from slavery?" asks Child's friend and colleague Eliza Lee Follen in an essay in the *Liberty Bell* (Follen 7).[11] Black women suffer from being their masters' sexual property; white women suffer from their husbands' sexual betrayal. "The moral corruption, which grows out of this degradation of women, spreads far and wide, and all around breathe a tainted atmosphere; and the pale, sensitive, fine lady of the South, knows this too well" (ibid. 8). The plantation lady is not blameless; the slave is not what *she* has been assumed to be either, that is, a "naturally" seductive woman, an almost-unconscious temptress. Child challenges reduction of the black woman, which was practised even by those opposed to slavery. Frederick Law Olmsted sees in black women "a good deal of that voluptuousness of expression which characterizes many of the women of the South of Europe" (Olmsted 47). Mary Chesnut, commenting on Charles Kingsley's mulatta romance *Two Years Ago* (1857) sniffs: "There will never be an interesting book with a negro heroine down here" (Woodward 243).[12] Child tries simultaneously to combat the erotic "romance" of black women in fiction *and* to name slavery as a vicious system of sexual exploitation and moral degradation. In *The Right Way, the Safe Way* (1860), on emancipation in the West Indies, she says that before slaves were freed "too often a gentleman's house was a kind of brothel" (Child, *The Right Way* 41). She goes very much against the grain in her insistence on the black woman's chastity; her heroines are, contrary to sentimental convention, not virgins: Mary Conant has had a child by an Indian, Rosalie is not married to Xarifa's father, and Rosa is pregnant when she dies. This requires a reordering of the very idea of female chastity, an idea which Child's nineteenth-century middle-class, genteel readers held most dear.

One of the most important attempts to redefine chastity for the slave woman was not written by Child but edited by her. The refugee slave Harriet Jacobs' *Incidents in the Life of a Slave Girl, Written By Herself* (1861) presents in autobiographical form the harem South with all its potential for "degrading" both the white and black woman.[13] "Linda Brent's" story documents the continuous sexual harassment, threatened rape, humiliation and psychological terrorism that white slave masters could subject their black women slaves to. Jacobs argues for a new dispensation for black women, a more flexible definition of what a good woman might be, and Child endorses her call: "I am well aware that many will accuse me of indecorum for presenting these pages to the public. . . .This peculiar phase of slavery has generally been kept veiled; but the public ought to be made acquainted with its monstrous features." (Jacobs 8).

Here slavery is a sort of monster with a terrifying face (and body). Child's endorsement of Jacobs' narrative withdraws the veil of decorum that has kept "decent" Americans from hearing of the sexual atrocities of slavery, revealing it in its naked horror. Child's imagery is both gothic and erotic: she will reveal a "secret," a hidden curse at the heart of America. She will also unveil a *body*, inverting the conventional discourse of modesty which decrees that all bodies, especially female ones, be kept covered and mysterious. This inversion makes Child's point: as a crusader for the integrity of women's bodies, as a champion of chastity, she must show the "naked" truth – Harriet Jacobs must tell the true story of slave women's sexual torment by white men.

In a famous passage in W. E. B. Du Bois' *The Souls of Black Folk*, he says, "The Negro is a sort of seventh son, born with a veil and gifted with second sight in this American world" (Du Bois, *Souls* 3). Du Bois' veil refers to the sense of uncanny doubleness felt by people who must resolve their Africanness and Americanness. But the veil also speaks to a sort of *mask* of blackness, a secret self, a self hidden both voluntarily and involuntarily. The veil becomes a metaphor for the interdict nature of blackness, the essential disguise of race. Women are doubly veiled, their bodies circumscribed, their sexuality interdict; yet the veil also promises an *unveiling*, a revelation. Child forces the audience to confront the unmentionable subject of Jacobs' book: the Southern harem. She goes on to say, in the Introduction, "I do this for the sake of my sisters in bondage, who are suffering wrongs so foul, that our ears are too delicate to listen to them" (Jacobs 8). The middle-class, genteel female reader's ears may be "too delicate," yet Child knows that Jacobs goes on to detail those "foul wrongs" which slave women suffer. Yellin declares *Incidents* is "to my knowledge, the only slave narrative that identifies its audience as female" and "the only slave narrative written in the style of sentimental fiction" (Yellin, "Texts and Contexts" 263). The white woman is forced to contemplate *being* Linda Brent, being a candidate for sexual abuse, trapped in the plantation harem. However, Karen Sanchez-Eppler argues that such tactics might actually impede the purpose of gaining white sympathy for slave women:

> in the writings of antislavery women the frequent emphasis on the specifically feminine trial of sexual abuse serves to project the white woman's sexual anxieties onto the sexualized body of the female slave. Concern over the slave woman's sexual victimization displaces the free woman's fear of confronting the sexual elements of her own bodily experience, either as a positive force or as a mechanism of oppression.
>
> (Sanchez-Eppler 33)

Jacobs' narrative and Child's own writings mediate between the states of sexual black body and asexual white body. It seems to me that rather than distancing white women from the legal rape in slavery, the victimization of a woman, even a black woman, forces the white woman to come to terms with the subject: such is the ideological work of sentimental fiction. Women were aware of how precarious their economic status could be: an unmarried woman, a working-class woman, a suddenly-impoverished woman could all "fall" in a moral as well as material sense. American cities and towns were full of prostitutes who sold their bodies through lack of other work. Certainly reading of slavery's abuses of women by a New England fireside was "safer" than being a black woman in Alabama, but Child and Jacobs work very hard to make their audience, trained in identification with a sentimental heroine, crying *with* as well as *over* Charlotte Temple or Clarissa, understand the position of the female slave.

In Jacobs' narrative, Child saw a vehicle to challenge chastity as defined in the sentimental or "True Womanly" conventions of Victorian America. Jacobs both claims the position of sentimental heroine and critiques it. As Yellin says, Jacobs does not "mouth the standard that a woman's self-esteem is a simple function of her adherence to conventional sexual mores. Although she discusses her efforts to preserve her virginity in connection with the struggle to maintain her self esteem, she presents these as related, not identical, goals" (Yellin, "Texts and Contexts" 273). Linda Brent demands a place in the category of True Woman. She says:

> Pity me, and pardon me, O virtuous reader! You never knew what it is to be a slave; to be entirely unprotected by law or custom. . . . I knew I did wrong. No one can feel it more sensibly than I do. The painful and humiliating memory will haunt me to my dying day. Still, in looking back, calmly, on the events of my life I feel that the slave woman ought not to be judged by the same standards as others.
>
> (Jacobs 86)

Editing *Incidents* was part of Child's testing of the boundaries of gender decorum and redefining chastity, opening up previously rigid definitions of purity and goodness to women who are "entirely unprotected by law or custom." Jacobs' autobiography quotes and inverts the convention, just as Child's fiction does. In her last novel, *A Romance of the Republic*, she incorporates many of the elements from *Hobomok*, from her "Tragic Mulatta" stories, and from Jacobs' narrative, to reclaim a woman who would, in conventional fiction, be considered "lost."

AMERICA'S MANY-COLOURED GARDEN

Rosabella Royal in *A Romance of the Republic* is a rewriting of Rosalie in "The Quadroons," and Rosa in "Slavery's Pleasant Homes," a "flower" of ladyhood: genteel, accomplished, refined, retiring and one-eighth black: legally a slave. When her white father dies, having neglected to manumit her, she is bought by Gerald Fitzgerald, a young Georgian she loves, and set up in a hidden cottage on his plantation. He, too, refuses to free her.

141

Child, writing during Reconstruction when the fleshpots of the South had theoretically been destroyed, demonstrates the wreck of the Southern plantation garden and plots the coming of the New Jerusalem – an American republic where women are no longer property and race is no longer the chief signifier of status, a nation where the bodies of its legal chattel, wives and slaves, are finally free. *A Romance of the Republic* realigns nineteenth-century middle-class views of chastity, imagining an inclusive America according black women the place Harriet Jacobs demands for them. Nevertheless, Child does not look past middle-class Victorian gender roles. She prescribes ladyhood for her ex-slave heroines, privileging their white genteel heritage rather than their African heritage; neither Rosa nor Flora draws strength from the ways black women were "excused" from ladyhood, as demonstrated by Sojourner Truth's famous speech demanding "Arn't I a woman?," while pointing out that slave women were never held to be fragile or delicate like white ladies.[14]

Rosa and Flora oscillate between the positions of lady and slave. Their owner, Gerald Fitzgerald, fancies himself master of a harem including Rosa, her younger sister Flora and a white heiress called Lily. Fitzgerald compares himself to the "Grand Bashaw" in his exclusive sexual access to his wife, his *placée*, and her sister. The slave South is, more fully than before in Child's fiction, an orientalized site of sensual suggestion. The New Orleans home of the Royal sisters is as garden-like as their names, with flowers on the walls, on the carpet, on the china and on the clothes of Rosa and Flora, implying a lush, excessive, fertility. Even their maid is called "Tulipa." They are surrounded by fountains, perfume and peacocks, and confined to their father's house for fear that their true status as slaves will be revealed. Child evokes the harem at every turn: Rosa and Flora read *Lalla Rookh* (Flora imagines herself "the Persian princess"), and Alfred King, the upstanding New Englander, cautions Mr Royal with his father's story of seeing Turkish women "wrapped up like bales of cloth, with two small openings for their eyes, mounted on camels and escorted by the overseer of the harem," chattering and giggling with an "animal sound" (Child, *Romance* 24). Words like "overseer" and even the image of bales of cloth (the South's slave fortunes largely rested on cotton) connects the oriental world with the South. Mr Royal's "protection" of his daughters is perverse: they enact a virginal version of the harem in his home, dancing, singing, dressing for his, and his male guests', pleasure. Rosa and Flora were commodities in the womb, slave daughters of a slave; their mother was a debt-relieving asset for their grandfather (Nelson 80). Life in Mr Royal's house is simply a prettily-disguised version of the lives of those baled, restricted Turkish women. Their father is as much an aspiring "Grand Bashaw" as Gerald Fitzgerald. Once the sisters reach Georgia, even though Rosa assumes she is legally married to Gerald, they must stay as hidden as they did in New Orleans, and go about heavily veiled. On the plantation, Gerald stops pretending that his relationship with Rosa is exclusive, despite the "marriage" ceremony they went through:

> Sometimes he would laugh, and say: "Am I not a lucky dog? I don't envy the Grand Bashaw his Circassian beauties. He'd give his biggest diamond for such a dancer as Floracita; and what is his Flower of the World compared to my Rosamunda?"
> (Child, *Romance* 84)

Gerald toys with an interesting inversion here, comparing himself favourably with the Grand Bashaw, an oriental (dark) man with white slaves (as the "Lustful Turk" had his English victims). Gerald is a white man with slaves who might *look* "Circassian" (Caucasian) but are legally *black*. Child at once forces her readers to imagine themselves in an oriental harem and to confront the reality of slave-state harems which national fantasies of postwar reunion and reconciliation were fast erasing from the white mind. Even when Flora escapes to the "free" North, her adopted mother insists that she go around veiled, lest agents of Gerald's find her. I wonder, too, if Child might have Hiram Powers' *Greek Slave* in mind: the narrative of the white Christian girl sold to "sensual" Turks to be raped and brutalized underscores the national fascination with the slavery of women – and, in particular, the Tragic Mulatta. The naked *Greek Slave* is, as various commentators insisted, clothed in her purity (Kasson 181). Her chastity itself (about to be violated) is a veil. Rosa and Flora are also veiled in chastity (which can be rent) but their veils, literal and figurative, both hide and signify their mixed race. They are both white and black, in danger of defilement and exemplars of True Womanhood struggling in a slave society.

It is hard to miss Child's point: the conventions of the South, the laws of the country which allow slavery, and the popular acquiescence in the system, "veil" the harsh truths of slavery. But as she intended promoting Jacobs' narrative, Child means to withdraw the veil from the mystified body of the slave woman, no matter what "indelicacies" might be revealed. In constantly using images of the harem, Child colludes in eroticizing the slave's body. Yet the burden of her novel is to negotiate a way out of the confinement of expectations that force the black woman to be signified only in her dark, suggestive flesh. Like Harriet Jacobs/Linda Brent, Rosa and Flora wish to claim True Womanhood and purity, asserting the right to dispose of their own bodies.

Rosa Royal is a highly-romanticized version of Linda Brent, a slave who must make difficult sexual choices in order to maintain some sense of her own integrity, both physical and spiritual. She is not allowed to choose virginity: she is an octoroon and her society has decreed that she be a sexual commodity. After her father's death, facing the sale of herself and her sister for his debts, she chooses to go with Gerald Fitzgerald, thinking their "marriage" will free her and Flora; her other choice is to be sold to the unsubtly-named Mr Bruteman. Gerald imagines Rosa on the auction block, vulnerable as the *Greek Slave*, gazed on by "men, whose upturned faces were like greedy satyrs . . . calling upon her to open her ruby lips and show her pearls" (Child, *Romance* 66). The implications of Rosa's "opening" herself to other men both distresses and excites Gerald; of course, he wants to be the one to "own" this "entirely new and perfectly sound [virgin] article" (ibid. 66). For his part, he is happy thinking that in saving her "from such degradation, he had acquired complete control of her destiny" (ibid. 67). If there is any degrading to be done, Gerald wants to do it himself.

For her part, Rosa thinks she is marrying the man she loves, despite the secrecy attached. The shadowy life Gerald offers is better than Bruteman's advances. As Linda Brent says, "It seems less degrading to give one's self than to submit to compulsion" (Jacobs 84–85). Rosa's "marriage" with Gerald, like countless "marriages" of *placées* to their patrons, has no legal status and acts more or less as a sop to the "fine feelings" and inhibitions of carefully-brought-up girls. White men find mulattas attractive because they combine the reticence and purity of white ladies with the availability and powerlessness of slaves. When Rosa discovers Gerald has a legal white wife, the shock of her true status almost kills her. She falls ill; the slave Chloe says "'De sperit hab done gone somewhar'" (Child, *Romance* 174). In Rosa's catatonic state even her eyes seem "strangely veiled" (ibid. 173). It is as if Rosa tries to destroy her body, the object of such strife and "pollution." Child's expansion of the boundaries of chastity begins to focus less on the body and more on the soul, though the "veil" remains a part of Rosabella's identity. Following Jacobs, Child insists that spiritual integrity is more important than bodily purity and "reputation;" she spends the rest of this long novel redeeming Rosa's life in her own sight, unveiling her as a virtuous woman, as a wronged wife and, eventually, as a *black woman*.

As in Jacobs' narrative, sexual morality for slave women in *A Romance of the Republic* is situational, not absolute: Linda Brent had to choose between two evils: being raped by Dr Flint or giving herself to Mr Sands. Rosa chooses to give herself to Gerald Fitzgerald. There is power in a woman's choosing: Mary Conant took herself out of the patriarchal economy by having two forbidden lovers; Rosa *thinks* she is removing herself from a literal traffic in women's bodies with a man she cares for. This is a limited power. Gerald *owns* Rosa and Flora: they are not his companionate equals in law. Rosa searches throughout the novel for emancipation and the unveiling of her real self, and for a sexual relationship in which she is respected as a partner, not chattel. In Alfred King, she finds a man (like Charles Brown in *Hobomok*) who can overcome the layers of erotic history that her race and status conjure up, though their marriage conforms to the patriarchal pattern and he struggles against his own prejudices about being in love with, as he puts it, an opera singer who "has twice been on the verge of being sold as a slave, and who has been the victim of a sham marriage!" (ibid. 245–46). She is black and she is the mother of an illegitimate mixed-race child: in conventional Tragic Mulatta fiction this heroine could redeem herself only in death. But in Child's novel and Jacobs' narrative, the heroine is not destroyed. She triumphs over her society's attempts to "veil" her. Rosa succeeds as an artist, a wife and a mother – she receives the reward of the *white* heroine. Jacobs/Linda, interestingly, does not, and calls attention to this: "Reader, my story ends with freedom; not in the usual way, with marriage . . . it is a vast improvement in *my* condition. The dream of my life is not yet realized. I do not sit with my children in a home of my own" (ibid. 302). Child, in recasting the black woman's journey through sexual exploitation to freedom, seems to lack the confidence or authority to show her, as Jacobs does, struggling alone to realize her dream. But Child, learning from Jacobs, and building on her own career's work, does assert a new dispensation for slave women that gives them a place in the American pantheon of good women, a renewed chastity for a reborn nation.

In the aftermath of the Civil War, Child imagines an America in the process of solving its racial problems, not by the race war threatened by pro-slavery Southerners or by colonization or by the perpetual legal and social subjugation of blacks but by miscegenation. In *An Appeal in Favor of that Class of Americans Called African*, Child had soothingly reasoned to whites: "With regard to marrying your daughters, I believe the feeling in opposition to such unions is quite as strong among the colored class, as it is among white people" (Child, *Appeal* 132). She went on to argue "While the prejudice exists, such instances [of miscegenation] must be exceedingly rare, because the consequence is degradation in society . . . Shall we keep this class of people in everlasting degradation for fear one of their descendants *may* marry our great-great-great-great-grandchild?" (ibid. 133). *An Appeal* was published at the beginning of the abolitionists' struggle against slavery. Child argued for immediate emancipation, but she seemed to feel that the most vexed issue of black and white sexuality could be deferred to a distant future. Perhaps her subsequent work convinced her that the fire next time was here: the Civil War had created a future where blacks and white *ought* to be on terms of "social equality" if the nation was to survive. *A Romance of the Republic* initially gives us the history of Rosa and Flora Royal as typical Tragic Mulattas, similar to Child's own stories of the 1830s and 1840s. Yet neither octoroon is called on to enter prostitution, languish with a broken heart, commit suicide or go insane. On the contrary, they go through great hardships (as sentimental heroines must) to find good husbands (and a career in Rosa's case) and eventually have beautiful children, beautiful homes, money and political righteousness on their side. Instead of allowing the Tragic Mulatta to remain a victim, patronized and isolated in her beauty, her whiteness and her suffering, Child's heroines assimilate into the American middle class and make common cause with other ex-slaves. It is as if Child dismantles the very genre she is often credited with inventing.

Rosa and Flora seed a new American garden – the characters are all, in a sense, cross-pollinated. Everyone is a flower: Rosa, Flora, Florimond (Flora's name for her husband), Lila, Lily, Rosen Blumen, Tulipa, Madame Guirlonde. The spaces they inhabit are floral: as I pointed out before, the Royals' parlour in New Orleans has flowers on the curtains, on the vases, on the walls, on the ceiling, on the furniture. It is essentially a garden. Flora makes Lila Delano's plain house like a floral bower as well. Child's national garden is promiscuous, permitting all varieties of growth. The walled, oriental Southern garden inhabited by the slaves Rosa and Flora is transformed to an open space of democratic vigour.

Child also expresses her amalgamated America through the complex (and rather incestuous) relationships between the Fitzgeralds, the Blumenthals, the Kings, the Delanos and the Bells. In a plot that anticipates Twain's *Puddn'head Wilson* by twenty-seven years, Rosa switches her newborn son with Gerald Fitzgerald's and Lily's in revenge (and pity).[15] Unlike Twain, Child does not use this to explore the debate between nature and nurture, proving that if a white child is brought up as a slave, he will behave as a slave. Rather, she seems more concerned with the arbitrariness of race as a defining category. Both Gerald, Rosa's son by Gerald Fitzgerald, and George Falkner, Lily's son by Gerald Fitzgerald, are equally noble, brave, intelligent and kindly. Child may have another point as well: until he knows the truth of his parentage, Gerald wants to marry Rosa and Alfred's daughter Eulalia, his sister. The threat of incest warns against facile racial divisions as well as argues for the inclusion of blacks into the American family.[16] The novel pairs off characters divided by race yet joined by experience. Rosa and Lily mirror each other; George and Gerald are doubles. As Shirley Samuels points out, Gerald sees his "mirrored likeness" in the Virginia campaign: "I thought I had seen myself," and, in this "fraternal war," he has (Samuels,"The Identity of Slavery" 170–71, Child, *Romance* 404). The meeting is uncanny, portentous: racial doubles "offer a running theoretical commentary on each other" (Sundquist, *To Wake the Nations* 259). But here, though young Gerald has met his (officially) "dark" brother George, it is *he* who is legally the mulatto: George is legally white. Their twinship, like Rosa and Lily's both being "married" to their father, pushes at the limits of racial definition, forcing a crisis in the ways the Bells, Fitzgeralds, Kings, Royals and Blumenthals – and, by extension, America itself – understand family and race.

Darkening the complexion of the American family, in Child's vision, promotes democracy and includes the excluded. The names of the characters may be full (along with the flowers) of Royals and Kings but Child does not endorse aristocracy. Instead, she underlines the democratic rhetoric of citizen nobility, the empowered voter in a participatory society, and the limitlessness of possibility in America – as Huey Long would later express in his Louisiana campaign slogan, "Every Man a King." Mixed blood extends the franchise (in a sense) and spreads American wealth around. In explaining to Gerald that his mother was his father's slave, Alfred King attacks the aristocratic model on which the South justified slavery:

> "I believe that Mr. Fitzgerald's sins were largely attributable to the system of slavery under which he had the misfortune to be educated. He loved pleasure, he was rich, and he had irresponsible power over many of his fellow-beings, whom law and public opinion alike deprived of protection."
>
> (Child, *Romance* 358–59).

The slave South allowed the abuse of other human beings, particularly women: the subtext of Alfred King's remarks is that an aristocratic and autocratic society encourages the sexual exploitation of women. In her essay "Women in Slave Holding Countries," Child remarks, "female virtue is a thing not even supposed to exist among slaves," and slavery is itself conducive to vice, as all the abolitionists agreed (Child, *History of the Condition of Women* II 213). But in the new America, that former exploitation of women slaves will be a *felix culpa*, resulting in a new citizen embodying the various elements of the republic, who will rise through merit, not birth. King tells the "dishonoured" Gerald:

> "I think it would be a more legitimate source of pride to have descended from that truly great man, Toussaint L'Ouverture, who was a full-blooded African, than from that unprincipled filibuster called William the Conqueror, or from any of his band of robbers who transmitted titles of nobility to their posterity."
>
> (Child, *Romance* 358).

Child imagines not only a mulatto America but an America brought back to its revolutionary roots: the preferred ancestor is a freedom fighter, not a land-grabbing invader. Child critiques not only the class system of the South but the imperialism of the nineteenth century that designates some cultures more "worthy" than others. Child, in so many ways a daughter of the Puritans, believes in individual responsibility, citizenship and morality: out of a slave ancestry comes a new generation of exemplary Americans, product of a new revolution (the Civil War).

Of course, Child's revolutionary postwar America is thoroughly middle-class: there is no sense of the descendants of African slaves engaging in their working-class culture. Instead, the race must be uplifted. Rosa and Flora own the genteel accomplishments of Victorian ladyhood, as do their daughters, no matter what their legal status or racial makeup. They are, as they are aware, privileged. When the Kings and the Blumenthals locate Lily and Gerald Fitzgerald's lost son, George, who had been living as a slave and married to a slave woman, their impulse is to "educate" them up to the Kings' standards. They employ Henriet, George's wife, as a seamstress to watch "'over her morals, and [furnish] her with opportunities to improve her mind'" (ibid. 415), not letting her know that she is married to the heir of the millionaire Mr Bell until she suits her station in life.

Child's revolutionary postbellum America is not very black. It is hardly black at all. As Jean Fagan Yellin points out: "Although proposing miscegenation as the solution to the American race problem, *A Romance of the Republic* colors the multiracial American family not from white to black, but only from white to beige" (Yellin, *Women and Sisters* 75). In the *olla podrida* of Rosa's and Flora's language, their cultural references, their customs, their education, the African is largely (though not entirely) suppressed. Even Henriet, the comparatively-dark mulatta who has had the actual labouring experience of slavery, is to become a middle-class lady who can find a place in, if not pass in, society with the help of Rosa and Flora's refinements.

Child fails to solve the perpetual problem of the Tragic Mulatta story: in order to get her white readers to identify with her heroines, they must be white enough to fit stereotypes of "beauty," "cultivation" and "virtue": their blackness must be hidden, like a gothic secret, almost metaphorical. This convention attacks the arbitrariness of racial categorizing in America but also leaves out the vast majority of more obviously African women whose rapes do not excite so much white sympathy. Moreover,

> By dictating a romance plot involving refined heroines, by proscribing frank treatment of sexuality and violence, and by imposing a white middle-class code of values as the ideal toward which all were to aspire, antislavery fiction reproduces and may well have reinforced the ideological assumptions that marginalized the masses of American blacks and circumscribed the freedom of white women.
>
> (Karcher, "Lydia Maria Child's *Romance*" 81)

The subversiveness of mixed marriages is undercut by Child's unrelenting commitment to assimilation: Charles Hobomok Conant Brown becomes just Charles Brown, no longer half-Indian but a European educated member of the elite. The "beigeness" of the King and Blumenthal children ensures that *their* children will be indistinguishable from all the other *olla podrida* European Americans. The invisible African in Child's miscegenous America allows her to avoid, in *A Romance of the Republic* at least, the vexed question of how to educate and empower the multitudinous freed slaves who had not the benefit of a polyglot family and rich friends.

A novel published the year after *A Romance of the Republic* endorses miscegenation yet takes a far dimmer view of its prospects in a racist America. Anna E. Dickinson's *What Answer?* (1868) is angry and pessimistic. Francesca Ercildoune, the mulatta heroine, is much more politically aggressive than Rosa and Flora; she is a radical, refusing to sing "The Star Spangled Banner," and discoursing in public on the evils of slavery. *What Answer?* shows the multiple misreadings of race and class in America. Francesca, dancing with the young aristocrat Will Surrey, is assumed by New York society to be a true lady. With his fair hair and her dark hair, they are characterized by an onlooker as "Saxon and Norman," evoking Sir Walter Scott's *Ivanhoe*, a central text in the South's romanticization of itself. Will Surrey's father says of Francesca, "'She's a thoroughbred. Democratic or not, I will always insist blood tells. . . no one needs to ask who *she* is. I'd take her on trust without a word'" (Dickinson 53).

Blood *does* tell: when the Surreys discover that their son Will is marrying a mulatta, they disown him. They feel cheated. Yet Francesca's wry description of her father as a "Virginia gentleman" is no lie: he is a member of one of the First Families of Virginia in the same way that Roxy in *Pudd'n head Wilson* is a member of the FFVs. A *male* mulatto marrying a white woman (an Englishwoman) marks an interesting twist on the usual parentage of the Tragic Mulatta whose legacy of slavery comes through her mother and bears with it the threat of rape. Perhaps this is why Rosa and Flora are comparatively passive and retiring. Francesca, however, is a new kind of Tragic Mulatta, politically-sophisticated, argumentative and strong (though with the usual self-sacrificing streak that marks her as a True Woman). She is also a free woman, since her mother was white. Yet the marriage of the "mongrel" – her future father-in-law misreads her as "a thoroughbred" – to Will signifies both a necessary rebellion and inevitable destruction. Francesca and Will's scandalous story is played out in the gutter press; and while Will is stirred from his life of indolence into raising a black brigade for the Union in the Civil War, he finally dies in a New York race riot. Even the "free" North cannot shelter those who transgress racially; no bright day of tolerance dawns in Dickinson's postwar society.

Child's final word on race, by contrast, declares it is morning in America. There is a new dispensation for a "new" (to borrow Joel Williamson's term for mulattoes) people. Eulalia King, Rosen Blumen Blumenthal (both "passing" daughters of octoroons) and Benny (son of a slave) stage a tableau in the last scene of *A Romance of the Republic*:

> Under festoons of the American flag, surmounted by the eagle, stood Eulalia, in ribbons of red, white, and blue, with a circle of stars round her head. One hand upheld the shield of the Union, and in the other the scales of Justice were evenly poised. By her side stood Rosen Blumen, holding in one hand a gilded pole surmounted by a liberty-cap, while her other hand rested protectingly on the head of Tulee's Benny, who was kneeling and looking upward in thanksgiving.
>
> (Child, *Romance* 440)

In Child's version of the chastened republic, the previously-excluded now exemplify freedom and the rule of law. It is true that, as Karcher says, Child's assimilation strategy does not "challenge a social order that subordinates women to men, people of color to whites, and the working classes to the bourgeoisie" (Karcher "Lydia Maria Child's *Romance*" 83). And it is true, as Yellin says, that "this assignment of the role of liberator to the light-skinned girl and the role of grateful, kneeling ex-slave to the dark child suggests an endorsement of white superiority that contradicts egalitarian claims" (Yellin, *Women and Sisters* 75). None the less, it is worth remembering that the girls who impersonate the goddesses of liberty are the daughters of ex-slaves. That they can "pass" does reinforce the stereotype of the sensitive mulatta (as opposed to the "simple" African), and the dark-skinned Benny is in an inferior position. But this patriotic set-piece represents the complex negotiations of what Child hopes is a transformed America. The book Child produced the year before *A Romance*, *The Freedmen's Book*, acts as a Bible of the new dispensation, beginning with the "genesis" of the African in the Americas and ending with

151

the apocalyptic "Day of Jubilee," with stories and biographical sketches designed to "uplift" the ex-slave and create a place for him or her in post-slavery America. It is occasionally patronizing (there are sections on "Kindness to Animals" and personal hygiene) but teaches the dignity of dark skin to its audience. Slave ancestry, in this revolutionary Bible, becomes a badge of honour.

The African is suppressed in the bodies of Rosa's and Flora's children but it returns in other bodies, in Tulee and Benny, Henriet and Little Hetty. Near the end of the patriotic celebration scene, Child says "All the family, of ages and *colors* [my emphasis], then joined in singing 'the Star-spangled Banner'" (Child, *Romance* 441). This all takes place in an America where the more common understanding echoed this declaration from Madison Grant's *The Passing of the Great Race* (1916): "the cross between a white man and an Indian is an Indian; the cross between a white man and a Negro is a Negro" (Grant 8). Child counters the idea of pollution with her endorsement of amalgamation in the American melting pot – the *olla podrida*. The American family has been expanded to include a range of colours it never had before. Child's revolution of sensibility is incomplete and limited, rooted as it is in the Victorian attachment to true womanhood and bourgeois values. But it calls for the overthrow of America's most cherished division – the violent, destructive hierarchy of white over black.

6

JEMIMA AND JEZEBEL IN THE NEW SOUTH

Twentieth-century women on race

And the edgy blackness and whiteness of things . . . the breathing symbols we made of the blackness and the whiteness . . . the metaphors we created and watched ourselves turning into . . . the shaky myths we leaned on even as we changed them into weapons to defend us against external events.

Lillian Smith, *Killers of the Dream*

Lydia Maria Child's progressive vision of an America whose racial problem would be resolved in the part-black, part-white bodies of its moral middle class faded almost as she published *A Romance of the Republic*, just after the Civil War. During Reconstruction the definitions of blackness and whiteness, challenged in the abolitionist project, were solidly reinscribed for the nation by an outraged, beaten white South. The union at the end of the nineteenth century was "predicated upon Northern acquiescence in Southern control of the 'Negro problem'" (Sundquist, *To Wake the Nations* 275). The Ku Klux Klan, which first appeared about the same time as Child's most radical novel, reasserted the absolute interdiction of black contact with white. Freed slaves, legally possessors of the rights of citizens, were terrorized back into virtual slavery or at least invisibility. The anxiety over interracial sexual liaisons and their mixed-race offspring, denied by pro-Southern writers and rehearsed with pathos by abolitionists, reemerged as a cultural hotpoint. The body was again the battleground. But this time, the anxiety was not simply directed at defining the opposition of black and white female bodies, but also enforcing separation of black *male* and white *female* bodies. Miscegenation became not just an antebellum tool for abolitionists but an active terror for postbellum whites. The sexual exploitation of black women by white men continued after slavery to some extent; but the white South worried most about revenge-minded free black men determined to sexually exploit white women.[1]

I cannot, of course, fully document the Reconstruction or what white Southerners called "Redemption" (the withdrawal of federal troops) and the creation of the "New South" and the "Jim Crow" South in the early twentieth century. Some events, relevant to the representations of both black and white, do bear noting. For example, legal definitions of "black" actually tightened between 1910 and 1930; prior to the turn of the century, most states designated a person as black if he or she were one-eighth black or more. Later on, states broadened the field to people 1/32nd part black, or even people with what whites called (evoking pollution) a "drop of ink" (Davis, *Who is Black?* 55–56). Paralleling this narrowing of racial boundaries was the institutionalizing of segregation in the 1920s and 1930s and the shocking number of lynchings between 1880 and 1950.[2]

As in the days of slavery, Southern society was officially racially polarized; the same discourses of high and low, pure and tainted, drew the representations of white and black, and the competing constructions of white and black bodies proved crucial to the South's legal structure and social customs. It seemed that the Civil War and abolitionists' attempts to reeducate America had done nothing to undermine Southern society's understanding that white and black were, and had to be, utterly separate.

In this chapter, I examine some white women writing fiction in the 1920s, 1930s and 1940s, playing out the anxieties over race and some possible solutions to the problem of race in their work. It is not that women (and men) were not writing on race in the four decades after the Civil War. But it seems to me that the early twentieth-century South's, and to some extent the nation's, scrambling to revivify old racial oppositions – Jim Crow laws, lynching, miscegenation statutes – to ensure that white and black could not, in any way, touch, is particularly fertile. This period also marks a struggle over the history of the South, when revisionist works by the Fugitives, Howard Odom, Rupert Vance, Ulrich Phillips, Wilbur J. Cash and others worked to demythologize the plantation at the same time as the Klan, the Daughters of the Confederacy, popular writers and Hollywood were reimagining the Old South as a kingdom of aristocratic grace and racial decorum.

The basic paradigm of white bodies represented by the classical statue, and black bodies represented by the grotesque body, flourished in the early twentieth-century South. Blacks were invested with sexuality and all its incumbent, "low" threats. Virginia Foster Durr, an Alabama aristocrat who later became a prointegration activist, said she was brought up to think sex "was something that happened in the basement;" her mother was always concerned that the cook was spending the night down there with men: "You cannot imagine the ideas that built up in us about sex. It really was something that black people did in the basement" (Durr 26).

The body of the white woman, particularly the white lady, was held to be the farthest removed from sexuality, yet was also the most endangered by it, specifically black sexuality, at every level from the "low talk" of black servants to the physical threat of the "black beast rapist." The consequence of contact with the grotesque body is "a continual shifting from top to bottom" (Bakhtin 11). Nell Irvin Painter points out that, in the postwar South, as in the slave South, upper-class white women were identified with civilization: black sexuality imperiled the very fabric of society itself (Painter 49). Political speechifying warned that the "white race" could become mongrelized; books like Myrta Lockett Avary's *Dixie After the War* (1906) portrayed a pure white South threatened by black pollution, and Madison Grant's *The Passing of the Great Race* (1916) theorized that only the Nordic or Anglo-Saxon white "races" had the capacity for leadership and morality: all others, especially Africans, were degenerate. Southern legislation was built upon the suppression of black sexuality. Josephus Daniels of North Carolina warned that black voting would jeopardize "the sanctity of [white] women," and Charles Manigault of South Carolina predicted that "social equality" would encourage "Cuffy" to dance "with the Governor's daughter" and presumably to have sexual access to her as well (Painter 50, 55).

Virginia Foster Durr recounts how another segregationist politician in the 1930s, "Cotton" Ed Smith of South Carolina, "would always go on about the sex thing. If anything happened to change the Southern system, the white women would just rush to get a black man" (Durr 175). So it was not just black sexuality that had to be controlled, it was white women's sexuality as well. Durr's analysis of the situation is that it was repression and transference:

Every black man wanted to rape a white woman and every white woman apparently wanted to be raped. If you read those speeches today, you would really be shocked by them because they showed a kind of sickness, a Freudian illness. I really

155

think those fears came from the fact that the white men of the South had had so many sexual affairs with black women. And they just turned it around.

(Durr 175)

In the circular logic of segregation, blackness equalled sexuality and sexuality was, in all senses, *black*. Black bodies inhabited the "low," socially, economically and, in white society, spiritually. In the hierarchy of purity to pollution, blackness was dirt. The black body was signified, like Bakhtin's grotesque, by its protuberances and orifices: mouths, breasts (for Mammy), belly, genitals: "it is blended with the world, with animals, with objects" (Bakhtin 27). Some parts of the white body even partook of blackness; the genitals were always black, even on a white body. Lillian Smith describes the way the Southern white body was politicized, telling how she as a child was taught that "parts of your body are segregated areas which you must stay away from and keep others away from . . . you cannot associate freely with them any more than you can associate freely with colored children" (Lillian Smith, *Killers* 87).

The language of segregation applies to human bodies, and bodies reside at the centre of segregation as a social policy. The world of the New South revolved around contested bodies and bodily states: "the shape and plasticity of the human body is indissociable from the shape and plasticity of discursive material and social norm in a collectivity" (Stallybrass and White 21). The white South struggled to keep control of the definitions of *pure* and *polluted* which formed the central binary of its structure: the body, sexuality and race were the enmeshed elements which the white South fought to define and contain with the object of keeping all taint, all "pollution," even the smallest "drop of ink" from the pristine whiteness it equated with goodness and order. Racial integration of any kind, any "touching" of black and white, miscegenation, especially sexual contact between black men and white women, caused a crisis. As Mary Douglas points out, "our pollution behaviour is the reaction which condemns any object or idea likely to confuse or contradict cherished classifications" (Douglas 48). In the collapse of slavery, the white South reinvented its racial binaries and reimagined the psychosexual world of blacks and white, elevated white ladyhood even higher into a bodiless realm, while black men and black women, cast out from the "moral order" of slavery, sank deeper into depravity.

156

Much of this ideological work was done in fiction.[3] Thomas Dixon, Jr's radical racist trilogy, *The Leopard's Spots* (1902), *The Clansman* (1905) and *The Traitor* (1912), basis for D. W. Griffith's *Birth of a Nation* (1915), lent a vocabulary to the "rape complex," spurred on segregation legislation and inspired sympathy for the South in the rest of the country.[4] Dixon's representation of black men and white women is crude but effective. Over and over again in his fiction he presents the Southern problem as the righteous order gone awry, with black men in the Reconstruction assuming sexual access to white women the way they demanded access to land and the vote. There are several lurid rapes in Dixon's Ku Klux Klan novels, always a young white virgin victimized by an ape-like black man who pollutes her and imprints on her officially spiritualized, or classical, body, his degraded physical, or grotesque, self. For Dixon, this is the vilest of inversions, one his fiction almost salaciously details, then rectifies by showing the white Christian "knights" of the Klan wreaking revenge on the rapist, reasserting the purity and bodilessness of the (now dead) defiled heroine by erasing the agent of her defilement.

The reinvention and hardening of the racial hierarchy of white over black, bodiless over embodied, however well-served it was in fiction, did not go entirely unanswered, nor was it always as straightforwardly unambiguous as Dixon presented it. White women writers, largely though not entirely from the South, debated the reconfiguration of race and gender in their fiction as energetically as they had slavery before the Civil War. And white women took as many political positions in their fiction as before, ranging from the progressive Lillian Smith to the conservative Margaret Mitchell.

The old types, Aunt Jemima and Jezebel particularly, were still resonant representations of black women, now recast for the struggles of the twentieth century. Aunt Jemima had been reinvented as a repository of Old South romance and "modern" domestic convenience. She appeared at the 1893 Columbian Exposition promoting ready-mixed food: "her condensation of racial nostalgia, national memory and progressive history was a symptomatic . . . vehicle for post Civil War national consolidation" (Berlant 122). The black mother was, no less than for Harriet Beecher Stowe and her critics, a figure of unexamined romance and comfort, even to liberals like Lillian Smith and Virginia Foster Durr, and a saint to conservatives like Margaret Mitchell.

The mixed-race woman is still with us in twentieth-century fiction as well, though no longer the indictment of sexual anarchy under slavery. The mulatta becomes an objectification of America's racial history and, in some cases, its racial future. Representations of the mulatta, found in the work of such white writers as Ellen Glasgow, Edna Ferber, Willa Cather, Lillian Smith and others, are necessarily complicated by her dominating presence in black writers such as Charles Chesnutt, and especially Frances E. W. Harper, Nella Larsen and Jessie Fauset. While they are really outside the bounds of my study here, it is essential to note that their appropriation of a figure used in fiction by blacks working towards emancipation in the nineteenth century (William Wells Brown and Harriet Jacobs among others) takes the mulatta in new directions, undermining the sentimental, romanticized figure found in white, and older black, writers. Harper, Larsen and Fauset, in particular, subvert the passive image of the mulatta by having her align herself fully and freely with the black community instead of existing in limbo between definitions of white and black. None the less, the mulatta works in fiction by both black and white women as an agent disrupting the simple categories of white and black, high and low, pure and polluted – just as she always has. As Berlant notes, the mulatta is "the most abstract and artificial of *embodied* citizens . . . occupying the gap between official codes of racial naming and scopic norms of bodily framing conventional to the law and to general cultural practices" (Berlant 113).

In this chapter, I examine a number of white women trying to understand the "official codes" of race in their culture and the means through which those codes may be broken down. The writers I concentrate on do not form as cohesive a group as the women who debated slavery in the nineteenth century and identified themselves as abolitionists or pro-slavery. Ellen Glasgow and Julia Peterkin were part of the first wave in what became the much-hyped "Southern Renaissance." The play of gender and racial politics in their fiction reflects their Southern milieu and the concerns that gripped the violence-torn, tradition-bound region they lived in. But writers like Edna Ferber and Willa Cather had much more peripheral connections to the South as it wrestled with the hardening of racial attitudes and the enforcement and institutionalization of segregation in the 1920s and 1930s; race and gender in their fictions become a means to explore stories of origins and identity. Margaret Mitchell and Lillian Smith, both Georgia writers, occupy two sides of a racial and historical debate, though Mitchell denied any political content to her famous tale and Smith longed to escape the label of polemicist and activist to be simply an artist. None the less, they display the negotiation of racial definition, gender role and representation of the body that haunts all writers who have tried to confront America's ghosts.

THE SECRET SISTERHOOD OF BLACK AND WHITE WOMEN: EDNA FERBER, JULIA PETERKIN, ELLEN GLASGOW, WILLA CATHER

For reasons of their own, some white writers of the 1920s and 1930s insisted in their fiction on the links between black and white women. In the period when Jim Crow was invented and implemented in its harshest forms, and the separation between races was the legally-enforced social policy of the South and general custom in the North, Ferber, Peterkin, Glasgow and Cather wrote novels that suggested, in greater and lesser degrees, a commonality of gender. Not that these women would have had identical politics on the matter of race: their backgrounds and aesthetics differed widely. But all attempt to read the white female body as implicated in the black female body and the black female body as a point of origin for the white female body.

In the 1920s, white intellectuals wanted to partake of the black, the Other. As has been well-documented, New York *salons* had their pet "Negro artists," and whites fervently participated in the Harlem Renaissance. Carl Van Vechten and other white critics saw in fashionable blackness a liberating force, a world of play, humour and sexuality which defied, or perhaps by-passed, white decorum. Writers such as Sherwood Anderson romanticized black "promiscuity" in works like *Dark Laughter* (1925), celebrating black women's "natural" attitude towards sex and child-bearing as a corrective to white America's Victorian prudery. Julia Peterkin's work can be read in this context, but she pushes beyond the fantasies of pliant (and silent) black women lusciously described in fictions by Anderson, and her fellow Southerners T. S. Stribling and William Faulkner. The black woman in Peterkin's work presents the complex possibilities inherent in an insistently sexual body.

Peterkin was a coast aristocrat who said that she learned to speak Gullah, the creole language of the Georgia and South Carolina coast, before she could speak English. Like a number of whites of her class and generation, Peterkin was brought up by a black nurse and, though a child of privilege, spent much of her early life in a world Lillian Smith called "the yard," where white children and black women could, for a while, avoid the strict segregation of bodies and classes on which official Southern society rested. As an adult, Peterkin observed black life from her plantation Lang Syne, wrote novels and non-fiction, and received praise for her sensitive treatment of African-American folklore and culture and her un-stereotyped characters.[5]

Peterkin's position as the lady in the Big House watching ex-slaves and the children and grandchildren of ex-slaves around her replicates the antebellum plantation order. Yet her fiction attempts to avoid colonizing its black characters. Peterkin's blacks live in a black, not white, community. She strives for what Alice Walker says Zora Neale Hurston accomplishes in *Their Eyes Were Watching God*: that is, to create "Black people as complete, complex, *undiminished* human beings." The white world of law and power is almost invisible; the plantation world is dead. In *Scarlet Sister Mary* (1928), Peterkin reaches back to the gothic South – the Big House is a ruin: "Ghosts can be heard at sunset rattling the closed window-blinds upstairs, as they strive for a glimpse of the shining river that shows between the tall cedars and magnolias" (Peterkin 13). The old order of the South has vanished, but the vibrancy of black life is undiminished.

Scarlet Sister Mary lyrically and comically endorses female sex-uality. Mary the heroine shocks her strict pillar-of-the-church grandmother by going pregnant to her wedding, and flouts her community by philandering as hard as the no-'count she married. The novel is also a celebration of female strength: Mary can chop wood, pick cotton, cook, clean and build. The world of liberating sexuality, physical frankness, spirituality and superstition does intersect with conventional white representations of black culture, especially black women. Wilbur J. Cash speaks of the "natural" black woman who welcomed sex while her "puritanical" white counterpart did not (Cash 87). Both racial conservatives and pro-gressives tended to characterize black women as promiscuous, or accommodating, or helplessly earthy, focusing attention on the body, not the mind. White women were placed in the realm of the spirit; black women in the realm of the flesh. In so doing, each defined the other.

It could be argued that Peterkin comes dangerously close to ratifying the bottom half, at least, of this mind/body split in the way her Mary "sins" without punishment, celebrating female desire. Yet Mary's hard-won sexual freedom is not portrayed as a foil to white "purity." Writing within a black context, Peterkin figures the plantation South as only a ghost, a dead past; she expresses the female body on its own terms, divorced, or at least distanced, from judgemental models of gender. Mary is a "scarlet" woman, a sexual transgressor; black skin implies licence, sensuality. Desire is figured as black; the body itself, the excessively physical, the insistently present, is figured as black. Mary is both black and red. In Mary, Peterkin makes reference to conventional representations of black women, using them in her attempt to create a female language of sexuality, trying to get outside of the binary of white over black, complicating the racial language of purity and pollution. Even when Mary decides to rejoin the church, claiming to repent her life of "sin," her life of the body, she does not give up the love charm conjure man Daddy Cudjoe made for her. Mary negotiates between a patriarchal tradition which tries to contain and limit expressions of sexuality and a pagan or "feminist" tradition which gives free play to sexuality. The novel's title carries Mary's dual selves: the "sister," member of the Christian community, adherent to its sexual codes, and "scarlet" (as in Woman of Babylon), the outsider, the breaker of those codes.

Mary's moving between the world of the church and the world of pleasure subverts white readings of black sexuality as threatening or merely animalistic, even while it seems to reinscribe certain stereotypes, long held to be sociological truth. I would not argue that Peterkin creates an "authentic" black world in her Blue Brook novels: however careful an observer of the life of the Quarters, her whiteness, her position as lady of the Big House, would always have an effect on the blacks she watched. So while Peterkin cannot be said to show the "truth" of black life, the importance of her use of the black community as an imaginative realm where she can play out the issue of sexuality and female power is central. Peterkin capitalizes on cultural associations of blackness with sexuality to write not about the problems of being black in a white world but about being female in a world where the female body is seen as a dangerous entity needing to be controlled, regulated and erased.

If Mary inhabits familiar racial ground, she none the less undermines gender conventions. Black women were exempt from (or denied) white rules of ladyhood; especially under slavery, this exposed them to the dangers of rape, torture and other forms of

161

abuse. Yet the gender conventions which "protected" white female bodies also locked them into rigid *bodilessness*; black women were left unprotected, but they were also not subject to the same suppression of the physical. Mary is sexually attractive in the terms of her world because she works:

> toil and carrying heavy loads had hardened her sinews and lengthened her wind and kept her body lean and slim. She could swing an ax and cut the toughest wood for hours at a time without a taint of weariness. She could jerk a hoe day after day through the hottest sunshine. She could pick cotton with the best and come home at night as cheerful and fresh as when she waked at dawn.
>
> (Peterkin 249)

Mary's version of womanhood outlasts the white women of the plantation garden. Peterkin underlines this in the way that Mary takes over the old plantation garden, claiming it as her special place to be alone and think. Mary feels the ghosts of the place, almost expecting "one of the fine ladies" to challenge her. But, in reality, "the white people were gone. The forest had taken back many of their fields, the river had swallowed their rice fields, but the black people were used to hardship and they lived on here and throve" (ibid. 250–51). As a model for survival, the white lady, represented by the statue on the pedestal, is extinct, while the black woman, her body immediate, strong and desiring, triumphs. Julia Peterkin, the white upper-class writer, the white lady, commits her own act of subversion in erasing her kind in favour of the black woman, the liberated body free to work, free to accept and give pleasure.

The partaking of blackness by white women is also centrally important in Edna Ferber's *Show Boat* (1926). Magnolia Hawks Ravenal becomes a successful singer principally because of her early immersion in black culture; she sings work songs and spirituals and performs them so convincingly that people constantly ask her if she is part black herself. But Magnolia is white, the white lady implied by her first name and part of the "chivalric" culture of the South as implied by her married name: Ravenal.[6]

Magnolia and the other characters in *Show Boat* live in a world of disguises: Magnolia herself has several names, including Maggie and Nola. She grows up on the *Cotton Blossom* show boat, a sort of floating emblem of America itself working the Mississippi, the quintessential American river, with both blacks and whites, farmers, "gentlemen," gamblers and, most importantly, actors. They are never what they seem: an actress billed as Lenore La Verne is really named Elly Chipley; an actress called Julie Dozier looks white but is legally black. They move between worlds of glamour and sordidness, official culture and underground culture, as the show boat wheels up and down the river, journeying from South to North and back again.

Magnolia exhibits the same shifting of selves. She is sometimes the flower-lady signalled by her name, her body all but erased. After having her daughter Kim, she almost disappears: "So white, so limp, so spent was she that her face on the pillow was startlingly like one of the waxen blossoms whose name she bore. Her slimness made almost no outline beneath the bedclothes" (Ferber 3). At other times, Magnolia's body is very present indeed, insistent and sexual. In the same post-childbirth scene her mother chides her for her cries during labour, saying "'I never saw anything so indelicate as the way you carried on and your own husband in the room.' Here Magnolia conveyed with a flutter of the lids that this had not been an immaculate conception" (ibid. 7).

Like Faulkner, Edna Ferber tries to deconstruct the image of the lady; unlike Faulkner she does not destroy the woman in the process. Magnolia can navigate between bodiless ladyhood and embodied sexuality because she has been presented with alternative models of the feminine. Her mother is like Miss Ophelia in *Uncle Tom's Cabin*: the archetypal Yankee schoolmarm dedicated to the mortification and suppression of the flesh. On the show boat, however, Magnolia lives among the black maids, "pert yellow wenches," the black cook–mammy Queenie and, her idol, Julie Dozier. Julie is a stock character, the Tragic Mulatta whose "fatal mark" is revealed when a Mississippi sheriff threatens to arrest her for violating a miscegenation statute. Julie's mother was black, her father white, and her husband, Steve, white. Before the sheriff comes to take her away, Steve cuts her hand and sucks up some of her blood, thus making it possible for him to swear he, too, has "mixed blood."

Ferber's treatment of Julie is quite conventional: the mulatta represents the breakdown of the white/black binary, "the living emblem of a social taboo" (Gross 67). Once her secret is out, she must endure the prejudice of her former friends who, like Elly Chipley, now see her as a "nasty yellow wench" (Ferber 149). Like many of her literary antecedents, Julie disappears from the white world. What is interesting about the episode is the way Ferber uses it to insist on integration in the face of a society that practises segregation. Steve chooses to define himself as part black; you could also say that Magnolia chooses to define herself as part black, not literally but culturally. Ferber shows Magnolia as a child clinging to the departing Julie in inverting language that deliberately collapses the opposition of black and white: "[Julie] dropped on her knees in the dust of the road and gathered the weeping child to her and held her close, so that as you saw them sharply outlined against the sunset the black of the woman's dress and the white of the child's frock were one" (ibid. 153). Julie wears the black that signifies her race and Magnolia wears the white that signifies hers, but the two merge, marking Magnolia with Julie's blackness. Magnolia is marked with blackness in other ways as well. She prefers to hang around the show boat kitchen: "It was here that she learned Negro spirituals from Jo and cooking from Queenie, both of which accomplishments stood her in good stead in later years" (ibid. 118). Her mother tries to impose whiteness on Magnolia with piano lessons, insisting that she practise "The Maiden's Prayer" instead of "the Negro plantation songs, wistful with longing and pain; the folk songs of a wronged race, later to come into a blaze of popularity as spirituals" (ibid. 120). Despite her mother's attempts to enforce young ladyhood on her by censoring her experience, Magnolia knows a great deal of black life from spirituals to fights to "ring shouts" in Louisiana because of her own life on the Mississippi.

Magnolia learns not only the words to these "Negro plantation songs," she learns to sing with "the hoarsely sweet Negro overtone – purple velvet muffling a flute" (ibid. 120). When her husband Gaylord Ravenal, a gambler and supposed broken-down Tennessee aristocrat who says he is a descendant of "black sheep" and himself is "black as pitch," leaves her, she puts aside her white lady persona and takes on, literally, a black voice in an audition: "She threw back her head then as Jo had taught her, half closed her eyes, tapped time with the right foot, smartly. Imitative in this, she managed, too, to get into her voice that soft and husky Negro quality." (ibid. 361). She sings "Go Down, Moses" to a young producer who is almost too thoroughly convinced:

His pale shrewd eyes searched her face. "You a nigger?"
The unaccustomed red surged into Magnolia's cheeks, dyed her forehead, her throat, painfully. "No, I'm not a – nigger."

"Well, you cer'nly sing like one. Voice and – I don't know –
way you sing. . . . No offense. I've seen 'em lighter'n you."

(ibid. 361–62)

Like so many white musicians after her from Al Jolson to Elvis
Presley, Magnolia becomes rich and famous singing "black." While
she does not literally put on the blackface of the "Coon Show," her
"nigger-sounding" voice partakes of the minstrel world which,
according to Sundquist, sent the message that all was well with the
races in America: "Minstrelsy was the cultural work for a national
reunion built upon an escalation of racial discrimination and violence" (Sundquist, *To Wake the Nations* 275). A generation before
Ferber published *Show Boat* in 1926, the "American century" had
been ushered in with the Wilmington and Tampa race riots in 1898,
the Robert Charles riots in New Orleans in 1900 and the Atlanta
riots in 1906.[7] By the time Ferber was writing, lynchings in the
South, while down from their previous peak, were frequent
(McMillen 206–38). Yet she tries, not simply to "mask" the violence
in negro spirituals sung for whites by a white woman, but to posit
a kind of private mediation in Magnolia's own body. She is simultaneously the white blossom and the "black" entertainer, a sort of
mulatta of the spirit, emblem of the way white popular culture in
America always steals from black subculture. The doubleness exhibited by the show boat life, the disguised names and hidden
selves, signifies the doubleness of America itself: black and white,
sometimes the blackness concealed in apparent whiteness. Magnolia becomes a star; her daughter Kim Ravenal becomes an even
bigger star. But in the end, Magnolia chooses to go back to the show
boat, the old *Cotton Blossom*, the floating emblem of her dual self,
with, as Kim says, "'flies and Negroes and mud and all this yellow
terrible river that you love more than me'" (Ferber 397). The white
woman returns to the miscegenous world that sustained her; Ferber envisions an integrated America and an integrated self where
the white woman becomes more truly herself through appropriating the black.

The erasure of the white in favour of the black seen in Peterkin's
novel and the integrated self seen in Ferber's are optimistic possibilities compared to the altogether more painful assessments of
race relations in Ellen Glasgow's *The Sheltered Life* (1932) and Willa
Cather's *Sapphira and the Slave Girl* (1940). Glasgow is so aware of
the long history of sexual exploitation of black women by white
men and of the jealousy white women feel toward black women

165

that she names her enigmatic mulatta Memoria. Even more than Peterkin and Ferber, Glasgow is part of the Southern revisionist project, aimed most pointedly at recovering and celebrating female sexuality – freeing white women from the pedestal, or at least displaying the debilitating effect of what Lillian Smith calls "playing statue." Like Peterkin, Glasgow came from the Southern upper class, a Virginian. But where Peterkin chose to imagine the life of the Quarters, Glasgow concerned herself with the people who once lived in the plantation house – people who are just ghosts in Peterkin's work. They are sometimes near-ghosts in Glasgow's: men who cannot bear the fall of the Old South, women who do not understand that the ideal of the plantation mistress no longer has a place in the modern world. In *The Sheltered Life*, old families like the Archbalds and the Birdsongs, stubbornly staying in their crumbling houses even when the neighbourhood is no longer the best, see the New South as "a second invasion," literally figured in "that bad smell" from the just-built chemical factory down the road (Glasgow 6–7).

Glasgow draws a contrast between Eva Birdsong, the Queenborough belle married to the charming philanderer George, and Memoria, the "superior negro" washerwoman with whom George has had an affair. Again, the white writer draws a contrast between white and black bodies: Eva spends her life corseting her "sacred" body and disguising her feelings of rage and betrayal in perfect behaviour until an unspecified gynaecological problem nearly kills her. Memoria washes clothes for the old white families of the town, representing a knowledge of the physicality and "filth" they will not admit. Glasgow is not primarily interested in the racial binary in her fiction: she reinscribes traditional representations of black women as Aunt Jemima in the many mammies and aunties who tend to be part of the furniture of the *haute bourgeois* South. And her central concern in *The Sheltered Life* is not the story of George and Memoria but of George and Eva's marriage and how Eva finally chooses not to be blind to his betrayal of her. Nevertheless, Memoria haunts the narrative just as the black woman Mandy haunted Glasgow's much earlier novel, *Virginia* (1913). Black women stand for the suppressed history of the South. White women can be desexualized and deprived of desire because black women are invested with all the sexuality and "passion" white culture denies them. White men go to black women because the culture claims to be divided: the underground world of blackness offers the white

166

man something "he could not find in his white life" (Lillian Smith, *Killers* 128).

Eva Birdsong and Memoria have parallel lives: they rarely meet yet they are bound together as the official and unofficial partners of George Birdsong. At one point in the novel, Eva tells Jenny Blair, the girl who will be George's last betrayal, that she fell in love with him when, as a boy, he rescued the child Memoria from a fire in the Quarters. There is no vision of integration in *The Sheltered Life*: only the description of white and coloured clothes hanging together on a line at Memoria's house. Memoria is a shadow of Eva, a "memory" of slavery, a reminder of the split between white women, absolved from sexuality, and black women, sexual before all.

In Willa Cather's *Sapphira and the Slave Girl*, the problem of how white men exploit black women and how white women collude in that exploitation moves to the foreground. Like Glasgow, Cather was, by birth, a Virginian, though she is best known, of course, as a novelist of Nebraska and the plains west. In *Sapphira*, her last novel, Cather returns to the South of her childhood, attempting to understand its history through the intertwined lives of three women: Sapphira Colbert, a slaveholding Virginia aristocrat, Rachel Blake, her anti-slavery daughter, and Nancy, a slave. They act out the drama of divided selves and disputed bodies that is the secret women's history of the Old South.

Toni Morrison reads *Sapphira and the Slave Girl* as, "in some ways ... a classic fugitive slave narrative" (Morrison, *Playing in the Dark* 20).[8] Like Linda Brent in Jacobs' *Incidents*, Nancy is threatened with rape, though she finally escapes. *Sapphira* is also like an old-fashioned abolitionist novel, making clear its relationship with *Uncle Tom's Cabin* from the outset, beginning with a discussion of selling a slave, underscoring the instability of the slave system and exposing the hypocrisy of the family model of the plantation. But instead of Mrs Shelby, representing the maternal feeling which Stowe suspected fired abolitionist sentiment, pleading against selling any of the "family," the plantation mistress Mrs Colbert takes the "masculine" role advocating the sale of Nancy while Mr Colbert says, "'We don't sell our people'" (Cather 6). The echoes and inversions of Stowe continue with Sapphira Colbert behaving sometimes like Marie St Clair and sometimes like Simon Legree. Her anger is focused on Nancy, whose presence constitutes both a sexual threat and a dynastic affront. She says nastily to her husband: "'black Till bore a yellow child, after two of your brothers had been hanging around here so much. . . . Perhaps you have a kind of family feeling about Nancy?'" (ibid. 8–9).

As in *Uncle Tom's Cabin*, and in Jacobs' *Incidents in the Life of a Slave Girl*, *Sapphira* plays out a psychological drama of sexual menace, unknown parentage and a final escape to freedom in Canada. It is as if Cather, as well as striving to explore her own personal history, wishes to remind the nation that the work of Stowe and the abolitionists was unfinished in 1940; the South was more segregated than ever, racial violence enforced the code of separation, and the hysteria over the scandalous touching of black and white bodies remained unabated.

Like Glasgow, Cather portrays the anxiety over white men and black women that terrorized Southern culture. And like Peterkin, Ferber and Glasgow, Cather implies an opposition of black and white bodies, with the black body standing for strength and desire and the white body standing for suppression and denial. Cather plays this literally: Sapphira is a cripple, living in a wheelchair, her body no longer sexual. "She can, and does, remain outside the normal requirements of adult womanhood because of the infantilized Africanist population at her disposal" (Morrison, *Playing in the Dark* 26). Sapphira, too, is infantilized, with slaves to feed, bathe and dress her like a baby:

> She escapes the necessity of inhabiting her own body by dwelling on the young, healthy and sexually appetizing Nancy. She has transferred its care into the hands of others. . . . The surrogate black bodies become her hands and feet, her fantasies of sexual ravish and intimacy with her husband, and, not inconsiderably, her sole source of love.
>
> (ibid. 26)

Sapphira illustrates Orlando Patterson's point about the total need of white masters for their slaves: "The slaveholder camouflaged his dependence, his parasitism, by various ideological strategies. Paradoxically, he defined the slave as dependent" (Patterson 337). Sapphira, like all slave mistresses, complains about her slaves but literally cannot move without them. She lives isolated like an invalid child in the antiseptic atmosphere of the Big House; her husband sleeps at his mill. Nancy, on the other hand, is vigorous, attractive and, to young white gentlemen, accessible because of her race. Sapphira is represented by her perfectly coiled hair and her white lace caps, the cold statue icon of the Southern lady, white as marble and hard as the stone she is named for. Conversely, Nancy is fleshy and soft with "slender, nimble hands, so flexible that one would say there were no hard bones in them at all." She is a "pale gold" colour, displaying her mixed heritage, though we never know whether Nancy's father is one of Henry Colbert's brothers or the Cuban artist who came to paint the Colberts' portraits (Cather 18).

The trouble in the Colbert household is the kind of sexual jealousy Mary Chesnut described in her Civil War diary when she inveighed against "beastly negress beauties" seducing white men. Ella Clanton Thomas also deplores master–slave sexual liaisons ("Southern women are I believe all at heart abolisionists [sic]") and rages covertly about her own husband's misdeeds (Burr 168, 56–63). Linda Brent tells of Mrs Flint's jealousy and distress when she learns of Dr Flint's desire for her: "She pitied herself as a martyr; but she was incapable of feeling for the condition of shame and misery in which her unfortunate, helpless slave was placed" (Jacobs 53). Sapphira Colbert fears that Nancy, as Lizzie the cook says, might be making the master's "'bed cumfa'ble fur him'" (Cather 61). Sapphira's first impulse is to rid the place of Nancy altogether, but since Henry vetoes it, her second solution is to encourage Henry's nephew Martin, son of one of the ne'er-do-well Colberts, to rape or seduce her. Here the novel intersects closely with *Incidents in the Life of a Slave Girl*. Martin dogs Nancy's steps, trying to get her alone, touching her, frightening her. He assumes that she is not only a body to be used but that she may have already been used by his uncle: "'By God, if I thought that old sinner had been there before me – '"(ibid. 186). Martin reduces Nancy to a desired *location*, "there," the intimate space of her body which Martin wishes to colonize and claim. Sapphira thinks that when Nancy has been taken by Martin, she will be seen as tarnished by Henry and no longer a threat to their cold marriage. Morrison points out the logical flaw here: "If Mr. Colbert is tempted by Nancy the chaste, is there anything in slavocracy to make him disdain Nancy the unchaste?" (Morrison, *Playing in the Dark* 25). For Morrison, the answer comes back to a fundamental white/black split in expectations: Sapphira's moral universe decrees sex "ruins" a woman. She cannot enter the slaves' world where sex cannot be the sole, or even a central, criterion for female goodness. As Harriet Jacobs argues, "the slave woman ought not to be judged" as a free white woman (Jacobs 86). Sapphira can only read chastity from her point of view and thus her plot against Nancy is not so much "vindictive" as "desperate" (Morrison, *Playing in the Dark* 25).

For Henry, the realization that his nephew is trying to rape Nancy, his favourite, is not an occasion for dramatic and righteous anger. He is disillusioned to find that he can no longer see Nancy as a child but as a sexual being: "Now that he must see her as a woman, enticing to men, he shrank from seeing her at all" (Cather 193). So long in a sexless marriage with Sapphira, Henry opts out of the world of desire. Nancy as a desirable body is distasteful to him; he has successfully infantilized her until Martin threatens her. Ironically, his final solution is to help his daughter Rachel get her away via the Underground Railroad. He must erase her troubling body and so evade the fact of the black woman's sexual availability under slavery. Though for different reasons, both Henry and Sapphira accomplish the same end – ridding their little world of any disruptive bodies.

Cather schematizes the great discomfort in white culture over the black body. Like Glasgow, she identifies the white woman's fear of her husband's response to the open bodies of black women as a central anxiety in a racist society. Unlike Peterkin, she does not celebrate black sexuality as liberating; Nancy's only defence from Martin the potential rapist (we know he has previously assaulted a lower-class white girl in the mountains) is in adopting "white" Victorian standards of decorum and virginity. Sexuality for her is not liberation but circular entrapment in a system that values her only for her sexuality. And unlike Ferber, Cather does not play out a comedy of integration where white culture is shown as dependent on black culture for its impetus. The Old South runs on mutual antipathy so deep that separation is the only safety for Nancy and the only peace for Sapphira.

Yet in the end, Nancy comes back to Virginia, the return of the repressed, the return of the secret blackness of the South. The voice of the novel shifts to a child "I" who could be the young Cather herself, finally seeing the woman who had figured in so many of her family stories. Nancy comes back dressed in furs and silk with a gold watch chain – an obvious material success. She has earned the sort of fine clothes that symbolized her former mistress', Sapphira's, place in the ruling class. And the child-narrator's mother asks Nancy to sit down, like an honoured visitor, breaking one of the chief social codes of the Jim Crow South. Nancy has transformed herself into something Other, something outside the class and race spectrum of the South. Even her language is different. The child says "Her words seemed to me too precise, rather cutting in their unfailing distinctness.... Nancy spoke of the his-to-ry of Canada. I didn't like that pronunciation. Even my father said 'hist'ry'" (ibid. 284). Nancy and her mother Till outlive the plantation system and Sapphira Colbert. They live on strong while all that is left of her is "lace caps and fichus, and odd bits of finery such as velvet slippers with buckles" (ibid. 291). As in Peterkin's fiction, the plantation system survives only in fragments, but its victims, ex-slaves and their dependents, remain. The romance of the indomitable black body is played out in these white women's fictions as they dramatize the debilitating separation of white and black bodies which still ruled the society out of which they wrote.

"HOW BLACK WAS RHETT BUTLER?" HOW WHITE IS SCARLETT?

Margaret Mitchell once said that she was glad if her novel helped to "correct" the errors and false impressions of the South put forth in Harriet Beecher Stowe's great bestseller. Eighty-five years after *Uncle Tom's Cabin*, seventy years after Appomattox, sixty years after "Redemption," the white South still debated slavery, gender and class. *Gone With the Wind* (1936) counters the integrationist fiction of writers like Glasgow, Cather and Peterkin and the revisionist history of the Old South coming out of North Carolina (and some other universities). *Gone With the Wind* reinvents the war over the body in a rewriting of the War Between the States, challenging some rosy assumptions of the plantation novel but reaffirming many of its verities.[9]

Mitchell displays a mixture of conservatism and feminism: she critiques ladyhood yet punishes her protagonist for deviating from it. She avoids the ugly, obvious racism of Thomas Dixon's Ku Klux Klan romances (which she, none the less, quite enjoyed in her youth) yet her novel represents blacks as faithful mammies, stupid servants or masterless, violent aggressors – when she deals with blacks at all. Maybe the most interesting aspect of *Gone With the Wind*'s blacks is their scarcity. Joel Williamson observes: "Margaret Mitchell was born into a social universe that was obsessed with blackness, and yet she wrote a novel that seemed so totally white" (Williamson, "Rhett Butler" 87).[10]

Despite the strange invisibility of blacks in a novel about the slave-owning class in a society built on slavery, *Gone With the Wind* is concerned with race and its most explosive intersection with gender, playing out what Irigaray calls "the sexuality that subtends our social order."[11] To understand how this might work, it is necessary to know something of the "social universe obsessed with blackness" which was Margaret Mitchell's culture. She was born in 1900, right in the middle of the fifteen years (1892–1907) when the most lynchings occurred in the South.[12] Lynchings were, of course, part of white society's attempt to police contact between the races through violence, especially enforcing the taboo against black men having anything to do with white women. Southern legislatures resisted civil rights legislation, seeing any relaxation of black subordination as an opening for miscegenation. Lynching became "a regional ritual," purging the community of the "pollution" of blackness to the point that "between 1885 and 1907 there were more persons lynched in the United States than were legally executed" (Williamson, *Crucible* 185).

Williamson reminds us that the year before Mitchell was born, one of the most appalling and famous lynchings took place in Newnan, Georgia, not far from Atlanta.[13] Sam Hose was a black labourer accused of murdering Alfred Cranford, a white farmer who employed him, and then raping Mattie Cranford "within arm-reach of where the brains were oozing from her husband's head," as the Atlanta *Constitution* put it (Williamson, "Rhett Butler" 87). Hose was captured and taken to the woods near Newnan where he was stripped, chained to a tree, and parts of his body were cut off from his ears to his fingers to his genitals. Then he was burned slowly. After the fire cooled, the crowd took pieces of his body away – finger bones, teeth, slices of his internal organs – as "souvenirs," as if these monstrous relics would somehow show the power of whites to control the black body and, by extension, the black sexuality they deemed so dangerous.

As the lynching of Sam Hose was quite famous, especially in Georgia, there is every reason to assume that Mitchell knew of it and many other lynchings throughout the South that occurred with terrible regularity during her childhood and adulthood: she was, after all, a journalist. There were spectacular lynchings in Mississippi in 1918, 1920, 1925 and 1935.[14] In 1934 Claud Neal was lynched in Jackson County in north-west Florida for the rape and murder of Lola Cannidy, a young white girl. Neal was castrated and mutilated, then hung in front of the county court house.

Photographs were taken of Neal's body and postcards were later sold (McGovern 80–100). The murder charges and the build-up to the lynching were well-publicized nationally with Walter White of the National Association for the Advancement of Colored People (NAACP) and Mrs William P. Cornell, chair of the Florida chapter of the Association of Southern Women to Prevent Lynching, lobbying Governor David Scholtz to send in troops. News stories appeared in the Richmond *Times–Dispatch*, the Washington *Post*, and the Boston *Herald*, among others (ibid. 100ff.). But neither the publicity nor the National Guard could stop the violence towards blacks that ignited all over west Florida as whites rallied, according to the Klan, "to protect Womanhood" (ibid. 70).

Mitchell had not been born when the race riot in Wilmington, North Carolina, took place in 1898, but she was in Atlanta and quite aware of what was going on during the four days of rioting there in September 1906. Her father, Eugene Mitchell, wrote to his wife in New York that he and various members of the family, including children, sat up one night, terrified that their affluent section of Atlanta would be burned. Eugene Mitchell was concerned that he had nothing like a weapon but "Margaret suggested that Mr Daley's sword would be a good thing. I adopted the suggestion" (Eugene Mitchell to Maybelle Mitchell, 29 September 1906, quoted in Williamson, "Rhett Butler" 92). The riot was evidently caused by reports of assaults on white women by black men.[15] All over the city, blacks were beaten, shot and burned out. The lesson was very clear: blacks could not (except as servants) touch the white world. The violence underscored the determination of whites to enforce black subjugation, reinscribing whites' commitment to keep guarded and enclosed the sacrosanct bodies of white women.

As if this were not enough, Mitchell grew up hearing the rhetoric of white supremacy and female purity that fuelled not only the extramural violence of the South but its legislative practices, especially Jim Crow. Southern feminism frequently took the form of trying to protect white women from black men. One of her mother's fellow suffragists, and later the first female senator from Georgia, Rebecca Latimer Felton, gave a speech on Tybee Island where she said: "If it takes lynching to protect woman's dearest possession from drunken, raving human beasts, then I say lynch a thousand a week if it becomes necessary" (Williamson, "Rhett Butler" 89). According to Mitchell's latest biographer, Maybelle Mitchell did not go along with the more radical racist suffragists – Felton and her sister Mary Latimer McLendon – none the less, Mitchell would have been exposed to the hysterical impulse to define blackness, to expel it from any but the most menial spheres of Southern life, and to represent the black body as a potential polluter of the white (Pyron, *Southern Daughter* 41).

As a child, Mitchell enjoyed the Klan novels of Thomas Dixon, Jr. As a teenager, Mitchell staged Dixon's *The Traitor* with neighbourhood children (all scions of upper-class Atlanta families), taking the part of Steve, the "traitor" who turns out to be the most loyal Southerner of all.[16] As an adult, after the success of *Gone With the Wind*, she wrote rather breathless letters to Dixon about how she was raised on his books, and he wrote back in kind from New York, saying he was glad her novel was selling so well since "a lovely SOUTHERN girl has done it! The highbrows up here are calling it the new REBEL YELL. And thank God for it in these days of renewed slander of the South." (Thomas Dixon, Jr to Mitchell, 5 August 1936, quoted in Wood 134). Clearly, Dixon saw *Gone With the Wind* not only as a worthy weapon to combat the bad reputation of the South, but part of the struggle to counter revisionist history and the breakdown of gender, class and race roles embattled in the nervous postbellum South.

I cite all of this not to somehow "prove" that Margaret Mitchell was a racist or an adherent to the kind of lynch-law and white suprematism that fuelled the white South's most barbaric acts, but simply to display the racial *donnée* of the society that shaped her. Where Dixon betrays little ambivalence about blacks and blackness in his fiction, Mitchell's productions are filled with interesting inversions and contradictions. For example, an early story called "'Ropa Carmagin," written in 1926 and destroyed at Mitchell's direction, would seem to indicate a quite daring reading of race and sexuality. The memories of those who saw the story are somewhat unclear and patchy, but it sounds as though Mitchell in 1926 was, as Williamson says with pardonable exaggeration, "about to write a book about miscegenation that was not vastly different from the truly great novel that William Faulkner published a decade later under the title *Absalom, Absalom!*" (Williamson, "Rhett Butler" 103). One version of the story has it that a white plantation aristocrat called Europa Carmagin falls in love with a young mulatto man whose mother had been a slave on the Carmagin place and whose father might have been Europa's father. Naturally, all ends tragically.[17] Certainly, there is no hint that miscegenation is acceptable even in a romantic, tragic sense in *Gone With the Wind*; Mitchell's later literary production firmly rebuilds the barriers between black and white bodies.

Or does it? Sexuality itself is represented in Southern culture as something black. In Faulkner's *The Sound and the Fury*, Caddy Compson's sexual activities are "negro": *"Why must you do like nigger women do in the pasture the ditches the dark woods hot hidden furious in the dark woods"* (Faulkner, *The Sound and the Fury* 114). For Virginia Foster Durr, sex was something black people did in the basement; for Lillian Smith, sexual organs and sexual feelings were "dark," unspeakable, segregated from the white, expressible parts of the body and white official decorum. In the white Southern mind, there seems to be no breaking the metaphorical chain that links the body to pollution to sexuality to blackness to blacks themselves. In *Gone With the Wind*, those who are literally black – Mammy, Pork, Uncle Peter, Prissy, Sam, even the nameless would-be thief–rapist – all behave in stylized, conventional ways in a society which is quite successful in keeping them subordinate or erasing them altogether, something noticed by the novel's earliest critics.[18] Pyron points out that Mitchell

> neglects a brooding off-stage presence for blacks that she allows even her shadowy aristocrats – the invisible presence that lurks between the lines of most exemplars of the Southern mind.... Slaves are important only as individuals, and the primary black actors ... are "house servants," and by Mitchell's conventional definition, "members of the family," "pets," and thereby hardly slaves at all.
>
> (Pyron 191–92)

But there are characters in whom blackness and, I will argue, *redness* (femaleness, danger), lurks illicit, unsanctioned and threatening to a social order that divorces white women from black bodies, male bodies and their own bodies.

Mammy is the most prominent black character in *Gone With the Wind*, represented in a perfectly traditional manner from her very dark skin to her constant strictures on the behaviour of "Young Misses," particularly Scarlett, trying to make her conform to her station as a white lady: "Far more than Ellen O'Hara herself, Mammy voices the conservative views and values of her mistress" (Taylor 172). While some critics have argued that Mammy has

175

power over her white folks, that power seems to be a condescending white convention like the "power" a nineteenth-century mother, with no property rights, no legal existence and no vote, was said to have. Mitchell says "Mammy felt that she owned the O'Haras, body and soul" but of course *they* own *her* (24). Mitchell's Mammy fits into the long Aunt Jemima tradition with little or no deviation from type. As Gloria Naylor summarizes Mammy:

> Her unstinting devotion assuaged any fear that slaves were discontented or harbored any potential for revolt. Her very dark skin belied any suspicions of past interracial liaisons, while her obesity and advanced age removed any sexual threat. Earth Mother, nursemaid, and cook, the mammy existed without a history or a future.
>
> (Taylor 171)

Mammy is "a huge old woman with the small, shrewd eyes of an elephant"; in one phrase Mitchell renders her body as large (Mammy likes food and is associated with it in the Aunt Jemima legend) and likens her to the "jungle," to Africa, with her elephant's eyes (Mitchell 24). Indeed, Mammy is "pure African," with none of the ambivalence that mixed blood would carry. In her otherness, her association with the *animal*, Mammy's body is very present throughout. She touches Scarlett far more than Ellen O'Hara, her mother, does, even more than any of her husbands (for most of the novel Scarlett resists sex). Ellen is represented by the disembodied white Virgin Mary who becomes indistinguishable from her in Scarlett's prayers; Mammy's blackness signals her physicality where whiteness means spirituality, remoteness: the difference between the grotesque body with all its protuberances and the classical body with its closed orifices and marble coldness.

Black Mammy is an agent of white ladyhood; her job is to enforce the classical model on Scarlett. Eve Kosofsky Sedgwick remarks, Mammy is

> *totally* in thrall to the ideal of the "lady," but in a relation that excludes herself entirely: she is the template, the support, the enforcement, of Scarlett's "lady" role to the degree that her personal femaleness loses any meaning whatever that is not in relation to Scarlett's role.
>
> (Sedgwick, *Between Men* 9)

She literally tries to restrain Scarlett's bodily transgressions (as well as her more social sins) throughout the novel. When we first see Mammy, she is lecturing Scarlett about running outside without a shawl on her: "'Ah done tole you an' tole you 'bout gittin' fever frum settin' in de night air wid nuthin' on yo' shoulders. Come on in de house, Miss Scarlett'" (Mitchell 25). Mammy spends her life trying to get Scarlett to cover herself and come inside the house, one way and another, though Scarlett's nature is to uncover herself and free herself of the restrictions of the parlour. Mammy exhorts Scarlett to eat before she goes to the Twelve Oaks barbecue so that she will only pick at her food in public, affirming her ladyhood: "'You kin sho tell a lady by whut she *doan* eat. . . . An ain' never seed no w'ite lady who et less'n Miss Melly Hamilton'" (ibid. 79). Mammy tells Scarlett it would not hurt her to faint every once in a while because she is so "'brash,'" and tries to stop her from wearing "an afternoon dress at a morning barbecue" because "'You kain show yo' buzzum befo' three o'clock'" (ibid. 79).

Throughout the rest of the novel, Mammy works to contain Scarlett and define her in ladyhood, mostly to no avail. Scarlett has *appetite* – for men, for money, for power, for food, for all kinds of pleasure.[19] She effectively resists the disembodiment Mammy (and her mother) plan for her, asserting her body in the face of the convention that represents the lady as spirit, not flesh. Melanie Hamilton, who hardly eats, who seems perfectly asexual, is a "tiny, frailly built girl, who gave the appearance of a child masquerading in her mother's enormous hoop skirts" with hair "sternly repressed beneath its net" and a "childishly undeveloped" figure (ibid. 102). Having a baby nearly kills her. Melanie, like Ellen Robillard, embodies self-denial. And, in Mitchell's mind, she is the true heroine of the novel, the "great lady," as Rhett Butler describes her, who stands for the highest ideals of the white South, the perfect statue.[20]

Scarlett, on the other hand, has an irrepressible physicality. She is, at best, *disguised* as a lady: "The green eyes in the carefully sweet face were turbulent, wilful, lusty with life, distinctly at variance with her decorous demeanour. Her manners had been imposed on her. . . her eyes were her own" (ibid. 5). And her body is her own as well, also "wilful" in Mitchell's descriptions of Scarlett's mature breasts and half-understood desires. More than any other white female character, we have a sense of Scarlett's body; it imposes itself. Scarlett's physical needs, her immature passion for Ashley, her ravenous hunger at Tara when there is no food, her attempts to control her body in corseting her tiny waist, or through refusing sex to Rhett then wallowing in her own subjugation the night he rapes her, are constantly rehearsed for the reader. The tension between Scarlett's insistent appetites and her attempts to act like a lady, as her class and culture demand, results both in her financial successes and emotional disappointments.

Scarlett's physicality is linked throughout the novel to the land, also a constant, concrete presence. Several critics have noticed how Scarlett is identified with the city of Atlanta: she was born the same year it was founded, she is, like Atlanta, only superficially a part of the Old South, and she commits herself to it as a symbol of the New South.[21] It is more important, I think, to see how identified with rural Georgia she is. Not for nothing is she named "Scarlett," almost as if she is called after the colour of the earth her father teaches her to love above all else. In the plantation novel, depicting the South as Eden, the walled, contained paradisal garden, is a commonplace: the Southern landscape is represented as feminine, a receptive, fertile space. The landscape of Scarlett's world is lush, but it is far more red than green. Scarlett may like to wear green to match her eyes but she is surrounded by a very feminine redness: "The moist hungry earth waiting upturned for the cotton seeds, showed pinkish ... vermilion and scarlet and maroon" (ibid. 10). Around her everywhere are reddish peach blossoms, the roads she travels on look "blood-red," she notices cherokee roses, violets, pink crab apple and "scarlet and orange and rose" honeysuckle (ibid. 10, 29, 83–84). In Faulkner's novels *The Sound and the Fury* and *Sanctuary*, honeysuckle signifies female sexuality – a fairly obvious association. In *Gone With the Wind*, Mitchell's identification of her *red* heroine with her *red* landscape is at least as obvious. While the strictures of ladyhood and of whiteness tell Scarlett she must be closed, still and cold, the land practically exhorts her to the opposite: "It was a savagely red land, blood-coloured after rains, brick-dust in droughts" with its "red furrows and the gashed red road" (ibid. 10, 29). Red is the colour of the dress Rhett makes her wear to Ashley's party when she and Ashley have been caught kissing; red is the colour of genitalia, of childbirth, of menstruation, of sexual transgression, of the Scarlet Woman of Babylon – of all that challenges and subverts ladyhood.

So how white is Scarlett? Not very; she is, as her name implies, as red as her land and in her redness, her "scarlet(t) woman" potential for transgression, lies her femaleness, her physicality, her sexuality: all that is denied by whiteness. It is fitting that this woman who struggles between the red physical concreteness she desires and the white decorum she has been taught would take up with a man who also struggles with white decorum. I will pose Joel Williamson's question again: how black is Rhett Butler? Williamson effectively shows that Rhett is described over and over again as "black," "dark," "swarthy," and so on.[22] Like a black man (and like Scarlett, too) he is intensely present and physical: as Helen Taylor says, Mitchell describes Rhett "obsessively in terms of his shape, size, and the space his body occupies" (Taylor 114). He is compared to an Indian and to various animals: a hawk, a panther (ibid. 115). From the first time he turns up in the novel he is constructed as a rapist: he has "such wide shoulders, so heavy with muscles, almost too heavy for gentility" and "animal-white teeth" and eyes "bold and black as any pirate's appraising a galleon to be scuttled or a maiden to be ravished" (Mitchell 97). He looks at Scarlett in a way that does not accord her ladyhood but asserts his knowledge of female sexuality: "'He looks as if – as if he knew what I looked like without my shimmy'" (ibid. 99).

Rhett Butler is the most visible rapist in this novel, though rape is one of the postwar threats, the "peril of white women," which worry the Southern survivors. Tony Fontaine has to go away when he kills Wilkerson for saying "'niggers had a right to – to – white women'" (ibid. 640, 630). A black "buck" had tried to attack his sister-in-law. And there is a brief episode where a black man tries to rob Scarlett when she unwisely goes to Shantytown. Mitchell depicts him conventionally in terms identical to those in Dixon's work, comparing him to "a gorilla" (ibid. 770). He has a "black face twisted in a leering grin" as he attacks Scarlett: "she felt his big hand at her throat and, with a ripping noise, her basque was torn open from neck to waist" (ibid. 771). Scarlett evades this robbery (and implied rape) though the reaction of her enemies to it is interesting: India Wilkes says "'What happened to you was just what you deserved and if there was any justice you'd have gotten worse'" (ibid. 777). Since Scarlett is not properly "white," or, as India puts it, she has no "common courtesy" and "no gentility," "you aren't one of us and never have been," her body is acceptably at risk, except that Ashley and Frank Kennedy do see Scarlett as white, not red (or black) and put themselves in danger with the Ku Klux Klan to kill her attackers (ibid. 777).

Scarlett's rape is deferred; just as she is a "scarlet" woman occasionally disguised as a white lady, she is ravished by a "black" man who looks white.[23] If Joel Williamson is right about "'Ropa Carmagin," Rhett Butler is the descendant of the mulatto hero who loved the white heroine (Williamson, "Rhett Butler" 102–04). But that need not be so: the most compelling way to read Rhett Butler as "black" depends not on a tenuous recollection of Mitchell's lost story but on an understanding of how the discourse of sexuality – and especially of rape – in the South is "black."[24] Williamson moves in the right direction, suggesting Dixon's Klan romances as an influence, but he does not push his argument far enough. In the famous scene in *Gone With the Wind*, Rhett Butler is represented as a black man in very much the same descriptive terms as Gus in *The Clansman*. Rhett's "blackness" is reiterated in his drunkenness: "his face was dark and flushed." The "large brown hands" with which Rhett threatens to tear Scarlett to pieces echo the big hand of the black would-be rapist at Scarlett's throat and the "black claws of the beast" Gus on Marion Lenoir's "soft white throat" (Mitchell 913, 914; Dixon, *Clansman* 304). The violence of the scene where an angry Rhett chases her and carries her upstairs to force her is an eroticized version of the rape of Marion Lenoir. But where Marion wakes up the next morning preparing to kill herself out of shame – she is a true Southern lady – Scarlett remembers the "rapture, the ecstasy of surrender" (Mitchell 918). She knows that a "lady, a real lady, could never hold up her head after such a night." Scarlett and Rhett have been true to themselves, breaking through their disguises as white gentry to the sexuality that drives them together. And in Margaret Mitchell's Southern world, that sexuality is red fading to black:

> Up the stairs he went in the utter darkness, up, up, and she was wild with fear. He was a mad stranger and this was a black darkness she did not know, darker than death ... she was darkness and he was darkness and there had never been anything before this time, only darkness and his lips upon her.
> (ibid. 917)

I am not, as Williamson is not, arguing that Rhett Butler is in any way *literally* black, any more than Scarlett is literally red (or "darkness" here as she is caught up in the sexual moment). It is just that Margaret Mitchell uses the discourses of her culture to describe the central erotic event in her novel as a symbolic black on white rape, simultaneously reiterating the accepted images of black men and white women as charged taboos, and questioning the "whiteness" of instigator and "victim." By tingeing Rhett Butler with blackness *and* by challenging Scarlett's whiteness, Mitchell represents the struggle over sexuality that threatened to destroy white women. Her erotically-charged colours – red, black and white – never stabilize. In Rhett's "blackness" lies his attraction and in Scarlett's "redness" lies her freedom. Both of them, in the end, must compromise with whiteness: Rhett goes back to the very white, conventional aristocratic world of Charleston to reimmerse himself in tradition and certainty, and Scarlett goes back to the red earth of Tara where sits a white house with "white walls" and "white curtains" (ibid. 1011). Mammy is there, the one person who can impose whiteness upon Scarlett. Mitchell's novel tries to negotiate the worlds of whiteness and non-whiteness, the chasm the South has built between bodies, present and absent, polluted and pure, that is the central, if hidden, debate for women in Southern culture.

LILLIAN SMITH AND THE LOUD GHOSTS OF THE PAST

While Margaret Mitchell might have rejected any conscious intent in her novel of carrying out the ideological work of old and immutable definitions of race, sexuality and gender, Lillian Smith used texts to further her progressive agenda. For her, fiction could act as both an aesthetic enterprise and a political tool. Like Lydia Maria Child, Smith made American hypocrisy over race and racial definition the driving force of her best writing; both women saw themselves engaged in a political struggle over the future of America. At the heart of that struggle was the way blacks and women were treated in American society, and both Child and Smith saw integration as the moral way out of the radical division of American culture into categories of black and white, polluted and pure, low and high. The struggle is always over the representation of bodies: how women are defined, how ambiguities are negotiated.

Smith committed her writing to destroying Southern apartheid, which she saw as damaging to both blacks *and* whites. Like Child she worked to subvert the false opposition of black and white, bringing taboo bodies together in revolutionary miscegenation. Smith's work also goes back to the Grimké sisters and Harriet Beecher Stowe in her gothicizing of the South as a place of curses,

181

secrets, repression and violence, beset by a past of unspeakable cruelty that refuses to die. In *Killers of the Dream* (1949), one of her most famous books, Smith says the South's "trouble" is "like a ghost haunting an old graveyard or whispers after the household sleeps," and that the interaction of blacks and whites throughout Southern history are "ghost relationships" that obsess the New South (Lillian Smith, *Killers* 25, 116–35). Smith's fiction and non-fiction attempt to describe and exorcize the haunting of America by race and to untangle the repressed couplings of white and black which return so vehemently over and over in its culture.

Smith belongs in a small group of progressive Southern white women that includes Jessie Daniel Ames, founder of the Association of Southern Women for the Prevention of Lynching, and the Civil Rights activist Virginia Foster Durr. Like Ames, Durr, Julia Peterkin, Ellen Glasgow and Margaret Mitchell, Lillian Smith was born into the privileged class of the South, in 1897 in Jasper, Florida. While her family were not so obviously aristocratic as the Peterkins or even the Mitchells, Lillian Smith was connected to Tidewater Georgia planters on her mother's side, and while the Smiths suffered financial setbacks that caused Lillian Smith to spend time trying to repair their fortunes, her place as a white "lady" who understood the practices of the Southern class and caste system was never in doubt.

In her own life, Smith transgressed a great many of the boundaries set for white women. She never married, choosing to live for years with Paula Snelling, her friend and lover, with whom she ran various "little" magazines and the Laurel Falls Camp for Girls in Rabun County, Georgia. She was an isolationist and a pro-unionist who, unlike many integrationists of the 1930s, 1940s and 1950s, felt wary of both socialism and communism.[25] She saw segregation as "spiritual lynching," a "psychocultural" illness, and advocated breaking it down with acts of personal integration, crossing the colour line (Loveland 58). She brought black children for visits at Laurel Falls, she served on a black scholarship committee and always tried to eat with blacks (breaking one of the most obvious rules of segregation) at the black colleges she visited, and held integrated women's parties at her house on Old Screamer Mountain (ibid. 30, 129). She criticized the women's movement, feeling some ambivalence toward the term "feminist," yet acted as a feminist, attacking ladyhood in all her writings, advocating the teaching of sex education at Laurel Falls, trying to cure the Southern sense of the body as dirty.[26] Part of her house was destroyed by arson in 1955, probably because she had been seen "embracing" some of her black guests (ibid. 129). She earned the ire of Southern "moderates" like Hodding Carter and Ralph McGill as well as the scorn of communists who found her dramatic adaptation of *Strange Fruit* ideologically unsound; and while she laboured to challenge the stereotypes of race and gender in the South, she reinscribed the quintessential racist image of the Mammy, praising in much of her work the maternal black woman who loves all children, black or white, a source of comfort, though a "haunted" figure to the white child of privilege. Like the other writers I have looked at, Southern apologists or integrationists, Smith's interrogation of her culture is contradictory and her challenges to the racial hierarchy finally incomplete. My interest lies in her struggle.

Smith's first novel, *Strange Fruit* (1944), was a *succès de scandale*, lambasted from both the right and the left. The book was banned in Boston and banned by the United States Post Office from the mails as "obscene"; Bernard De Voto was arrested buying it in Cambridge, Massachusetts to publicize the ridiculousness of the obscenity statute.

Strange Fruit sold very well. As with *Uncle Tom's Cabin*, both praise and blame were heaped on the author's head. Smith wrote: "You are called bitch and saint, whore and heroine, you are praised for your courage and sneered at for your obscenity." (Loveland 72). W.E.B. Du Bois liked the novel, seeing in it expression of "the tragedy of the South" and its racial knots "that only evolution can untangle or revolution break" (*New York Times*, Book Review, 5 March 1944, 1). In (unsurprising) contrast, a Georgia newspaper, the *Hapeville Statesman*, charged on its front page that Smith portrayed "a romantic affair between a white Georgia boy and a negro girl ... in such glamour that will make such courtships between negroes and white appear attractive" (Loveland 70). This review (and others along the same lines) echoes the disapproval pro-slavery reviewers expressed over *Uncle Tom*: that it grew out of an unnatural sexual attraction for blacks held by the author and that it would promote "unhealthy" race mixing. But it was not just pro-segregation whites who were shocked at Smith's novel: several black leaders disliked it as well. Dean Gordon Hancock of the Associated Negro Press lamented, "it is difficult to imagine a more subtle indictment against the Negro race in general and Negro womanhood in particular than that presented in *Strange Fruit*" (ibid. 69). Hancock also charged that the novel was popular with whites because it showed blacks as subservient.[27]

From labelling it as "obscene" to labelling it as a libel on "Negro womanhood," problems with *Strange Fruit* focus on Smith's portrayal of sexual and racial transgressions. The novel illustrates the ways the South remained essentially unchanged since Emancipation as well as how the Civil Rights movement developed. It also demonstrates how old literary forms remained resonant. Smith's novel does not deviate far from the Tragic Mulatta narrative. Nonnie Anderson, a cultivated, college-educated, light-skinned black woman, gets pregnant by Tracy Deen, scion of one of the small Georgia town's old families. He thinks he loves her, but the imperatives of his class and his colour prove too strong. He thinks he can "keep" her by marrying her to his illiterate childhood playmate, Henry, son of his old mammy, while he marries the whiter-than-white girl next door, Dottie.

Strange Fruit rehearses the "mark" of the mulatta found in fiction from Lydia Maria Child's "The Quadroons" up through Stowe's Cassy to Robert Penn Warren's Amantha Starr in *Band of Angels*, published eleven years after Smith's novel. Nonnie's sister Bess reminds her of the "curse" (as James Fenimore Cooper's Cora also calls it) of her mixed blood: "'Just look at your skin! What does it mean to you, that color – just a pretty shade? You know what it meant to the women back of us – you've got to know, Non! Shame and degradation and heartbreak'" (Lillian Smith, *Strange Fruit* 83). Bess is an astute reader of how little her culture has changed; Nonnie assumes she can evade the implications of her colour, just as her lover Tracy does, for a while. Nonnie thinks she will be the one to subvert the Tragic Mulatta story because she thinks Tracy loves her for herself, not her as an idea of "Negro" sexuality that is the obverse of the white lack of sexuality in the world enforced by his cold, controlling mother. And though the novel kills off the young white man instead of the mulatta, nothing changes to bring the white and black worlds of Maxwell, Georgia, divided economically, culturally and geographically, any closer to integration.

Yet while Smith's story bleakly reiterates the tragedy of a region which, as one character puts it, is represented by "'a white man kneeling on a nigger's stomach'" where "'every time he [the white man] raises his arms in prayer, he presses a little deeper in the black man's belly'" (ibid. 238), it also questions the division of the world into black and white, male and female, and puts forth an integrationist vision by inverting all the codes the South builds itself upon. Southern culture insists on the regulation and definition of bodies – segregation at all levels, even of the single, apparently unified body, segregated from itself, from its sexuality, as Smith knows: "parts of your body are segregated areas which you must stay away from and keep others away from" (Lillian Smith, *Killers* 87). And she is aware that one of the South's sustaining stories about race says that the definitions are easy and absolute:

> I also knew that I was better than a Negro, that all black folks have their place and must be kept in it, that sex has its place and must be kept in it, that a terrifying disaster would befall the South if I ever treated a Negro as my social equal.
>
> (ibid. 27–28)

Yet *Strange Fruit* works to create that "terrifying disaster" for the ideology of racial, gender and bodily division on which the social order of the segregation rested. Smith implies that order is already shaky; whites' need for definition borders on the hysterical. What counts in the South are the "signs everywhere. *White . . . Colored . . . White . . . Colored*" (Lillian Smith, *Killers* 95). The signs of the Southern racial hierarchy try to mark the bodies of the South by allowing only certain ones into certain spaces, yet outside the official, legal, realm of segregated lunch counters and cinemas, subversion of the signs begins to render them meaningless.

From the very beginning of the novel, Smith undermines the supposed absolutism of white over black, the expected opposition of the elevated body over the degraded one. Nonnie is constantly described as *white* – she is "tall and slim and white in the dusk" and has "a face that God knows by right should have belonged to a white girl" (Lillian Smith, *Strange Fruit* 1–2). Nonnie appears in a white dress, appropriating one of the signs of white female purity. If black is white, sometimes white is black: Bess sees Tracy's hand in "dreams sometimes, white, with black hairs across it – touching the dirty floor, touching her sister" (ibid. 12). Pollution is figured as something dark, but its agency does not always belong to blacks.

Still, Maxwell, Georgia insists on colour definitions visible in the very demographics of the town: White Town and Colored Town are divided, different. Blacks walk to White Town to work as servants and labourers; whites, especially white men, drive to Colored Town to get "something you can't get here in White Town . . . well, they've got plenty of that!" (ibid. 65). Sexuality is *black* and purity

185

is *white*; black women are sexually accessible and white ladies are not. And yet there are confusing forces at work in Maxwell, resistance to absolutes, acts of transgressions, boundary crossings. Nonnie's lover Tracy compares her to his sister: *"In the dusk she's as white as Laura"* (ibid. 4). This move is destructive of the discourses of opposition where black and white cannot touch – they have, they do; comparing a black girl, even one who's been to Spelman College, to a white lady, violates class and colour conventions. Part of Tracy's attraction to Nonnie arises from the old romantic racist mulatta story: the white man finds the light black woman attractive (because she is nearly white) and also because she is legally black, carrying all the associations of "dark" sexuality, sensuality and licence which white women are not allowed to express. But Nonnie also erases in Tracy, at least at the beginning, the cultural impositions of black and white that divide them. In seeing Nonnie as white, or as no colour at all, Tracy subverts his society's laws. Nonnie's own status as black seems irrelevant to her. She says "Race is something – made up, to me. Not real. I don't – have to believe in it. Social position – ambition – seem made up, too" (ibid. 63). It is not hard to see why some black critics might be uncomfortable with Nonnie's declaration of colourlessness; Jessie Fauset, Nella Larsen and, a generation earlier, Charles Chesnutt and Frances E. W. Harper (among others), appropriated the mixed-race heroine of abolitionist romance and racially reclaimed her. Instead of dying for her "darkness" the mulatta began to assert her blackness not as a curse but as a gift. This heroine refused to "pass" and refused to be an erotic object.[28]

As long as Tracy can see Nonnie as white, or as of no race at all, he can resist the pressures to conform which White Town, personified by his mother, put on him to marry the acceptable white Christian virgin waiting for him to settle into the upper-middle-class profession which is his by inheritance. Tracy fights with Southern absolutes: "You can't love and respect a colored girl. No, you can't. But you do" (ibid. 65). Yet his resistance begins to fragment when he thinks of her as black: the words "colored girl" destroy his pleasure in loving her. Nonnie shifts from occupying an individuated space as a beloved, singular body: not quite represented by the Bakhtinian classical statue but none the less a person, not a category, to Tracy. But in his crisis over class, race and gender oppositions, he reduces her to a category, a generalized representative of her race. He calls Nonnie "Nigger" and tries to rape her: "He'd lead a respectable life from now on – but by God he'd have his nigger" (ibid. 131). The prayer song of the revival meeting is "*Whiter than snow. . . yes, whiter than snow. . . oh wash me and I shall be whiter than snow:*" yet the truth of the body is dark.

Colored Town is a transgressive area, a place where inversions, challenges to white power, occur, especially *for* whites. Without its own sense of Colored Town as a place housing the elements of sexuality and physicality purged from its domains, white Maxwell would not understand itself *as white*, and thus powerful. Smith reinscribes the cultural *donnée* that sexuality is something black, something "negro," showing how that construction entirely rules the South, setting up all the other oppositions of gender, class and racial roles. Maxwell is completely paralysed by its attempts to contain and control sexuality. Alma Deen finds a clay sculpture of a naked female torso in her daughter's drawer and feels violated herself. Laura's room had been like a temple of virginity where Alma could sleep apart from her husband, "escaping Tut's masculinity" (ibid. 45). But the torso sexualizes the room for her – and, by extension, Laura herself. It is not an idealized Greek goddess but an anatomically graphic, realistic version of a woman's body: hardly the smooth, perfect statue that represents the lady in Alma's world. Alma knows that Laura spends a lot of time with her friend Jane, an older, unmarried woman, against whom she has warned her daughter. Yet the compartmentalization of class and sexuality is so strong that Alma finally dismisses the sculpture as "a lump of wet dirt" which she destroys, and decides Laura "quite likely copied this thing out of a book without realising its – its – well, that it wasn't so *nice*" (ibid. 48). The reality of the female body, revealed as having genitals, challenges the image of the white lady which women like Alma, and Tracy's fiancée Dottie, cannot tolerate.

Everywhere in *Strange Fruit*, things that "aren't so nice," things that transgress racial and sexual codes, disrupt the community, then get covered over, ignored or violently suppressed. A young pregnant white girl, Grace, desperately wants an abortion. Dr Deen refuses to perform it, sending her to an old black woman, reaffirming the black world as the location of sexual life. Laura is in love with Jane but will have to repress it all her life. Alma Deen sends the revival preacher, Brother Dunwoodie, to explain the divisions of class and culture to her transgressing son. He gives the official version of the ways of black women: "Live a fairly decent, respectable life – that is, if a nigger woman can live a decent respectable life . . . you have to keep pushing them back across that nigger line" (ibid. 59). Brother Dunwoodie goes on to delineate gender roles as well; there are two worlds: "the woman's has to do with the home and children and love. God's love and man's. The man's world is different. It has to do with work. . . . Now, when a man gets over into a woman's world, he gets into bad trouble. . . . Too much love makes you soft" (ibid. 60).

Tracy breaks Maxwell's laws: until the end, he refuses to push Nonnie back across the "nigger line" and ventures into a woman's world of love. He transgresses class and gender codes by seeing Nonnie, for a while, not as "his nigger" but the person he loves. Brother Dunwoodie and Alma Deen win him back, however, though in his bitter passivity he knows that he is destroying the truth. As he makes up his mind to cave into his mother's demands, marry Dottie, join the church and take a job, he sees clearly the dividing line drawn by the South:

> Back of him White Town. Back of him white women. All the white women in the world. Yeah. . . they tie their love around you like a little thin wire and pull, keep pulling till they cut you in two. That's what they do. Back there, they're asleep now, stretched out on their beds asleep, ruling the town. White goddesses. Pure as snow. Dole out a little of their body to you – just a little – see – it's poison – you can't take but a few drops – don't be greedy – do as I tell you – do as I tell you now – be a good boy – .
>
> (ibid. 131)

The white woman doling out her body by the drop becomes the mother doling out her love by the drop; both make desire and gratification contingent on obedience to the Southern social order which constructs white women as goddesses, untouchable yet powerful. Tracy Deen had resisted the division of women's bodies into black and white, polluted and pure, but he is not strong enough to reject his class and his race. Nonnie becomes just a "nigger" he can sexually assault; he turns into the vicious boy Nat from her childhood who wanted to get under her dress because all black girls are available to white boys (ibid. 2). Yet to her own brother, Nonnie is a cherished body polluted by whiteness – a powerful inversion. Ed Anderson kills Tracy for "ruining" his sister: purity cuts both ways in *Strange Fruit*. But the fight is over "ownership" of Nonnie's body; she cannot negotiate the expectations of sexuality and availability Tracy has of her, or the middle-class aspirations her mother, sister and brother had for her. Chastity – or the absence of chastity – still governs and defines female worth. Though Nonnie tried to remove herself from the economy of good girl/bad girl that both her worlds, black and white, subscribe to, both her worlds conspire to limit her. She cannot live in the white world so she fades back into the black world, denied even the dignity of mourning for Tracy, denied celebrating her pregnancy. She spends the day after her brother murders her lover, dressed in her maid's uniform, disguised in blackness or, as Smith says of another character, buttoned into her "white folks manner," an invisible member of an invisible underclass, surviving in White Town as long as no one really sees her, like a sort of ghost.

Smith offers a useful reading of her own novel in her non-fiction *Killers of the Dream*, published five years after *Strange Fruit* at the end of the 1940s. One section is called "Three Ghost Stories" and deals with the forbidden sexual relationship between a black woman and a white man, the suppressed relationship between the white father and his mixed-race children, and the devalued relationship between the white child and the black mammy. Smith shows how the culture designates sexuality as the province of "low" black women while white women are elevated by the disembodying impulse of their culture into sexlessness. The South practises a "patriarchal puritanic system which psychically castrated its women" (118). White women were as divided from the body as White Town was from Colored Town:

> The more trails the white man made to backyard cabins, the higher he raised his white wife on her pedestal when he returned to the Big House. The higher the pedestal, the less he enjoyed her whom he had put there, for statues after all, are only nice things to look at.
>
> (Lillian Smith, *Killers* 121)

Here is the classical body of Bakhtin, closed, cold, untouchable. As Stallybrass and White point out, "we *gaze up* at the figure" (21). Alma Deen and Dottie in *Strange Fruit* have divorced themselves from their bodies and have become represented by stillness and coldness. Nonnie, on the other hand, acknowledges and enjoys her body, not realizing that it means, in the social order, she is "low," open, to be used sexually: this is why she can say, with pitiable

5

naïveté, that she does not believe in race. If so, she is alone: the South believes in little else. Smith employs the stereotypes of the very physical culture of blacks in order to present an alternative model of human sexual behaviour, sometimes coming dangerously close to trivializing when she speaks of the "dark people, natural, vigorous, unashamed, full of laughter" (ibid. 116–17). Yet for Smith this alternative is never taken on its own terms: sexual interaction between black women and white men is a "ghost" of the Southern past, a holdover from plantation days: one of many.

Yet sexuality, the touching of bodies, in Smith's scheme, *potentially*, at least, subverts the white-over-black hierarchy, just as it did in the integrationist fiction of Child. Nonnie will bear a child whose heritage is both White Town and Colored Town, though, like a ghost, he or she will have to wrap up in blackness, or invisibility, and never reveal that his or her father is Tracy Deen. It is true that Smith romanticizes the sexual relationships between white men and black women. She does not speak of the rape of slavery days but of "passionate affairs, relationships tender and rich" and "love affairs that made white women despair as competitors; delicate, sensitive, deep relationships in which mind and body and fantasy met in complete union" (ibid. 127). Smith dismisses "Marxist" interpretations of white/black sex under slavery as economic or exploitative in nature. Her denial of the ghosts of the past bears questioning:

> Whether or not the captive female and/or her sexual oppressor derived "pleasure" from their seductions and couplings is not a question we can politely ask. . . . Indeed, we could go so far as to entertain the very real possibility that "sexuality" as a term of implied relationship and desire, is dubiously appropriate, manageable, or accurate to *any* of the familial arrangements under a system of enslavement.
>
> (Spillers, "Mama's Baby" 76)

Smith represents Nonnie and Tracy's relationship as potentially a union of minds, bodies and fantasies warped by the Jim Crow South, refusing to see that, at one level, their affair reinscribes the power structure of white over black. And in *Killers of the Dream*'s third "ghost relationship," Smith also reinscribes the essential maternity of the mature black woman, though she insists that it is "a relationship without honor in his [the Southern child's] own mind and region" (Lillian Smith, *Killers* 128). Like sex with a black

190

woman, the mammy fulfils a need the white child "could not find in his white life" (ibid. 128). Smith indulges in familiar images of the mammy with her rich humour, her "ample breasts," her association with food. In *Strange Fruit*, Tracy Deen adores Mamie (even her name is essentially "mammy"), the woman who nursed both him and Henry and who had a "faint clean body smell like a pile of fresh ironed sheets," full breasts and a big lap to hold him in (Lillian Smith, *Killers* 72).

There is little deviation here from Mammy in *Gone With the Wind*, or Aunt Chloe in *Uncle Tom's Cabin*. Smith tries to politicize her representation in insisting that the white middle-class Southerner (it is a male here – Smith does not address white women's feelings toward their mammies any more than she addresses the hot-button issue of white women's sexual feelings toward black men) is divided from himself if he does not acknowledge the "blackness" of the South. Sedgwick asks: "Whose mother is Mammy?" (Sedgwick, *Between Men* 10). She is *ours*, white folks' – or so we assume when we keep her from her own children and her own home, cooking, cleaning, nurturing in ours. Smith speaks of the Southern child's two mothers: one looks at him, is distant from him, is desired by him but not possessed, while the other touches him, feeds him, cleans him, responds to his needs (Lillian Smith, *Killers* 132). Smith's point is that white Southerners have effectively split their world into White Town and Colored Town, and bodies into white and black, pure and polluted, estranged from themselves, as crippled as Sapphira Colbert and as dependent. Smith's integrationism demands that the culture bring its ghosts into the equalizing daylight – crossing the divide from White Town to Colored Town, no longer a transgression but a natural movement.

The divisions of high and low, white and black, in the South serve the political interests of a very few, as Smith points out: "white women had not profited in the least from the psychosexual profit system which segregation in the South supported so lavishly" (ibid. 143). White women appear to gain from being absolved from the pollution designated for black women but, for Smith, that is simply a rhetorical strategy to keep them powerless:

> washed-out women of the rural South whose bodies were often used as ruthlessly as was the land. . . . No wonder a demagogue talking on rural courthouse steps can buy the votes of these malnourished, worn-out, lonely women of the South with his talk of "sacred womanhood," and "purity" and

191

"protecting our women from the menace of negroes," for he is
buying votes with a dream.

(ibid. 169)

Or is he buying votes with the ghosts of a glamorous history that
hardly anyone in the white South materially benefited from but all
participated psychically in? Stowe constructed the South as a
haunted house, filled with the ghosts of the unjustly enslaved,
tortured, raped and killed. For Smith, the ghosts walk still in the
strategies of Southern politics; racism appeals "*not* to the conscience but to the mythic mind where the ghosts wander around"
(ibid. 172). Smith does not hold out much hope in *Killers*: she uses
the gothic image of the South as a region with skeletons in its
antebellum closets, the curse of slave history raining down, secrets
in its "dark" areas, and ghosts who will not be silent: "haunting the
mind of the South and giving shape to our lives and our souls"
(ibid. 135).

EPILOGUE
Making the word the thing

The word in language is half someone else's. It becomes "one's own" only when the speaker populates it with his own intention, his own accent. . . . [The word] exists in other people's mouths, in other people's intentions: it is from there that one must take the word and make it one's own.

Bakhtin, "Discourse in the Novel"

This is a story to pass on. At the end of Toni Morrison's *Beloved*, the living try to forget their dead: the slave child murdered out of furious love, the seductive, needy ghost. The ghost becomes a barely-acknowledged "bad dream," yet she is always present. Lillian Smith speaks of black–white interchanges as "ghost relationships," acknowledging that the black presence in America is at once powerful and invisible as smoke. The black body is a ghost, *disembodied*, in the white world. In Morrison's *Beloved*, the ghost is Sethe's child, but in Stowe's *Uncle Tom's Cabin*, the ghost could be Cassy's child, the one killed with an overdose of laudanum. Morrison gently, but firmly, takes over the gothic discourses about America's invisible ones. She answers Stowe and Faulkner, answers Hawthorne and Melville, too, in her *roman noir's* insistence on reclaiming the national ghost story for the ghosts themselves.

This has been the project for black writers in general, but especially for black women writers, who first borrowed, delicately modifying here and there, the words of white culture, but then increasingly made the words their own, shaping them with their mouths and pens, pronouncing them in new ways – and loudly.

White women's writing has sometimes served to silence black women and sometimes tried to set free their voices, but has always operated out of a set of assumptions that either distanced black

193

from white because black was too "low" to touch "high" white, or else tried to bring the two together (uplifting the race). Toni Morrison says, "For the most part, the literature of the United States has taken as its concern the architecture of a *new white man*" (Morrison, *Playing in the Dark* 14). The purpose of this book has been to show the history of these white women's texts as they debate fundamental questions of black and white in an America tainted by slavery, then Jim Crow, obsessed with definitions and boundaries. Sometimes the questions about race these women – comparatively privileged, comparatively well-educated – struggle with are not really about race at all but about being women who write. Whether they reinforce the walls that encircle them in a class, a race or a domestic sphere, or challenge the existence and efficacy of any walls at all, these women had to negotiate forces in their society that discouraged their even asking the questions in the first place. I have concentrated on white women because I think their centrality to the interrogation, disabling or shoring up of stories about blackness in the United States has been neglected or assumed to be a subset of white men's writing. Maybe looking at the transmission of these stories through the fictions of white women suggests more mysterious territory than it maps.

As even my slight evocation of writers like Harriet Jacobs and Toni Morrison shows, there is much work to be done, looking at the way black women (and men, of course, though that opens up a whole new can of worms) have tried to write themselves not only out of slavery, as Henry Louis Gates says, but out of the bondage that gender can be in American society. We are still interested in the stories black women tell about their lives; Sojourner Truth and Ellen Craft recounted tales of slavery to listeners in meeting halls and parlours, Anita Hill tells of her life as a woman harassed first by her boss, then by the United States senate, in university lecture theatres and law societies. Writers from Harriet Jacobs to Zora Neale Hurston to Alice Walker to Ntozake Shange to Gloria Naylor make fiction out of the urgent issues of both blackness and womanhood. All of them share a commitment to addressing historical representations of black women; all of them gather up the white-stamped images of themselves they inherit from the American album and recast them their own way. Debating the representations of blackness and femaleness which have been dominated by white texts is a vital debate – one which should be examined at length. I will only suggest here that black women

194

writers' riffs and significations on the old representations which veiled them need to be studied if we want to truly understand the tangle of fiction in race and race in fiction.

Aunt Jemima and Jezebel are but two of the "markers" representing and limiting black women: they are old-fashioned, white-generated terms but still in currency as part of the American national shorthand. Underneath them lie real women struggling with representations fixed in culture long before they were born. I cite Hortense Spillers' declaration once more: "Let's face it. I am a marked woman, but not everybody knows my name" (Spillers, "Mama's Baby" 65). The names white America has for black women are masks, aliases, constructions heavy with cultural baggage. When Oroonoko and Imoinda are renamed Caesar and Clemenc, they are "buried" beneath a set of expectations and prescriptions. Yet they insist on their own names (or at least the African names Aphra Behn imagines for them) at the end. In a new naming, perhaps the hidden will become visible, the spirits will turn flesh. *Beloved*, a story of both haunting and naming, warns that this is not easy, or painless, this mediumship – conjuring a ghost is not without cost:

> So they forgot her. Like an unpleasant dream during a troubling sleep. Occasionally, however, the rustle of a skirt hushes when they wake, and the knuckles brushing a cheek in sleep seem to belong to the sleeper. Sometimes the photograph of a close friend or relative – looked at too long – shifts, and something more familiar than the dear face itself moves there. They can touch it if they like, but don't, because they know things will never be the same if they do.
>
> (Morrison, *Beloved* 275)

Morrison insists "It was not a story to pass on," but she means just the opposite. The story *must* be passed on, for it is the still unfolding narrative of America and race. White women writers are part of that story, still trying to understand the parameters of whiteness with – or against – blackness. There is much more of the story to be spoken, many more ghosts to be laid to rest.

195

NOTES

INTRODUCTION

1 See Cathy Campbell, "A Battered Woman Rises" and Marilyn Kern-Foxworth, "Plantation Kitchen to American Icon: Aunt Jemima" on the history of Aunt Jemima as a brand image. The first "real" Aunt Jemima was Nancy Green, born a slave in 1834, hired by Charles Rutt, inventor of the pancake mix, to publicize it at the 1893 World Columbian Exhibition in Chicago, Illinois. The second Aunt Jemima – still the basis for the image – was Ethel Ernestine Harper, who had been a singer. Both women, as Campbell points out, were activists: "while Aunt Jemima was associated with Uncle Tom, behind the scenes Nancy Green and Ethel Ernestine Harper were cooking up antipoverty programs."

2 Margaret Ferguson's essay "Juggling the Categories of Race, Class and Gender" uses the image of juggling to illustrate the difficulties inherent in dealing with the categories of race, gender and class.

3 I should point out that the extreme polarization of white over black is a feature of the plantation classes. Poor whites and small farmers may have been aware of the "elevation" of the white woman, based on the degradation of the black, but ladyhood was the prerogative of the rich; poor white women worked in the fields as slaves did. Certainly, however, poor whites still felt a sense of *racial* superiority to blacks, a division of the lower classes along racial lines which served powerful whites long into the twentieth century.

4 I do agree with bell hooks that white women's oppression and blacks' oppression are not equivalent: "Theoretically, the white woman's legal status under patriarchy may have been that of 'property,' but she was in no way subjected to the dehumanization and brutal oppression that was the lot of the slave" (hooks 126).

5 In his magisterial *To Wake the Nations: Race and the Making of American Literature*, Eric Sundquist speaks of "the general failure of American writers to confront the nation's most pressing moral challenge. . . . Or, one should say, the failure of white writers, not of black" (29). *Or*, I should say, *male* writers, not *female*. During the nineteenth century, hundreds of women writers, not just the two mentioned by Sundquist

NOTES

(Stowe and Jacobs) confronted the "moral challenge" of race in America. I deal with a few here – there are many, many more yet to be studied.

6 My colleague Harold Weber rightly reminds me that along with these old-fashioned images, American culture now has Michael Jordan, Colin Powell, Diana Ross and Prince, and suggests that Michael Jackson is really the best-known image of a black woman in America. Of course this is true (though I think Michael Jackson represents both black and white, both male and female, in a way far too complex to sort out here). None the less, behind these black achievers, these exceptions that prove the rule, lies our assumption that most blacks conform to certain negative or positive constructions. For example, Prince can be read as a Jezebel: promiscuous and exotic. This is not to reduce all representations of blacks to stereotypes but simply to suggest that far too many of these old categories are still in operation. We have only to turn on the nightly television news to see another unexamined "bad nigger" robbing or raping or murdering. And on prime time, we get long-suffering black mothers in sitcoms or even blatant recollections of the Tragic Mulatta as in the recent mini-series *Queen*, based on material by Alex Haley.

7 See Karen Newman, "'And Wash the Ethiop White'" on representations of Africa and blackness in Renaissance England. See Jordan 30–40 on early depictions of blacks, early attitudes and reports of rampant sexual behaviour. See also Davis 461–62. Davis cites Edward Long's *History of Jamaica* (1744) where there are stories of chimpanzees carrying off black women to rape them.

8 The anarchist critic George Woodcock said in *The Incomparable Aphra*: "Mrs. Behn appears, if not strictly the first abolitionist, at least the first novelist to expose in grim and vivid detail the horrors of slavery, and thus ranks as the precursor of that succession of writers which led directly to Harriet Beecher Stowe and helped greatly hasten the abolition of slavery in England, and, eventually, in the United States" (9).

9 Ferguson follows Janet Todd in pointing out that in Behn's 1677 play *The Rover*, she turns the whore-label on itself by naming her prostitute character Angelica Bianca, bearing Behn's own initials. See Todd 1.

10 The exact dates and circumstances of Behn's visit are unclear. See Goreau 49–69, and Ferguson, "Whose Dominion" note 8.

11 *Othello* has had a difficult history in the United States. The actress Frances Kemble reports that John Quincy Adams, whom she met at a dinner in Boston, "talking to me about Desdemona, assured me with a most serious expression of sincere disgust, that he considered all her misfortunes as a just judgment upon her for having married a 'nigger'" (105). This was by no means an uncommon sentiment in America in the nineteenth century. J. Q. Adams had something of an obsession with *Othello* which led him to publish several essays on it. In the *New England Magazine* 9, 1835, he said the "great moral lesson of *Othello* is that black and white blood cannot be intermingled without a gross outrage upon the law of Nature." There were minstrel show versions of *Othello* and parodies, including "Dars de Money," "Old Fellow, or the Boor of Vengeance," and "Desdamonium." See Tilden G. Edelstein, "*Othello* in America".

197

12 See Ferguson, "Whose Dominion" 3, and Ballaster 69–113. Behn used "Caesar" as a name for Charles II in "A Farewell to Celadon on His Going into Ireland" (1684) and also as a name for James II in "Poem to Her Most Sacred Majesty Queen Mary" (1689).

13 Eroticism, orientalism and the Caribbean were associated well before Behn wrote. Ligon describes a black belle in suggestive detail, up to her eyes, "the largest and most orientall that I have ever seen" (12).

14 One of the first things the narrator tells us about Surinam is the variety of curious or desirable goods that come from there, such as parrots, a snake skin for "His Majesty's antiquary's," and feathers. See *Oroonoko* 28. And see Laura Brown "The Romance of Empire" 47–55; her essay aims, she says "to demonstrate the contemporaneity of issues of race and gender in a particular stage in the history of British capitalism associated broadly with commodity exchange and colonialist exploitation" (47).

15 This is not to say that white women did not sleep with black men. Indeed, Ferguson points out how David Brion Davis, in *The Problem of Slavery in Western Culture*, says that at one point Maryland actually reversed the common law doctrine of *partus sequitur ventrum*, where children follow the condition of the mother, so that white women would cease sleeping with black men (96–97). See Ferguson, "Whose Dominion" 5–6. Generally, though, because the child follows the condition of the mother, a slave woman having a child by a white man had far fewer social consequences than the other way around; the child was, after all, a commodity, a slave. Free blacks were tolerated in parts of the South, especially before the 1830s, as well as in the Caribbean, but not encouraged. And the social consequences for a white woman who slept with a black man were far greater than for a white man who slept with a black woman.

16 The term "lynching" does not refer only to hanging but to any vigilante murder. Many times in the killings of blacks by whites in the South, hanging was almost an afterthought to the burning, mutilation and other tortures.

17 Lynching almost always had a sexual aspect: even if the black man in question did not commit rape, the focus of mob violence was often on his genitals. See Trudier Harris, *Exorcising Blackness*; James R. McGovern, *Anatomy of a Lynching*; Neil R. McMillen, *Dark Journey*; Joel Williamson, *The Crucible of Race*.

18 See Toni Morrison, *Race-ing Justice*.

1 *UNCLE TOM'S CABIN*: AN AUTHENTIC GHOST STORY

1 I am indebted to Bruce Boehrer for pointing out that 16th- and 17th-century legal documents used the term *famulus* for "servant." This sense of "family" survived in the slave South. Plantation owners and plantation mistresses in particular were encouraged to think of their households and slaves as so many children. In the Southern ideology, the mistress was seen as "mother" to all. See Fox-Genovese 24–27; Thomas Nelson Page, *The Old Dominion*; Margaret Mitchell, *Gone With*

the Wind; Frances Ann Kemble, *Journal of a Residence*, chs 4 and 5. Even some Southern women viewed this "Old Testament" model with some scepticism and anger over the sexual availability of female slaves to white masters. Mary Boykin Chesnut quotes an acquaintance: "Mr. Harris said it was so patriarchal. So it is – flocks and herd and slaves – and wife Leah does not suffice. Rachel must be *added*, if not *married*. And all the time they seem to think themselves patterns – models of husbands and fathers" (Woodward 31).

2 Spillers' essay challenges the idea that it is somehow harmful for black culture to be a "matriarchy" as defined in Daniel Patrick Moynihan's famous 1965 report. Fatherlessness is the legacy of slavery, a legacy which has contributed to a kind of empowerment for black women who are *"out* of the traditional symbolics of female gender" (Spillers, "Mama's Baby" 80).

3 See John Pendleton Kennedy, *Swallow Barn* (1832); Caroline Gilman, *Recollections of a Southern Matron* (1838); William Gilmore Simms, *Woodcraft* (1854), *The Yemassee* (1835), *Katherine Walton* (1851); Richard Hildreth, *The Slave* (1836); J. H. Ingraham, *The Quadroone* (1840); Lydia Maria Child (see Chapter 5), "The Octoroons" (1847); Harriet Martineau (see Chapter 3), "Demerara," in *Illustrations of Political Economy* (1832–34); and Frances Trollope (See Chapter 3), *The Life and Adventures of Jonathan Jefferson Whitlaw* (1836). See also the slave narratives of Mary Prince, Harriet Jacobs, Olaudah Equiano etc.; Harriet E. Wilson, *Our Nig* (1859); and Frederick Douglass, *Narrative of the Life* (1845). See especially C. Peter Ripley ed., *The Black Abolitionist Papers*, vols I–V on challenges to Stowe's "invention" of blacks. Ripley's extraordinary series covers Britain, Canada and the United States from 1830 to 1865 and contains a wealth of information on the dynamic role played by blacks in their struggle to liberate themselves. Often we have the impression that Harriet Jacobs and Frederick Douglass were exceptions in a white-run movement. Ripley's work corrects this, and Henry Louis Gates' article, "From Wheatley to Douglass: The Politics of Displacement" shows that blacks were writing prolifically in both the eighteenth and nineteenth centuries. Gates suggests that James Williams' "Narrative," serialized in 1838 in *The Anti-Slavery Examiner* and later shown to be a complete "fabrication," was, in fact, the "first negro novel" (59).

4 A number of critics have discussed Stowe's South as gothic, though without making the claims for the significance of this that I will make. See Fiedler, *Love and Death in the American Novel* 262–65; Gilbert and Gubar 533ff.; Karen Halttunen, "Gothic Imagination and Social Reform"; Hortense Spillers, "Changing the Letter." See also Kari Winter, *Subjects of Slavery, Agents of Change*; Winter says the gothic and slave narratives "focus on the sexual politics at the heart of patriarchal culture, and both represent the terrifying aspects of life for women in a patriarchal culture" (13). Sundquist also discusses the gothic in *Uncle Tom's Cabin* and in Frederick Douglass' *My Bondage* (*To Wake the Nations* 108–09).

5 See Louis Montrose, "The Work of Gender in the Discourse of Discovery"; 10–25. There are many early modern narratives which

represent the "New World" as feminine: see Ralegh's *Discoverie of the Large, Rich, and Beautiful Empire of Guiana* (1596), Robert Johnson's *Nova Britannia* (1609) and Arthur Barlowe's "The First Voyage Made to the Coasts of America" (1584).

6 Stowe was not the first to use these themes in abolitionist fiction; indeed, she may have been influenced by Frances Trollope's *The Life and Adventures of Jonathan Jefferson Whitlaw* (1836). Trollope's novel features a villainous overseer, so like Simon Legree he could be a close relative; a mulatta woman of occult power who wants revenge on Whitlaw, the overseer; and a young mulatta girl Whitlaw threatens with rape. There is no direct evidence that Stowe read Trollope's novel. Various critics have dismissed the idea of influence, pointing out that there was no American edition, though Charles Foster, in *The Rungless Ladder*, says *Uncle Tom's Cabin* was influenced by *Jonathan Jefferson Whitlaw* (13). However, such a book-loving (and politically-minded) family as the Beechers might have had access to a British edition. Frances Trollope was a very well-known writer in America: she was notorious for her 1832 *Domestic Manners of the Americans*. See Kirkham 78–79.

7 For discussions of Calvinism in Stowe's work, see: Edward Wagenknecht, *Harriet Beecher Stowe*; Jeanne Boydston, Mary Kelley and Anne Margolis, eds, *The Limits of Sisterhood*; Gayle Kimball, *The Religious Ideas of Harriet Beecher Stowe*; Charles Foster, *The Rungless Ladder*.

8 See Gillian Brown, "Getting in the Kitchen with Dinah." Brown's thesis that Stowe's strategy for reform involves women's renunciation of desire and restoration of the domestic centre follows Elizabeth Ammons and others. See also Jane Tompkins' "Sentimental Power: *Uncle Tom's Cabin* and the Politics of Literary History" in her book *Sensational Designs* 122–46. Spillers, in her essay "Changing the Letter," disagrees.

9 The origins of the "Oriental Tale" in English actually go back to mediaeval times, but its modern incarnation dates from the appearance of *The Arabian Nights* in English in 1705. There was a great fashion for oriental tales in the eighteenth and nineteenth century, many of which were extremely popular in the United States, including Johnson's *Rasselas* (1759), Beckford's *Vathek* (1781), De Quincey's *Confessions of an English Opium Eater* (1822) and Irving's *Legends of the Alhambra* (1832). Byron's orientalist poems *Don Juan* (1819–24), *The Giaour* (1813) and *The Bride of Abydos* (1813) were scandalously celebrated in the states, both North and South, and Thomas Moore's *Lalla Rookh* (1817) remained popular in the South until the turn of the century.

10 This paradox was not lost on anti-*Uncle Tom* reviewers like Louisa S. McCord who pointed out that, by Stowe's logic, slavery must be benign because it produced such an angelic being. See Chapter 2.

11 See entries in Weld, *American Slavery As It Is* by Nehemiah Caulkens (16), Sarah Grimké (23), Angelina Grimké (53), "Testimony of Messrs. T. D. M. and F. C. May" (107) and Hiram White (51).

12 See Woodward 168. Chesnut makes a number of outraged or sardonic comments on slaveholders' use of female slaves as a harem. As do Sarah Gayle Gorgas (see Fox-Genovese 9), Ella Gertrude Clanton Thomas (see Burr 168) and a number of other Southern slaveholding

women. Like many women of her class, Chesnut blames white men
and black women ("beastly Negress beauties") equally.

13 *Lalla Rookh* lasted as a theatrical subject at least until the 1870s when
even such a morally-upright authoress as Augusta Jane Evans staged
it starring young members of Mobile society (see William Perry Fidler
163). I am indebted to George Starbuck for the suggestion that these
slaveholding ladies were sending their husbands a sexually and
morally radical message in their play-acting.

14 Joy S. Kasson's "Narratives of the Female Body" discusses *The Greek
Slave* as an "orientalist" work and a focus for national anxieties over
sexuality, women's subjugation and the body.

15 Frederick Law Olmsted's two-volume *The Cotton Kingdom* and, to a
lesser extent, William H. Russell's *My Diary North and South* are good
sources on New Orleans' own "peculiar institution" of *plaçage*. While
white men kept mulatta mistresses on their plantations and in other
towns and cities in the South, it was in New Orleans that the practice
was virtually codified and given its own vocabulary and manners. See
Olmsted I 300ff. for a thorough description of *plaçage*.

16 Philip Fisher locates radicalism in Stowe's use of the sentimental, a
move which raises the traditionally powerless – the child, the slave –
to an importance which challenges the hegemony of the state. When
Sundquist in *To Wake the Nations* calls Little Eva "saccharine," he misses
the point. See "Making a Thing into a Man" (Fisher 87–127), and Jane
Tompkins, "Sentimental Power" – she argues most forcefully for the
grandeur and importance of Eva and Tom's story.

17 Lydia Maria Child wrote to Esther Carpenter (20 March 1838) about
how pro-slavery agitators and those loudly disapproving of women
speaking in public called Angelina Grimké "Devilina" and "Miss
Grimalkin," underscoring the gothic. See Lydia Maria Child, *Selected
Letters* 71.

18 *The Slave* is a very strange novel; it makes much of the threat to the slave
Cassy from her lustful white father/master while ignoring the fact that
Cassy marries, and has children by, her half-brother Archy.

19 It is worth noting that Marie St Clare is commodified in a similar way;
Augustine "became the husband of a fine figure, a pair of bright dark
eyes, and a hundred thousand dollars" (*Uncle Tom's Cabin* 240). Slavery
does not degrade only black women. Indeed, the balkanization of
heroines is standard in fiction. Perhaps Stowe was making a point
about patriarchy as well.

20 See Jeanne Boydston, Mary Kelley and Anne Margolis, eds, *The Limits
of Sisterhood* on Isabella Beecher's radicalism. See Jane Tompkins,
"Sentimental Power" 141–46; Elizabeth Ammons, "Stowe's Dream of
the Mother–Savior"; and Elizabeth Ammons, "Heroines in *Uncle Tom's
Cabin*" on the maternal in Stowe's novel.

21 Jean Fagan Yellin, in "Doing It Herself," intriguingly suggests that
Little Evangeline is a version of Angelina Grimké, noting the closeness
of their names and similar childhood horror of slavery.

22 At the beginning of her article "Mama's Baby," Hortense Spillers says
"Let's face it. I am a marked woman." Spillers goes on to discuss her
"marked" status as black and as female.

23 The connection with Charlotte Brontë's *Jane Eyre* is interesting. Bertha Mason is a West Indian, a "Creole," and, though Brontë does not explore this possibility, might be, like Cora Munro, part black. Her rage destroys her in *Jane Eyre*; in *Uncle Tom's Cabin*, Cassy's rage is what keeps her alive.

24 See Kate Ferguson Ellis, *The Contested Castle*, on how the gothic transforms domestic spaces into "haunted houses."

25 See James Baldwin, "Everybody's Protest Novel" (1949) in *Notes of a Native Son* 13–23; Tompkins 134–41; Fisher 91ff.; Elizabeth Ammons, "Heroines" 152 ff; Leslie Fiedler, *Love and Death* 262ff.; Yarborough 55; and Elizabeth Ammons, "Stowe's Dream."

26 In *Northanger Abbey* Jane Austen both parodies and employs gothic discourse. Catherine Moreland is not in danger of ghosts or demons at the abbey, or even in danger of a wife-murderer. But General Moreland *is* a spiteful old snob who endangers Catherine by turning her out of his home, forcing her to make a journey home alone. Austen's point is that there are real dangers to women enough in the world without constructing supernatural ones.

2 "INSTIGATED BY THE DEVIL:" THE SOUTH AND HARRIET BEECHER STOWE

1 See C. Peter Ripley, ed., *The Black Abolitionist Papers* on the vastness of the debate in the US, Canada and Britain, 1830–1865.

2 For a comprehensive list of anti-*Tom* novels, see Gossett 185ff. and 430ff., and Jane Gardiner, "The Assault on Uncle Tom." Elizabeth Moss, in *Domestic Novelists in the Old South*, lists some of the ways important pro-Southern women writers like Caroline Gilman, Caroline Lee Hentz and Maria McIntosh respond to *Uncle Tom's Cabin*, though almost entirely without analysis of their work. Moss' naive treatment continually refers to *Uncle Tom's Cabin* as a "diatribe" and seems to regard slavery as a neutral, almost arbitrary, dividing issue. For example, she says "unlike these Southern writers [Hentz, Gilman, McIntosh etc.], Stowe did not struggle to keep an open mind when it came to political controversy; neither did she attempt to moderate her partisanship" (106). Moss almost begins to sound like her Southern apologists when she dismisses Stowe's account of slavery on the grounds of Stowe's unfamiliarity with the South and its defining institution. A thorough and thoughtful study of antebellum Southern women novelists remains to be written.

3 See Burr 169; Fox-Genovese 359–63.

4 Stowe's attackers did not read *Uncle Tom's Cabin* as an oriental fiction, despite her obvious borrowings from and references to the genre. The gothic was what they fixed on to refute. Perhaps an orientalized South was not, to them, such an ideological threat; after all, elite Southerners themselves participated in orientalizing their culture, play-acting *Lalla Rookh* and cultivating an upper class of women who made indolence and leisure a positive virtue.

5 Novels and magazines played a part in producing the ideology of the

slave South throughout the 1830s, 1840s, and 1850s. Fiction by the New England-born Caroline Gilman (*Recollections of a Southern Matron*, 1838), Caroline Lee Hentz, Maria McIntosh, William Gilmore Simms (and the whole plantation school) displayed the sunniest aspects of slavery, though some also brought out conflicting views of women's roles. Articles in Gilman's *Southern Rose* advocated education for women (22 December 1838) and opportunities for a career (4 March 1837). Yet as early as 1835, Gilman felt she had to defend Southern slavery from Northern calumny. In her editorial for 31 October 1835, two fictional girls debate Catharine Sedgwick's novel, *The Linwoods*, in which a slave longs for freedom. One girl, "Medora," says "We will show them [Northern writers] happy black faces enough, particularly on plantations, to modify their views; but we will not be satisfied with a *traveller's glance*... [or with] ladies who sit at home with a fair sheet of paper and write only of what they feel" (quoted in Jan Bakker, 15).

6 Progressive political positions continue to be linked with sexual transgression. Communism in twentieth-century America was condemned not only as "godless" but as a promoter of "free love." Recent issues involving the pro-choice movement are accused of propagating "promiscuity" by their fundamentalist opponents. And proponents of lifting the ban on homosexuals in the military are charged with wanting barracks overrun with lust-filled queens and paedophiles. One gets the uncomfortable feeling that many political debates in America are really about sex.

7 See Chapter 3.

8 The story of Eliza and George's escape in disguise is a good example of the way categories are violated. Eliza dresses as a young man and her son Harry as a little girl. They are not only cross-dressed but "passing" as white. This episode in *Uncle Tom's Cabin* was probably based partly on William and Ellen Craft's escape from slavery in which Ellen dressed as a white man and William became her black "boy." Garber points out that Ellen herself violated accepted categories: she was so light in colour that it annoyed her white owners and they gave her away as a wedding present. See Garber 282, and Ripley IV 36–37.

9 See George F. Holmes in the *Southern Literary Messenger*, 18 October 1852, 630–38; William Gilmore Simms, Review of *Uncle Tom's Cabin* 214–54; Maria McIntosh, *Letter on the Address of the Women of England*; Louisa S. McCord, Review of *Uncle Tom's Cabin*; see also Gossett and Gardiner on pro-slavery reactions to Stowe.

10 One review of Stowe's second novel, *Dred*, by "A Young Lady of New England" in *The Southern Literary Messenger*, 27 October 1858, ends "Were she a woman, we should blush for the sex – luckily she is only a Beecher."

11 Subverting the subversive, *Uncle Tom's Cabin* became a popular nineteenth-century minstrel show sometimes acted entirely by men. A number of minstrel shows lampooned feminism and abolitionism as well, focusing on women wearing bloomers or trousers. Of course, these were often men playing women dressing like men and white men

playing blacks playing whites. Garber points out that minstrel shows both "quoted" and "erased" "black" and "woman" (277).

12 Underlining Stowe's scandalous connection to blackness, the *Charleston Courier* in 1852 reported a rumour that Stowe was to be godmother to the infant "black prince of Haiti" (Hirsch 305).

13 *The Devil in America* (1859) is the title of a compendium of dangers besetting America (including also women's rights, spiritualism and mesmerism). Satan strives to "blacken" every heart so as to "negrify" the nation. For a fascinating discussion of this see Shirley Samuels, "The Identity of Slavery".

14 But Southern women did read *Uncle Tom's Cabin*, some of them, like Mary Chesnut, almost obsessively, over and over. There are at least twenty references to Stowe in her diary – many of them reflective, astute and not particularly bombastic. For example, she remarks that "Mrs. Stowe did not hit the sorest spot. She makes Legree a bachelor" (Woodward 168). In other places, Chesnut is more critical, accusing Stowe of romanticizing slaves and revelling in the subject of white men's mulatta concubines: "It is not a nice topic" (ibid. 307). Yet as the war wore on, she kept up a sort of dialogue with the novel: "tried to read *Uncle Tom*. Could not. Too sickening. A man send his little son to beat a human being tied to a tree? It is bad as Squeers beating Smike in the hack. Flesh and blood revolts" (ibid. 381). See Fox-Genovese 359–60 on Chesnut and Stowe. See also Ella Clanton Thomas, who read Stowe with great attention (*Secret Eye* 169).

15 True to her conservative ideas of "woman's sphere," McCord signed her numerous articles only with "L.S.M.," suppressing her name and her gender, revealing discomfort with authorship and women's "intrusion" into the public arena.

16 Several anti-*Tom* novels attack abolitionism by writing about the dreadful conditions of workers in Great Britain, responding to the enormous popularity of *Uncle Tom* and the prevalence of Anti-Slavery societies there. See especially 'Dr Pleasant Jones,' *The Slaveholder Abroad, or Billy Buck's Visit, With His Master, To England* (Philadelphia 1860) and Lucien B. Chase, *English Serfdom and American Slavery, or Ourselves as Others See Us* (New York, 1854). The latter, an attack on the rigidities of the British class system, argues that abolitionism is a British plot to destroy American democracy.

17 See Annette Kolodny, *The Lay of the Land*. The Civil War was figured as a rape in much Southern writing as well; see my study *Faulkner and Southern Womanhood* Chapter 5; Kathryn Lee Seidel, *The Southern Belle in the American Novel* Chapters 2 and 11.

18 See sympathetic "Tragic Mulatta" or "Tragic Octoroon" fiction such as James Fenimore Cooper's *The Last of the Mohicans* (1826), William Wells Brown's *Clotel* (1853), J. H. Ingraham's *The Quadroone* (1840), Dion Boucicault's *The Octoroon* (1859), Albion Tourgee's *Toinette* (1874), Charles Chesnutt's *The House Behind the Cedars* (1900), Lydia Maria Child's "The Quadroons" (1842), William Faulkner's *Go Down, Moses* (1942) and Robert Penn Warren's *Band of Angels* (1955).

19 Crissy appears to be a response to Stowe's Eliza: both are attractive and

intelligent mulattas who escape via dramatic scenes on the Ohio River. See *Northern Bride* II 82.

20 In addition to novels discussed, see also J. Thornton Randolph, *The Cabin and the Parlor;* Mrs Henry R. Schoolcraft, *The Black Gauntlet;* Mrs G. M. Flanders, *The Ebony Idol* (New York, 1860); Robert Criswell, *"Uncle Tom's Cabin" Contrasted With Buckingham Hall;* Caroline Lee Hentz, *Marcus Warland;* W. L. G. Smith, *Uncle Tom's Cabin As It Is;* "Xariffa" (Mary Ashley Towsend), *The Brother Clerks;* Martha Haines Butt, *Antifanaticism: A Tale of the South* (Philadelphia, 1853); J. H. Ingraham, *The Sunny South* (Philadelphia, 1860); Maria J. McIntosh, *The Lofty and the Lowly* (New York, 1853).

21 Mary Chesnut concurs: "These negro women have a chance here women have nowhere else. They can redeem themselves. The 'impropers'. They can marry decently – and nothing is remembered against them, these colored ladies" (Woodward 307).

22 The plantation as Garden of Eden remained a strong theme in Reconstruction fiction by such Old South mythologizers as Thomas Nelson Page, Marion Harland, Joel Chandler Harris and Thomas Dixon, Jr. By the time modernism hit the South, writers like William Faulkner, Ellen Glasgow, Allen Tate and others revised (though they never quite eradicated) the paradisal plantation. Slavery became original sin. See Glasgow's *Barren Ground* (1925), Tate's *The Fathers* (1938) and Faulkner's *Absalom, Absalom!* (1936), *The Unvanquished* (1938) and *Go Down, Moses* (1942).

23 This is also a common motif: slaves who are kidnapped by abolitionists, seduced into running away or freed generally come back to the plantation begging to be re-enslaved. Perhaps the most extreme example is found in Simms' *The Sword and the Distaff* (his response to Stowe) where *his* Tom, slave to the ridiculous Captain Porgy, is so devoted to his master that he almost goes along with Captain Porgy's rather Egyptian idea of a suicide pact. Porgy insists when he dies Tom should be buried with him (203–04). See also W. L. G. Smith 19ff., and "Xariffa" (Mary Ashley Towsend) 163.

24 Along with "Cassy" and "Eliza," "Cora" is a popular name for mulatta characters. The first Tragic Mulatta in American literature, Cora in *The Last of the Mohicans,* may have inspired her successors. William Wells Brown's lost sister is called Cora, as is Harry's sister in Stowe's second slavery novel, *Dred* (1856).

3 MISS WRIGHT, MRS TROLLOPE AND MISS MARTINEAU: OR, THREE BRITISH WOMEN LOOK AT AMERICAN SLAVERY

1 See Sacvan Berkovitch, *American Jeremiad;* Cathy N. Davidson, *Revolution and the Word;* Jane Tompkins, *Sensational Designs;* Leslie Fiedler, *Love and Death in the American Novel;* Toni Morrison, *Playing in the Dark;* and Eric J. Sundquist, *To Wake the Nations.*

2 See C. Peter Ripley, ed., *The Black Abolitionist Papers,* I: *The British Isles, 1830–1865.*

NOTES

3 See *Orientalism* 22ff. on representations of the Orient, 162ff. on writing about the Orient.
4 Some Victorian Britons seemed as obsessed with blacks and blackness as Americans. Diarist Arthur Munby sometimes had his white maid (later his wife) Hannah Cullwick blacken her skin and wear a headrag like a slave. In *her* diary, she records him sitting on her lap and "nursing" like a baby with his mammy – she also called him "massa." See Leonore Davidoff, "Class and Gender in Victorian England"; and Stallybrass and White, 155–56.
5 Of course, there was a vast corpus of British anti-slavery writing, dating from the 17th century when Quakers like Alice Curwen protested the treatment of Africans in the American and West Indian colonies; see Ferguson, *Subject to Others* 56ff. But abolitionist attention really began to focus on the United States after Britain could tell itself slavery had been "solved" in its own lands.
6 See Celia Morris Eckhardt, *Frances Wright*; and A. J. G. Perkins, *Frances Wright*.
7 Frances Wright was also called, in the popular press, "the Whore of Babylon." See Clinton 65–67.
8 See Eckhardt, chapters 10 and 11 on Wright's marriage (in 1831) to her lover Phiquepal d'Arusmont, her divorce, and her bitter return to America and estrangements from friends and family.
9 See Rose O'Neal Greenhow, *My Imprisonment and the First Year of Abolition Rule at Washington* (London, 1863) 7; Virginia Clay-Clopton, *A Belle of the Fifties* (New York, 1904) 171; and Woodward 419.
10 For what it's worth, there was (and is) a story that Thomas Jefferson fathered children on his wife's slave, Sally Hemings. This was the subject of a novel, *Clotel, or, the President's Daughter* (1853) by William Wells Brown, a refugee slave. It is probable that Trollope heard it, underlining the irony of her anti-hero's name: Frances Wright was aware of it. See Eckhardt 84.
11 Some American novelists of the 1830s saw the South as a home of disordered passions, filled with brooding, angry gothic types. In Catharine Sedgwick's 1835 novel *Home*, a little boy struggling with his violent temper is exhorted not to be like the ungovernable whites of the slave South.
12 It is worth noting that, for Donne as well, his "America's" sexuality is somewhat oriental: the mistress brings with her "a heaven like Mahomet's paradise."
13 See James Fenimore Cooper, *The Last of the Mohicans* (1826); Lydia Maria Child, "The Quadroons" (1842); Charles Chesnutt, *The House Behind the Cedars* (1900); and Robert Penn Warren, *Band of Angels* (1955). Cora, Rosalie, Rena and Amantha are all mixed-race women whose central crises have to do with the (usually tragic) coming to terms with the fact of their "blackness" in a white America. I include novels across such a broad spectrum of time (there are plenty of others) to show the persistence of the mulatta as a fictional type.
14 Martineau took a dim view of Frances Trollope, saying she "had thought proper to libel and slander a whole nation." She found Frederica Bremer tiresome and called Frances Kemble "vexatious."

Excessive behaviour on the part of abolitionist women could, she thought, bring the whole movement into disrepute. See her *Autobiography* I 317–18, 364–65, 400, 427.

15 "Drivers" were slaves given authority to oversee field work. They were often accorded extra privileges and were depicted in abolitionist writing as identifying with the power of their white masters. Simon Legree's two drivers, Quimbo and Sambo, are particularly vicious. Fanny Kemble also writes of some abusive drivers in her *Journal of a Residence on a Georgian Plantation*.

16 See Harriet Jacobs, *Incidents in the Life of a Slave Girl*.

4 THE STRANGE CAREER OF FANNY KEMBLE

1 Abolition circles were tight in the 1830s: some of Kemble's opinions of slavery may well have been informed by talking with Harriet Martineau in Philadelphia during Martineau's 1835 visit. Kemble was enthusiastic about Martineau but the feeling was not mutual. Martineau disapproved of Kemble's American *Journal* and of Kemble's flamboyance:

> I really strove hard to like and approve her; and I imposed on myself for a time ... the belief that I did so: but I could not carry it on long. There was so radical an unreality about her and her sayings and doings and so perverse a sporting with her possessions and privileges in life, and with other people's peace, that my interest in her died out completely in a way which could not have happened if I could have believed her notorious misfortunes to have been other than self-inflicted.
>
> (*Autobiography* I 365)

2 Two burlesques of Kemble's American *Journal* were published within a year of its appearance, *Fanny Kemble in America* and *My Conscience!*. See Wister, 146.

3 There were a few aristocratic abolitionists, most notably the Duchess of Sutherland, who entertained Harriet Beecher Stowe on her visit to Britain. Other upper-class members of the British and Foreign Anti-Slavery Society included Lady Byron and the Earl of Shaftesbury. See Ripley, vol. I.

4 See Kemble's response to *The Times* review of *Uncle Tom's Cabin* in the Appendix to the *Journal* 347–68; and W. E. Gladstone's speech at Newcastle, 7 October 1862, reported in *The Times*, 9 October 1862.

5 See Katheryn Lee Seidel, *The Southern Belle in the American Novel*; Wilbur J. Cash, *The Mind of the South*; Bertram Wyatt-Brown, *Southern Honor*; Goodwyn Jones, *Tomorrow is Another Day*; Diane Roberts, *Faulkner and Southern Womanhood*; Elizabeth Fox-Genovese, *Within the Plantation Household*; Clinton, *The Plantation Mistress*.

6 Elizabeth Fox-Genovese says that the "passionlessness" for women prevalent in the North, which Nancy Cott has written about, was not necessarily in force for Southern women. In the South, she says, white female sexuality was acknowledged, especially by women, who

express much concern over its regulation. Clearly there was anxiety over the possibility of white ladies *degenerating* into black women. Fox-Genovese deals mainly with expressions of sexuality in a private sphere – I am concerned here with the cultural construction of a *social image* around which plantation ideology and much of the pro-slavery argument was erected. See *Within the Plantation Household*, 235–41.

7 See Kemble's *Journal* 88 and 271 on plantation clothing allowances for slaves.

8 The first edition of the Georgia *Journal* omitted chapters 2 and 3. They were originally written to Harriet St Leger from Georgia in January 1839 and originally appeared in *Records of a Later Life* I 170–218.

9 What Kemble calls the "low Irish" throughout the *Journal* occupy, for her, something of the same place as blacks for Southern whites, even though she is far more analytical about *why* she dislikes them and why they "smell." Curiously enough, the Kemble family was, several generations back, from Ireland.

10 See Chapter 2 on the pro-slavery and plantation novels which "answered" Harriet Beecher Stowe's *Uncle Tom's Cabin*, trying to wrest the moral high ground away from the abolitionists. There were plantation novels from the 1830s, however, beginning with John Pendleton Kennedy's *Swallow Barn* (1832). See also Caroline Gilman, *Recollections of a Southern Matron* (1838).

11 Books, pamphlets, literacy itself were central to the abolitionist project. As Shirley Samuels shows, children were exhorted by such juvenile organs as the *Slave's Friend* to save their money to buy books and pamphlets to spread the anti-slavery message ("The Identity of Slavery" 164).

12 See Una Pope-Hennessy, *Three Englishwomen in America*; Fanny Kemble Wister, ed., *Fanny, the American Kemble*; Margaret Armstrong, *Fanny Kemble, a Passionate Victorian* (New York, 1938), esp. chs 21–23; Henrietta Buckmaster, *Fire in the Heart* (New York, 1948). For an assessment of the relative accuracy and usefulness of these biographies, see Kemble 409–10.

13 Pierce Butler's attempt to regulate his unruly, independent, abolitionist wife included a "contract" she had to follow in order to see her children. Butler demanded that she not speak to or correspond with her friends the (abolitionist) Sedgwicks, she was not to allude to the past and she was not to speak of or to Butler himself. Meanwhile, Butler was apparently carrying on a rather public affair with a married woman. See Wister, 189–92.

14 Sarah (b. 1835) and Frances Butler saw little of their mother from the mid-1840s, when their parents' marriage exploded, until they were of legal age. After that, Sarah maintained a constant relationship and Fan a more difficult one, as she had adored her father. Still, I am reminded by a reader, Fan and her mother lived together for a while and visited back and forth after Fan's marriage to Canon Leigh – they must have effected a truce.

5 *OLLA PODRIDA* AMERICA: LYDIA MARIA CHILD AND RADICAL MISCEGENATION

1 Yellin points out that Child was too radical too soon: see her *Women and Sisters* 192, note 3. Carolyn Karcher says:

> the American public of the 1830s simply would not tolerate controversy over slavery. The economic prosperity of the nation rested on the partnership between southern cotton planters and northern textile manufacturers, merchants and financiers. These elites governed public opinion, and in the years following the publication of Child's *Appeal*, they used every means at their disposal. . . mob attacks against abolitionist lecturers and editors, the destruction of antislavery presses, censorship of the mails to prevent dissemination of antislavery literature, and even a 'gag' law stipulating that antislavery petitions submitted to Congress be tabled without discussion.
>
> ("Rape, Murder and Revenge" 325).

2 Child does have several stories, including "The Quadroons" and "Slavery's Pleasant Homes," in which mulattas meet tragic ends. Indeed, Susan Koppelman, Jean Fagan Yellin and Carolyn Karcher credit Child with introducing "into American literature the archetype of the 'tragic quadroon,'" via her *Juvenile Miscellany* in the 1830 "St. Domingo Orphans" (*Hobomok* xiv). This depends on how strictly the character is defined. James Fenimore Cooper's Cora Munro in *The Last of the Mohicans* (1826) has a claim to being the first Tragic Mulatta in American literature as well: her mixed blood dooms her to death instead of an appropriate marriage. Certainly by 1840, tragic mulattas were everywhere, including in British novels such as Frances Trollope's *Jonathan Jefferson Whitlaw* and J. H. Ingraham's *The Quadroone*.

3 In Ligon's *History of Barbados* (1657), he variously refers to *olio podrido*, an element in beef recipes, and *ollo podrido*, a stew. *Olla podrida* literally means "rotten pot."

4 Child refers to the difference between slave state law and English Common Law with its democratic (though rather patriarchal) bent in *An Appeal in Favor* 39–40. King Alfred is credited in folklore as being the establisher of Common Law.

5 See Karcher's introduction to *Hobomok* as well as her "Lydia Maria Child's *A Romance of the Republic*," and "Rape, Murder and Revenge." Karcher has done more – and better – work on Lydia Maria Child than anyone else. I am indebted to her research throughout this chapter.

6 See Karen Sanchez-Eppler's fine article, "Bodily Bonds," in which she argues that "the social and political goals of both feminism and abolition depend upon an act of representation"(29). The identifications made between women and slaves in radical texts, she says, tend toward exploitation of the slave.

7 *Hobomok* seems to have been inspired by at least a review of (and possibly the thing itself) *Yamoyden*, a narrative poem by James Wallis Eastburn and Robert Sands about the wars of "King Philip" (the

Wampanoag sachem Metacom) sympathetic to the Indians. See Karcher's Introduction to *Hobomok* (xvii).

8 There is a modern statue of Roger Conant, an historical founder of Salem, Massachusetts, in front of the Salem Witch Museum.

9 See Karcher's Introduction to *Hobomok* (xviii): she shows how Child also uses *Othello*.

10 "The Quadroons" was originally published in the abolitionist magazine, the *Liberty Bell*, 3, 1842, 115–41. "Slavery's Pleasant Homes" appeared in the *Liberty Bell*, 4, 1843, 147–60.

11 Child was involved in the editing, writing and production of many gift books, most notably *The Oasis* (1834) and the *Liberty Bell* (1839–58). Her earliest anti-slavery stories were published in the *Juvenile Miscellany* (September 1830) and the *Liberator* (beginning in 1831). See Ralph Thompson, "The *Liberty Bell* and Other Anti-Slavery Gift-Books."

12 Kingsley's novel has a mulatta character, an actress, who goes by the name of La Cordifiamma. She may well have influenced Child's portrayal of Rosabella as La Señorita Campaneo, the opera star, in *A Romance of the Republic*.

13 Harriet Jacobs had, at first, considered letting Harriet Beecher Stowe "use" her story. She had wanted her daughter Louisa to accompany Stowe on a trip to England in 1853 in order to interest Stowe in her story and to benefit Louisa. Stowe rather rudely (to Jacobs) declined. In 1859, she met Lydia Maria Child through abolitionist mutual friends (Jacobs, along with her brother John S. Jacobs, was active in anti-slavery circles in Rochester, New York) and Child agreed to provide a preface for the book. For a full account of the genesis of *Incidents* and its authentication, see Jean Fagan Yellin, "Texts and Contexts."

14 The ex-slave Isabella Van Wagener renamed herself Sojourner Truth in 1843. In 1851 she spoke at the Akron Women's Rights Convention and delivered her famous speech on the plight of women in slavery. At the end of the speech, she displayed her muscular arm while still demanding "Arn't I a woman?," thus complicating American culture's insistence that women are physically inferior. See Yellin's chapter on Sojourner Truth in *Women and Sisters* 77–96.

15 J. H. Ingraham's *The Quadroone* (1840) also has an interracial baby-switch.

16 Incest is used in miscegenation fiction on both political sides: in Richard Hildreth's *The Slave*, a slaveholding father threatens to rape his own daughter, refusing to acknowledge her as his. But in Thomas Dixon, Jr's *The Sins of the Father*, incest is used as a weapon by an evil mulatta. Faulkner's *Absalom, Absalom!* and *Go Down, Moses* both use incest as an emblem of the tragedy and "curse" of slavery.

6 JEMIMA AND JEZEBEL IN THE NEW SOUTH: TWENTIETH-CENTURY WOMEN ON RACE

1 See Williamson, *Crucible* 111–326 on the South after the Civil War and the "rape complex" (as Wilbur J. Cash called it) which drove much of Southern politics. See also Kathleen M. Blee, *Women of the Klan*; James

F. Davis, *Who Is Black?*; Jacquelyn Dowd Hall, *Revolt Against Chivalry*; Neil R. McMillen, *Dark Journey*.

2 See C. Vann Woodward, *The Strange Career of Jim Crow* (New York, 1955); Trudier Harris, *Exorcising Blackness*; and Neil McMillen, *Dark Journey*.

3 I do not, of course, claim to be comprehensive in this brief survey of the ideological work of fiction and the importance of representations. There were an enormous number of (white) writers from 1870 to 1920 who refought the Civil War, reinvented the Old South and healed the political and racial rifts of the nation in their novels. Thomas Nelson Page, for example, wrote romances of the Old Plantation where ex-slaves refused to abandon "Ole Miss" and Yankee officers married Virginia belles, uniting the country in a political marriage which, while it destroyed slavery, converted the country to the Southern point of view. Marion Harland, E. D. E. N. Southworth, Francis Hopkinson Smith, Mark Twain, George Washington Cable, James Branch Cabell, J. W. De Forest, Thomas Dixon, Jr and Albion Tourgee contributed to the inventory of Southern stories. Some black writers, such as Charles Chesnutt and Frances E. W. Harper also made fiction which engaged the legacy of slavery and the racial divide of the nation.

4 My use of the term "radical" comes from Joel Williamson's fine examination of American race relations after the Civil War, *The Crucible of Race*. Radical Racists were those who believed that blacks were essentially savages, that miscegenation would destroy the "Anglo-Saxon race" which rightfully ruled America, and that the South had been misunderstood in its attempts to save civilization from a mob of bestial freed slaves during Reconstruction. See *Crucible* 111–39.

5 Various figures of the Harlem Renaissance and black leaders praised Peterkin's work, including Langston Hughes, Countee Cullen and Walter White. See "Julia Peterkin," *Encyclopaedia of Southern Culture*; Thomas Landess, *Julia Peterkin* (Boston: Twayne, 1976); Houston A. Baker, *Afro-American Poetics: Revisions of Harlem and the Black Aesthetic* (Madison: University of Wisconsin Press, 1988); Arna Bontemps, *The Harlem Renaissance Remembered* (New York: Dodd, Mead, 1972).

6 The name Ravenal may well come from John W. De Forrest's famous novel of 1867, *Miss Ravenal's Conversion from Secession to Loyalty*, in which an aristocratic Southern lady (named Lilly, of course) forgives the North for the war.

7 See Sundquist, *To Wake the Nations* on the Wilmington riots and Charles Chesnutt's fiction (275–76, 407–46). See Williamson, *Crucible* 195–223 on race violence in the "New South."

8 In Morrison's *Playing in the Dark*, she offers a reading of *Sapphira* in terms of "fugitive" states, seeing Nancy as a fugitive in Sapphira's house and Sapphira as a fugitive from her own body. The text itself is also a fugitive. See 18–28.

9 See Richard King, "The 'Simple Story's' Ideology: *Gone With the Wind* and the New South Creed" (167–84); Louis Rubin, "Scarlett O'Hara and the Two Quentin Compsons" (81–104); and Kenneth O'Brien, "Race, Romance and the Southern Literary Tradition" (153–66), all in Pyron, *Recasting*, on the place of *Gone With the Wind* in the plantation novel tradition. Most of these scholars see Gone with the Wind as

NOTES

fundamentally different from what Thomas Nelson Page or Joel Chandler Harris were trying to do. While I agree that Mitchell wants to demythologize the Old South, she also reinscribes some of the plantation novel's fundamental class, race and gender assumptions. Scarlett herself is a subversion of ladyhood but Melanie Wilkes and Ellen Robillard O'Hara are well within Page's realm of Madonna-like plantation mistresses, for example. And while Mitchell shows how North Georgia was not Tidewater Virginia with its two hundred years of "gentility," those with power continue to be white landowners.

10 I am indebted to Williamson's ideas throughout this section, from the title – which I use and signify upon – to his symbolic reading of blackness in Mitchell's life and work.

11 Eve Kosofsky Sedgwick, in *Between Men*, agrees that blackness is a factor in *Gone With the Wind* but only in so far as it lines up with "white bourgeois feminism" to display strategies of power: "Black sexuality 'means' here only as a grammatic transformation of a sentence whose true implicit subject and object are white" (10). While I agree that Scarlett is educated in how to manipulate male-defined, male-controlled power in a world run on the iconography of ladyhood (gender roles), I think that black sexuality has more discursive power than Sedgwick gives it credit for, considering the society that produced Mitchell. For a full cultural study of *Gone With the Wind*, see Helen Taylor, *Scarlett's Women*.

12 See McMillen 206–35; Williamson, *Crucible 180–223; and McGovern 1–16.

13 See *Crucible* 204–05; "Rhett Butler" 87–88.

14 See McMillen 206–33. There were, of course, more lynchings actually happening than got reported.

15 See Williamson, *Crucible* 209–23; and on Williamson's reading of the violence, George M. Frederickson, *The Arrogance of Race: Historical Perspectives on Slavery, Racism, Social Inequality*, Middletown, Conn.: Wesleyan University Press, 1988.

16 See Pyron, *Southern Daughter* 56 and Edwards 31–32. Edwards' book contains photographs of Mitchell as Steve, hamming it up in trousers on the porch of her parents' house. Someone could do some interesting work on Mitchell and cross-dressing: she was dressed as a boy until she was school age because of a fire accident when a baby, with some voluminous petticoats, and insisted for much of her childhood on being called "Jimmy." See Pyron, ibid. 29.

17 Edwards cites a version close to this (129–30); Pyron dismisses the miscegenation aspect in favour of accounts that call it a "ghost story," based on the life of an old lady in Alabama who is more like Miss Emily Grierson than Judith Sutpen (*Southern Daughter* 215–17).

18 See Gerald Wood, "The Loss of American Innocence" (123–36), and Thomas Cripps, "Winds of Change" (137–52), in Pyron, ed., *Recasting*. See also Helen Taylor's most original book, *Scarlett's Women*, which details a great many responses, both early and contemporary, by the novel's readers and the film's viewers.

19 In *Scarlett*, the sequel by Alexandra Ripley, Scarlett seems to take very seriously her oath about never going hungry again. She eats fantastic

212

amounts of food in every episode. So much for ladyhood in a world of eating disorders.

20 See Harwell, Mitchell letter to Julia Collier Harris, 5–6; letter to Harry Edwards, 15. See also Taylor 75.

21 See Helen Deiss Irvin, "Gea in Georgia" (57–68) and Richard King, "The 'Simple Story's' Ideology" (167–84), in Pyron, ed., *Recasting*.

22 Kenneth O'Brien in his essay "Race Romance and the Southern Literary Tradition," suggests that Mitchell constructs Rhett Butler as black then pulls back from his analysis:

> The repeated use of the word *darkness* here [in the rape scene] suggests racial associations, but in this specific context, the sexual assault is being committed by Rhett Butler, the white husband and hero. In this sequence, Mitchell portrays rape as an integral facet of human sexual relations, having nothing to do with race.
>
> (Pyron, ed., *Recasting* 162)

This is a curious statement: while O'Brien struggles to absolve Mitchell of racism in his piece, he does not take into account how the discourses of blackness and rape are intertwined in Mitchell's – and *Gone With the Wind*'s – culture.

23 Helen Taylor does not think "rape" is the appropriate description of what happens between Rhett and Scarlett that night (130). Sedgwick agrees it is rape but says the terms are altered: "when it is white hands that scrabble on white skin, its ideological name is 'blissful marriage'" (*Between Men* 10).

24 Williamson, Pyron, Edwards and various commentators on Mitchell's life and work suggest her rendering of rape as sexual fulfilment might have something to do with her first marriage to Berrien "Red" Upshaw, a man known to assault her in front of guests. Red/Rhett can also be seen to partake of the "scarlett:" the slippage of names into colours and back again shows how vexed Mitchell's attitude towards sex was, perhaps owing to her early experiences with her first husband. There was even a suggestion of marital rape. See Williamson, "Rhett Butler" 96; Pyron, *Southern Daughter* 193–94.

25 See Anne C. Loveland, *Lillian Smith* on Smith's life and work. See also Margaret Rose Gladney, *How Am I to be Heard?*

26 Loveland 186. Loveland is generally defensive about Smith's feminism and her relationship with Paula Snelling: "she was clearly not a feminist writer, for lesbianism was only a minor theme in her novels and none of her works was written to promote women's rights or liberation" (191). This is a curious statement, considering the work Smith did all her life exhorting women to fight segregation and to fight against the empedestalled position Southern culture forced them into. As for lesbianism, Smith's novels *Strange Fruit* and *One Hour* deal with love relationships between two women in a sensitive, mature and positive manner that most would now call feminist. Smith herself was, no doubt, uncomfortable with the associations of the term. See Gladney, Introduction (especially 10–11, 16) on Smith's sexuality and the part it played in her work.

27 Smith wondered in *Killers of the Dream* if blacks, once so openly sexual, were not becoming puritanical (127). Smith was banned from the campus of Spelman College, because her unwed, pregnant, race-transgressing heroine Nonnie in *Strange Fruit* was a Spelman graduate, and this was interpreted as a slur on young black womanhood.

28 See Charles Chesnutt, *The House Behind the Cedars* (1900); Frances E. W. Harper, *Iola Leroy, or Shadows Uplifted* (1892); Jessie Fauset, *Plum Bun* (1928); and Nella Larsen, *Passing* (1929).

BIBLIOGRAPHY

American Criticisms of Mrs. Trollope's Domestic Manners of the Americans, London, 1833.

Ammons, Elizabeth, "Heroines in *Uncle Tom's Cabin*," in Elizabeth Ammons, ed., *Critical Essays on Uncle Tom's Cabin,* Boston: G. K. Hall, 1980, 152–65.

—— "Stowe's Dream of the Mother–Savior," in Eric Sundquist, ed., *New Essays on Uncle Tom's Cabin,* Cambridge: Cambridge University Press, 1986, 155–95.

d'Arusmont, F. S. G., *Memorial of Suffrage,* 3 February 1874.

Askeland, Lori, "Remodelling the Model Home in *Uncle Tom's Cabin* and *Beloved,*" *American Literature* 64, (4), December 1992, 785–805.

Bakhtin, M. M., *Rabelais and His World,* trans. Hélène Iswolsky (1965), Bloomington: Indiana University Press, 1984.

Bakker, Jan, "Another Dilemma for the Intellectual in the Old South: Caroline Gilman, the Peculiar Institution, and Greater Rights for Women in the *Rose* Magazines," *Southern Literary Journal* 17, Fall 1984, 12–25.

Baldwin, James, *Notes of a Native Son,* London: Pluto, 1985.

Ballaster, Ros, *Seductive Forms: Women's Amatory Fiction from 1684 to 1740,* Oxford: Clarendon Press, 1992.

Barnes, Gilbert Hobbs, *The Anti-Slavery Impulse,* New York: Appleton-Century, 1933.

Bartley, Numan V., ed., *The Evolution of Southern Culture,* Athens: University of Georgia Press, 1988.

Beckford, William, *Vathek,* ed. Roger Lonsdale, Oxford: Oxford University Press, 1970.

Beecher, Catharine, *Letters on the Difficulties of Religion,* Hartford: Belknap and Hamersley, 1836.

Behn, Aphra, *Oroonoko* (1688), ed. Maureen Duffy, London: Methuen, 1986.

—— *All the Histories and Novels Written By the Late Ingenious Mrs Behn,* London, 1705.

Berkovitch, Sacvan, *American Jeremiad,* Madison: University of Wisconsin Press, 1978.

Berlant, Lauren, "National Brands/National Body: *Imitation of Life,*" in H. Spillers, ed., *Comparative American Identities,* New York and London: Routledge, 1991.

Blee, Kathleen M., *Women of the Klan: Racism and Gender in the 1920s*, Berkeley: University of California Press, 1991.

Boydston, Jeanne, Mary Kelley and Anne Margolis, eds, *The Limits of Sisterhood: The Beecher Sisters on Women's Rights and Woman's Sphere*, Chapel Hill: University of North Carolina Press, 1988.

Bremer, Frederika, *The Homes of the New World*, 3 vols, London: A. Hall, 1853.

Brown, Gillian, "Getting in the Kitchen With Dinah: Domestic Politics in *Uncle Tom's Cabin*," *American Quarterly* 36 (4), Fall 1984, 503–23.

Brown, Laura, "The Romance of Empire: *Oroonoko* and the Trade in Slaves," in F. Nussbaum and L. Brown, eds, *The New 18th Century: Theory, Politics, English Literature*, London: Methuen, 1987, 47–55.

Brown, William Wells, *Clotel; or the President's Daughter*, London: Partridge and Oakey, 1853.

Buckmaster, Henrietta, *Fire in the Heart*, New York: 1948.

Burr, Virginia Ingraham, ed., *The Secret Eye: The Journal of Ella Gertrude Clanton Thomas, 1848–1889*, intro. by Nell Irvin Painter, Chapel Hill: University of North Carolina Press, 1990.

Campbell, Cathy, "A Battered Woman Rises: Aunt Jemima's Corporate Makeover," *The Village Voice*, 7 November 1989, 44–46.

Cash, Wilbur J., *The Mind of the South*, New York: Knopf, 1941.

Cate, Margaret Davis, "Mistakes in Fanny Kemble's Georgia Journal," *Georgia Historical Quarterly* 44, March 1960, 1–17.

Cather, Willa, *Sapphira and the Slave Girl* (1940), London: Virago, 1986.

Chapman, Maria, *Right and Wrong in Massachusetts*, Boston, 1840.

Child, Lydia Maria, *Hobomok and Other Writings on Indians* (1824), ed. Carolyn Karcher, New Brunswick: Rutgers University Press, 1986.

—— *An Appeal in Favor of that Class of Americans Called African*, Boston: Ticknor and Fields, 1833.

—— *A Brief History of the Condition of Women in Various Ages and Nations*, 2 vols, New York: C. S. Francis, 1835.

—— *The Anti-Slavery Catechism*, Newburyport: Charles Whipple, 1836.

—— "The Quadroons," *Liberty Bell* 3, 1842, 115–41.

—— "Slavery's Pleasant Homes: A Faithful Sketch," *Liberty Bell* 4, 1843, 147–60.

—— *The Freedmen's Book*, Boston: Ticknor and Fields, 1865.

—— *A Romance of the Republic*, Boston: Ticknor and Fields, 1867.

—— *The Right Way, the Safe Way* (1860), New York: Arno Press, 1969.

—— *Selected Letters of Lydia Maria Child*, ed. Milton Meltzer and Patricia G. Holland, Amherst: University of Massachusetts Press, 1982.

Clinton, Catherine, *The Other Civil War: American Women in the Nineteenth Century*, New York: Hill and Wang, 1984.

Cooper, James Fenimore, *The Last of the Mohicans* (1926), New York: Washington Square Books, 1960.

Cowdin, Mrs V. G., *Ellen; or the Fanatic's Daughter*, Mobile: S. H. Goetzel and Co., 1860.

Criswell, Robert, *"Uncle Tom's Cabin" Contrasted with Buckingham Hall*, New York: D. Fanshaw, 1852.

Davidoff, Leonore, "Class and Gender in Victorian England: The Diaries of Arthur J. Munby and Hannah Cullwick, *Feminist Studies* 5(1) (1979), 89–141

Davidson, Cathy N., *Revolution and the Word: The Rise of the Novel in America*, New York: Oxford University Press.

Davis, David Brion, *The Problem of Slavery in Western Culture*, Ithaca: Cornell University Press, 1966.

Davis, James, *Who is Black?*, Penn State Press, 1991.

Dew, Thomas R., *The Pro-Slavery Argument*, Philadelphia: Walker and Richards, 1853.

Dickinson, Anna E., *What Answer?*, Boston: Ticknor and Fields, 1868.

Dixon, Thomas, *The Clansman* (1905), intro. Thomas Clark, Lexington: University Press of Kentucky, 1970.

Douglas, Mary, *Purity and Danger: An Analysis of Concepts of Pollution and Taboo*, London: Routledge, 1966.

Du Bois, W. E. B., *The Souls of Black Folk*, New York, 1903.

—— Review of *Strange Fruit*, *New York Times* Book Review, 5 March 1944, 1.

Durr, Virginia Foster, *Outside the Magic Circle*, New York: Simon and Schuster, 1987.

Eastman, Mary H., *Aunt Phillis' Cabin*, Philadelphia: Lippincott, 1852.

Eckhardt, Celia Morris, *Frances Wright: Rebel in America*, Cambridge: Harvard University Press, 1984.

Edelstein, Tilden G., *"Othello* in America: The Drama of Racial Intermarriage" in J. Morgan Kausser and James M. McPherson, eds, *Region, Race and Reconstruction*, Oxford: Oxford University Press, 1982, 179–97.

Edwards, Anne, *The Road to Tara*, New Haven: Ticknor and Fields, 1983.

Eliot, George, Review of *Dred*, *Westminster Review*, 10 October 1856, 571–73.

Ellis, Kate Ferguson, *The Contested Castle: Gothic Novels and the Subversion of Domestic Ideology*, Urbana: University of Illinois Press, 1989.

Faulkner, William, *The Sound and the Fury* (1929), New York: Vintage, 1946.

—— *Light in August* (1934), New York: Vintage, 1942.

—— *Absalom, Absalom!* (1936), New York: Vintage, n.d.

Ferber, Edna, *Show Boat*, New York: Grosset and Dunlap, 1926.

Ferguson, Margaret, "Juggling the Categories of Race, Class and Gender: Aphra Behn's *Oroonoko,*" *Women's Studies* 19, 1991, 159–81.

—— "Whose Dominion, or News from the New World: Aphra Behn's Representations of Miscegenous Romance in *Oroonoko* and *The Widow Ranter,*" forthcoming in D. Miller, S. O'Dair, H. Weber, eds, *The Production of Renaissance Culture*, Ithaca: Cornell University Press, 1994.

Ferguson, Moira, *Subject to Others: British Women Writers and Colonial Slavery, 1670–1834*, London and New York: Routledge, 1992.

Fidler, William Perry, *Augusta Jane Evans: A Biography*, University of Alabama Press, 1951.

Fiedler, Leslie, *Love and Death in the American Novel*, New York: Stein and Day, 1966.

—— *Inadvertent Epic: From Uncle Tom's Cabin to Roots*, New York: Touchstone, 1979.

Fields, Barbara J., "Ideology and Race in American History" in J. Morgan Kousser and James McPherson, eds, *Region, Race and Reconstruction*, Oxford: Oxford University Press, 1982.

Fisher, Philip K., *Hard Facts*, Oxford: Oxford University Press, 1985.

Fitzhugh, George, *Cannibals All! or Slaves Without Masters* (1857), ed. C. Vann Woodward, Cambridge: Harvard University Press, 1960.

Follen, Eliza Lee, "Women's Work", *Liberty Bell* 3, 1842, 7–12.

Foster, Charles, *The Rungless Ladder: Harriet Beecher Stowe and New England Puritanism*, Durham, North Carolina: Duke University Press, 1954.

Fox-Genovese, Elizabeth, *Within the Plantation Household*, Chapel Hill: University of North Carolina Press, 1988.

Furnas, J. C., *Goodbye to Uncle Tom*, London: Secker, 1956.

Garber, Marjorie, *Vested Interests: Cross-Dressing and Cultural Anxiety*, New York and London: Routledge, 1992.

Gardiner, Jane, "The Assault on Uncle Tom: Attempts of Pro-Slavery Novelists to Answer *Uncle Tom's Cabin*," *Southern Humanities Review* 12(4), Fall 1978, 313–23.

Garrison, William Lloyd, (untitled) essay on intermarriage, *Liberator*, 7 May 1831.

Gates, Henry Louis, "From Wheatley to Douglass: The Politics of Displacement," in Sundquist, ed., *Frederick Douglass: New Literary and Historical Essays*, Cambridge: Cambridge University Press, 1990, 47–65.

Gates, Henry Louis, ed., *"Race," Writing and Difference*, Chicago: University of Chicago Press, 1986.

Gates, Henry Louis and Charles T. Davis, eds, *The Slave's Narrative*, Oxford: Oxford University Press, 1985.

Gilbert, Sandra and Susan Gubar, *The Madwoman in the Attic*, New Haven and London: Yale University Press, 1979.

Gilman, Caroline, *Recollections of a Southern Matron*, New York: Harper and Bros, 1838.

Gilman, Sander L., "Black Bodies, White Bodies: Toward an Iconography of Female Sexuality in Late 19th Century Art, Medicine and Literature" in Henry Louis Gates, ed., *"Race," Writing and Difference*, Chicago: University of Chicago Press, 1986, 223–61.

Gladney, Margaret Rose, ed., *How Am I to be Heard? The Letters of Lillian Smith*, Chapel Hill: University of North Carolina Press, 1993.

Glasgow, Ellen, *The Sheltered Life*, New York: Doubleday, 1932.

Goreau, Angeline, *Reconstructing Aphra: A Social Biography of Aphra Behn*, Oxford: Oxford University Press, 1980.

Gossett, Thomas F., *Uncle Tom's Cabin and American Culture*, Dallas: Southern Methodist University Press, 1985.

Grant, Madison, *The Passing of the Great Race*, New York: Scribners, 1916.

Grimké, Angelina, "Appeal to the Christian Women of the South," *Anti-Slavery Examiner*, September 1836.

Gross, Louis, *Redefining the American Gothic from Wieland to Day of the Dead*, Ann Arbor: University of Michigan Press, 1989.

Hall, Jacquelyn Dowd, *Revolt Against Chivalry*, New York: Columbia University Press, 1979.

Halttunen, Karen, "Gothic Imagination and Social Reform: The Haunted Houses of Lyman Beecher, Henry Ward Beecher, and Harriet Beecher Stowe," in Eric Sundquist, ed., *New Essays on Uncle Tom's Cabin*, Cambridge: Cambridge University Press, 1986, 107–34.

Harris, Trudier, *Exorcising Blackness: Historical and Literary Lynching and Burning Rituals*, Bloomington: Indiana University Press, 1984.

Harwell, Richard E., *Margaret Mitchell's Gone With the Wind Letters, 1936–1949*, New York: Macmillan, 1976.

Hentz, Caroline Lee, *Marcus Warland*, Philadelphia: T. B. Peterson, 1852.
—— *The Planter's Northern Bride*, 2 vols, Philadelphia: A. Hart, 1854.
Hirsch, Stephen A., "Uncle Tomitudes: The Popular Reaction to *Uncle Tom's Cabin*," in Joel Myerson, ed., *Studies in the American Renaissance*, Boston: Twayne, 1978, 303–30.
Holmes, George Frederick, Review of *The Key to Uncle Tom's Cabin, Southern Literary Messenger*, 19 June 1853, 321–30.
hooks, bell, *Ain't I a Woman? Black Women and Feminism*, Boston: South End, 1981.
Howard, Jean E., "Crossdressing, the Theatre, and Gender Struggle in Early Modern England," *Shakespeare Quarterly*, September 1988, 418–40.
Jacobs, Harriet, *Incidents in the Life of a Slave Girl* (1861), Oxford: Oxford University Press, 1988.
Jordan, Winthrop, *White Over Black: American Attitudes Towards the Negro*, Chapel Hill: University of North Carolina Press, 1968.
Kahane, Claire, "The Gothic Mirror," in Shirley Nelson Garner, Claire Kahane, and Madelon Sprengnether, eds, *The (M)other Tongue: Essays in Feminist Psychoanalytic Interpretation*, Ithaca: Cornell University Press, 1985, 334–51.
Karcher, Carolyn, "Rape, Murder and Revenge in 'Slavery's Pleasant Homes': Lydia Maria Child's Antislavery Fiction and the Limits of Genre," *Women's Studies International Forum* 9(4), 1986, 320–13.
—— "Lydia Maria Child's *A Romance of the Republic*," in D. McDowell and A. Rampersad, eds, *Slavery and the Literary Imagination*, Baltimore: Johns Hopkins University Press, 1989, 81–103.
—— "Lydia Maria Child and the Example of John Brown," *Race Traitor* 1, Winter 1993, 21–43.
Kasson, Joy S., "Narratives of the Female Body in *The Greek Slave*," in Shirley Samuels, ed., *The Culture of Sentiment*, Oxford: Oxford University Press, 1992, 172–90.
Kemble, Frances Anne, *Journal of a Residence on a Georgian Plantation in 1838–1839* (1863), ed. J. A. Scott, Athens: University of Georgia Press, 1984.
Kern-Foxworth, Marilyn, "Plantation Kitchen to American Icon: Aunt Jemima," *Public Relations Review* 16(3), Fall 1990, 55–65.
Kimball, Gayle, *The Religious Ideas of Harriet Beecher Stowe*, New York: Mellen Press, 1982.
Kirkham, E. Bruce, *The Building of Uncle Tom's Cabin*, Knoxville: University of Tennessee Press, 1977.
Kolodny, Annette, *The Lay of the Land: Metaphor as Experience and History in American Life and Letters*, Chapel Hill: University of North Carolina Press, 1975.
Kousser, J. Morgan and James McPherson, eds, *Region, Race and Reconstruction*, Oxford: Oxford University Press, 1982.
Lauretis, Teresa de, *Technologies of Gender: Essays in Theory, Film, and Fiction*, Bloomington: Indiana University Press, 1987.
Leigh, Frances Butler, *Ten Years on a Georgia Plantation Since the War*, London: R. Bentley, 1883.
Lerner, Gerda, *The Grimké Sisters from South Carolina*, Boston: Houghton Mifflin, 1967.

Lewis, Matthew, *The Monk* (1796), Oxford: Oxford University Press, 1973.

Ligon, Richard, *A True and Exact History of the Island of Barbados*, London, 1657.

Lombard, Mildred C., "Contemporary Opinions of Mrs Kemble's *Journal of a Residence on a Georgian Plantation*," *Georgia History Quarterly* 14(4), December 1930, 335–43

Loveland, Anne C., *Lillian Smith: A Southerner Confronting the South*, Baton Rouge: Louisiana State University Press, 1986.

McCord, Louisa ("L.S.M."), "Negro and White Slavery," *Southern Quarterly Review* 20, July 1851, 118–32.

—— "Enfranchisement of Women," *Southern Quarterly Review* 21, April 1852, 322–41.

—— Review of *Uncle Tom's Cabin*, *Southern Quarterly Review* 23, January 1853, 81–120.

McGovern, James R., *Anatomy of a Lynching*, Baton Rouge: Louisiana State University Press, 1982.

McIntosh, Maria, *Letter on the Address of the Women of England to their Sisters of America in Relation to Slavery*, New York: Appleton, 1853.

McMillen, Neil R., *Dark Journey: Black Mississippians in the Age of Jim Crow*, Urbana: University of Illinois Press, 1989.

Martineau, Harriet, "Demerara," in vol. II, no. 4, *Illustrations of Political Economy*, 9 vols, London: Charles Fox, 1832–34.

—— *Society in America*, 2 vols, New York: Sander and Otley, 1837.

—— *The Hour and the Man*, 3 vols, London: Edward Moxon, 1841.

—— *Autobiography*, 3 vols, London: Smith and Elder, 1877.

Melville, Herman, *Benito Cereno*, London: Chatto, 1926.

Milford, H., ed., *Letters of Matthew Arnold to A. H. Clough*, Oxford: Oxford University Press, 1932.

Mills, Bruce, "Lydia Maria Child and the Endings to Harriet Jacobs' *Incidents in the Life of a Slave Girl*," *American Literature* 64(2), June 1992, 255–72.

Mitchell, Margaret, *Gone With the Wind* (1936), London: Pan, 1974.

Morrison, Toni, *Beloved*, New York: Knopf, 1987.

—— *Playing in the Dark: Whiteness and the Literary Imagination*, Cambridge, Mass.: Harvard University Press, 1992.

—— *Race-ing Justice, En-gendering Power: Essays on Anita Hill, Clarence Thomas, and the Construction of Social Reality*, New York: Pantheon, 1992.

Montrose, Louis, "The Work of Gender in the Discourse of Discovery," *Representations* 33, Winter 1991, 1–41.

Moss, Elizabeth, *Domestic Novelists in the Old South: Defenders of Southern Culture*, Baton Rouge, Louisiana State University Press, 1992.

Nelson, Dana, *The Word in Black and White: Reading "Race" in American Literature, 1638–1867*, Oxford: Oxford University Press, 1992.

Newman, Karen, "'And Wash the Ethiop White:' Femininity and the Monstrous in *Othello*," in Jean E. Howard and M. F. O'Connor, eds, *Shakespeare Reproduced: The Text in Ideology and History*, New York and London: Methuen, 1987, 143–62.

Olmsted, Frederick Law, *The Cotton Kingdom*, 2 vols, New York: Mason, 1861.

Page, Thomas Nelson, *The Old South: Essays Social and Political*, New York: Charles Scribner's Sons, 1892.
—— *The Old Dominion*, New York: Charles Scribner's Sons, 1910.
Painter, Nell Irvin, "'Social Equality,' Miscegenation, Labor, and Power" in Numan V. Bartley, ed., *Evolution of Southern Culture*, Athens: University of Georgia Press, 1988, 47–67.
Parker, Alice, "Evangeline's Darker Daughters: Crossing Racial Boundaries in Postwar Louisiana," in D.H. Brown and B.C. Ewell, eds, *Louisiana Women Writers*, Baton Rouge: Louisiana State University Press, 1992, 75–97.
Patterson, Orlando, *Slavery and Social Death: A Comparative Study*, Cambridge, Mass.: Harvard University Press, 1982.
Perkins, A. J. G., *Frances Wright: Free Enquirer*, London: Harper, 1939.
Peterkin, Julia, *Scarlet Sister Mary*, Indianapolis: Bobbs Merrill, 1928.
Phillips, Ulrich B., *Life and Labor in the Old South*, Boston: Little, Brown, 1929.
Pope-Hennessy, Una, *Three Englishwomen in America*, London: Ernest Benn, 1929.
Pratt, Minnie Bruce, "Identity Skin Blood Heart," in E. Bulkin, B. Smith and M. Pratt, *Yours in Struggle: Three Feminist Perspectives on Anti-Semitism and Racism*, Brooklyn: Long Haul Press, 1984, 11–63.
Pyron, Darden Asbury, "The Inner War of Southern History," in Darden Pyron, ed., *Recasting: Gone With the Wind in American Culture*, University Press of Florida, 1983, 185–201.
—— *Southern Daughter: The Life of Margaret Mitchell*, Oxford: Oxford University Press, 1991.
Pyron, Darden Asbury, ed., *Recasting: Gone With the Wind in American Culture*, University Press of Florida, 1983.
Randolph, J. Thornton, *The Cabin and the Parlor; or Slaves and Masters*, Philadelphia: 1852.
Ripley, C. Peter, ed., *The Abolitionist Papers*, 5 vols, Chapel Hill: University of North Carolina Press, 1985–92.
Roberts, Diane, *Faulkner and Southern Womanhood*, Athens: University of Georgia Press, 1993.
Rush, Caroline, *The North and the South, or Slavery and Its Contrasts* (1852), New York: Negro Universities Press, 1968.
Russell, William Howard, *My Diary North and South*, 2 vols, London: Bradbury, 1863.
Said, Edward, *Orientalism*, New York: Vintage, 1979.
—— *The World, the Text and the Critic*, Cambridge, Mass.: Harvard University Press, 1983.
Samuels, Shirley, "The Identity of Slavery," in Shirley Samuels, ed., *The Culture of Sentiment*, Oxford: Oxford University Press, 1992, 157–71.
Samuels, Shirley, ed., *The Culture of Sentiment: Race, Gender and Sentimentality in Nineteenth-Century America*, Oxford: Oxford University Press, 1992.
Sanchez-Eppler, Karen, "Bodily Bonds: The Intersecting Rhetorics of Feminism and Abolitionism," *Representations* 24, Fall 1988, 28–59.
Schoolcraft, Mrs Henry, *The Black Gauntlet*, Philadelphia: Lippincott, 1860.
Sedgwick, Eve Kosofsky, "The Character of the Veil: The Imagery of Surface in the Gothic Novel," *PMLA*, March 1981, 255–70.

—— *Between Men: English Literature and Male Homosocial Desire*, New York: Columbia University Press, 1985.

Seidel, Kathryn Lee, *The Southern Belle in the American Novel*, Tampa: University of South Florida Press, 1985.

Simms, William Gilmore, Review of *Uncle Tom's Cabin*, *Southern Quarterly Review* 7, July 1852, 81–120.

—— "Stowe's Key to Uncle Tom's Cabin," *Southern Quarterly Review* 8, July 1853, 214–54.

—— *The Sword and the Distaff*, Philadelphia: Lippincott, 1853.

Smith, Lillian, *Strange Fruit* (1944), New York: Harcourt, 1944.

—— *Killers of the Dream* (1949), New York: Norton, 1961.

Smith, W. L. G., *Uncle Tom's Cabin As It Is*, London: W. Tegg, 1852.

Spillers, Hortense, "Mama's Baby, Papa's Maybe: An American Grammar Book," *Diacritics*, Summer 1987, 65–81.

—— "Changing the Letter: The Yokes, the Jokes of Discourse," in Deborah McDowell and Arnold Rampersad, eds, *Slavery and the Literary Imagination*, Baltimore: Johns Hopkins University Press, 1989, 25–61.

Stallybrass, Peter, "Patriarchal Territories: The Body Enclosed," in Margaret Ferguson, Maureen Quilligan and Nancy J. Vickers, eds, *Rewriting the Renaissance*, Chicago: University of Chicago Press, 1986, 123–42.

Stallybrass, Peter and Allon White, *The Politics and Poetics of Transgression*, London: Methuen, 1986.

Stowe, Harriet Beecher, *Uncle Tom's Cabin* (1851), ed. and intro. by Ann Douglas, Harmondsworth: Penguin, 1981.

—— *The Key to Uncle Tom's Cabin*, Boston: John P. Jewett, 1854.

—— *Dred: A Tale of the Great Dismal Swamp*, 2 vols, Boston: Phillips, Sampson and Co., 1856.

—— *Religious Studies*, vol. XV of *The Writings of Harriet Beecher Stowe*, Boston: Houghton Mifflin, 1877.

Stowe, Harriet Beecher, and C. Beecher, *A First Geography for Children* (1833), Boston: Phillips, Sampson and Co., 1855.

Sundquist, Eric, ed., *New Essays on Uncle Tom's Cabin*, Cambridge: Cambridge University Press, 1986.

—— *Frederick Douglass: New Literary and Historical Essays*, Cambridge: Cambridge University Press, 1990.

—— *To Wake the Nations: Race in the Making of American Literature*, Cambridge, Mass.: Harvard University Press, 1993.

Taylor, Helen, *Scarlett's Women: Gone With the Wind and Its Female Fans*, New Brunswick: Rutgers University Press, 1989.

Thompson, Ralph, "The *Liberty Bell* and Other Anti-slavery Gift-books", *New England Quarterly*, 7(1), March 1934, 154–68.

Todd, Janet, *The Sign of Angellica: Women, Writing and Fiction 1660–1800*, New York: Columbia University Press, 1989.

Tompkins, Jane, *Sensational Designs: The Cultural Work of American Fiction 1790–1860*, Oxford: Oxford University Press, 1985.

Towsend, Mary Ashley ("Xariffa"), *The Brother Clerks*, New York: Derby, 1857.

Trollope, Frances, *Domestic Manners of the Americans*, London: Whittaker, Treacher, 1832.

—— *The Life and Adventures of Jonathan Jefferson Whitlaw; or, Scenes on the Mississippi*, London: Longman, 1836.

"The Views of Judge Woodward and Bishop Hawkins on Negro Slavery of the South, Illustrated from *The Journal of a Residence on a Georgian Plantation* by Mrs Frances Ann Kemble," Philadelphia, 1863.

Wagenknecht, Edward, *Harriet Beecher Stowe: The Known and the Unknown*, New York: Oxford University Press, 1965.

Wardley, Lynn, "Relic, Fetish, 'Femmage:' The Aesthetics of Sentiment in the Work of Stowe," in Shirley Samuels, ed., *The Culture of Sentiment*, Oxford: Oxford University Press, 1992, 203–20.

Waterman, William Randall, *Frances Wright*, New York: Columbia University Press, 1924.

Weld, Theodore, *American Slavery As It Is: Testimony of A Thousand Witnesses*, New York: The Anti-Slavery Society, 1839.

Wheatley, Vera, *The Life of Harriet Martineau*, London: Secker, 1957.

Williamson, Joel, *New People: Miscegenation and Mulattoes in the United States*, New York: Free Press, 1980.

—— *The Crucible of Race*, Oxford: Oxford University Press, 1984.

—— "How Black Was Rhett Butler?," in Numan V. Bartley, ed., *The Evolution of Southern Culture*, Athens: University of Georgia Press, 1988, 87–107.

Wilson, Charles Reagan and Bill Ferris, eds, *Encyclopedia of Southern Culture*, Chapel Hill: University of North Carolina Press, 1989.

Winter, Kari J., *Subjects of Slavery, Agents of Change: Women and Power in Gothic Novels and Slave Narratives 1790–1865*, Athens: University of Georgia Press, 1992.

Wister, Fanny Kemble, ed., *Fanny, the American Kemble: Her Journals and Unpublished Letters*, Tallahassee: privately printed, 1972.

Wood, Gerald, "From *The Clansman* and *Birth of a Nation* to *Gone With the Wind*: The Loss of American Innocence," in Darden Pyron, ed., *Recasting: Gone With the Wind in American Culture*, University Press of Florida, 1983, 123–36.

Woodcock, George, *The Incomparable Aphra*, London, 1948.

Woodward, C. Vann, ed., *Mary Chesnut's Civil War*, New Haven: Yale University Press, 1981.

Wright, Frances, *Views of Society and Manners in America*, London, 1821.

Wyatt-Brown, Bertram, *Southern Honor: Ethics and Behavior in the Old South*, Oxford: Oxford University Press, 1982.

Yarborough, Richard, "Strategies of Black Characterization in *Uncle Tom's Cabin* and the Early Afro-American Novel," in Eric Sundquist, ed., *New Essays on Uncle Tom's Cabin*, Cambridge: Cambridge University Press, 1986, 45–84.

Yellin, Jean Fagan, "Texts and Contexts of Harriet Jacobs' *Incidents*," in Henry Louis Gates and Charles T. Davis, eds, *The Slave's Narrative*, Oxford: Oxford University Press, 1985.

—— "Doing It Herself: *Uncle Tom's Cabin* and Woman's Role in the Slavery Crisis," in Eric Sundquist, ed., *New Essays on Uncle Tom's Cabin*, Cambridge: Cambridge University Press, 1986, 85–105.

—— *Women and Sisters*, New Haven: Yale University Press, 1989.

"A Young Lady of New England," Review of *Dred*, *Southern Literary Messenger*, 27, October 1858.

INDEX

225